How to control

Your anger, anxiety and depression
Using nutrition and physical activity

Renata Taylor-Byrne and Jim Byrne

~~~

Published by the Institute for Emotive-Cognitive Embodied Narrative Therapy
(E-CENT)

~~~

Copyright © Renata Taylor-Byrne and Jim Byrne, 2017

Published by the Institute for Emotive-Cognitive Embodied-Narrative Therapy, 27 Wood End, Hebden Bridge, West Yorkshire, HX7 8HJ, UK

Telephone: 01422 843 629

~~~

All rights reserved.

The right of Renata Taylor-Byrne and Jim Byrne to be the exclusive creators of this book, and its exclusive owners, have been asserted. This book is the intellectual property of Dr Jim Byrne and Renata Taylor-Byrne (at ABC Coaching and Counselling Services, and the Institute for E-CENT). No element of this work may be used in any way, without explicit written permission of the authors. The sole exception is the presentation of brief quotations (not for profit), which must be acknowledged as excerpts from:

Taylor-Byrne, R.E. and Byrne, J.W. (2017) *How to control your anger, anxiety and depression, using nutrition and physical activity.* Hebden Bridge: The Institute for E-CENT Publications.

Website: https://ecent-institute.org/

~~~

Early drafts of parts 1 and 2 of this book were originally published – in briefer, incomplete form - as appendices to a book titled *Holistic Counselling in Practice*, by Jim Byrne, with Renata Taylor-Byrne, in 2016, and the copyright of those documents rests with Renata Taylor-Byrne and Jim Byrne. (See Byrne, 2016).

~~~

Cover design: Charles Saul. Website: http://www.charles-saul.co.uk/

~~~

ISBN-13: ISBN-13: 978-1981216666

~~~

Copyright © Renata Taylor-Byrne and Jim Byrne, November 2017

~~~

Disclaimer

This book is intended for *educational* purposes only, and does not purport to be *medical* advice. Bear in mind that each individual body is probably pretty unique, because of its unique nutritional journey through life. We are changed by the foods we eat, and some experts would say we 'are what we eat'. (A recent refinement is this: We are what our food has eaten. When we eat animals that are fed on bad foods, we develop bad health!)

However, we also know that physical exercise changes the biochemistry of the body-brain, which changes moods and emotions, as well as promoting better cardio-vascular health, and oxygenation of the whole system.

Furthermore, there are many expert nutritionists and nutritional therapists available today, at reasonable fees; and you would be well advised to see a nutritionist, or some other kind of holistic health practitioner, if you are concerned there might be a link between your current emotional state and your diet. And there are increasingly available lifestyle coaches, health coaches, and exercises coaches and personal trainers, who can help to get you into a new set of healthier dietary and exercise habits which will promote greater physical and mental health and emotional wellbeing.

Nevertheless, despite the caveats and reservations above, there is undoubtedly a lot of very useful *educational* material in this book, based on recent, sound, scientific research, which could be helpful in guiding you towards your own answers to your questions about emotional health and wellbeing and the linkages from lifestyle choices. The ideas in this book will also be an invaluable resource for counsellors, psychotherapists, health and lifestyle coaches, self-help enthusiasts, students of these disciplines, and others.

~~~

Acknowledgements

We owe a great debt of gratitude to many authors who have helped us to understand the body-brain-mind-diet-exercise axis. They are too numerous to mention here. Many of them are listed in the Reference List at the end of this book. If we had to mention just a few, then we would choose Dr Dharma Singh Khalsa; Linus Pauling; Dr Kelly Brogan; Dr Abram Hoffer; Patrick Holford; Dr David Perlmutter; Michael Tse; Matthias Alexander; and Dr Giulia Enders.

~~~

About the authors

Renata Taylor-Byrne has an honours degree in psychology, plus diplomas in nutrition, stress management, CBT and other systems of coaching and counselling. She taught health and nutrition courses, as well as counselling, stress management, self-assertion, and other personal development courses, in further education, with adult students, during a thirty-five year teaching career. As a Lifestyle Coach, she has a very strong interest in the link between diet, exercise, health, and emotional wellbeing.

~~~

Jim Byrne has a doctoral degree in counselling and a master's degree in education; plus a diploma in counselling psychology and psychotherapy. He has been involved in counselling psychology and psychotherapy for almost twenty years; and he's studied optimum nutrition and balanced exercise approaches to improve his own physical and mental health for decades. He is the creator of Emotive-Cognitive Embodied Narrative Therapy (E-CENT), which emphasizes the interactionism of body-brain-mind-environment as a whole system, which is what underlies the phenomenon which some see as 'the life of the individual', and which he has characterized as *the embodied and embedded social-self*.

~~~

Contents Pages

Preface *9*

Foreword *15*

Part 1: Diet, nutrition and the implications for anger, anxiety and depression management *25*

    1. Introduction 25

    2. Why is nutrition important to the body-brain-mind? 26

    3. What would a *balanced diet* look like? 27

        (a) Types of diet 28

        (b) Some general dietary guidelines 40

    4. What kinds of foods should we avoid for the sake of our physical, mental, and emotional health and wellbeing? 44

        (a) Trans-fats: 44

        (b) Sugar 46

        (c) Alcohol 47

        (d) Caffeine 49

        (e) Processed food (or 'Junk food') 50

        (f) Gluten 51

    5. What kinds of regular supplements (of vitamins, minerals, etc.) should we take to support our physical health and emotional wellbeing? 54

        (a) The British National Health Service (NHS) view 54

        (b) A Nutritional Therapist's perspective 55

        (c) A dissenting voice 56

        (d) In favour of supplements 57

        (e) A critique of Holford's position 57

        (f) Additional forms of dietary supplementation 59

    6. How good is the evidence that anxiety, anger and depression can be created by the wrong kind of food and drink? 60

        (a) Anxiety and nutrition 61

        (b) Anger and nutrition 67

        (c) Investigating links between diet and depression 70

    7. Diet and good mental and physical health in general 76

...continued...

Part 2: Physical exercise and common emotional problems 79
   1. Introduction 79
   2. Anxiety disorders and the benefits of exercise 80
      Anxiety and physical exercise 81
   3. Exercise and its effect on depression 84
      Exercise for depression 86
      Exercise and stress: Get moving to manage stress 86
   4. Exercise and anger 87
   5. Indian and Chinese exercises for health 88
      Yoga 88
      Chinese exercise systems 90
   6. Exercise and the brain-mind 92

Part 3: Dr Jim's Stress and Anxiety Diet 95
   1. Introduction and disclaimer 95
   2. Personal experience of diet and emotional distress 95
   3. No universal agreement regarding diet 97
   4. Schools of thought on diet 97
   5. Stress management advice 99
   6. Proportions of food groups 100
   7. Food combining, or not 100
   8. Drinks and drinking 101
   9. Fats and oils 102
   10. Never skip breakfast 104
   11. Snacks, supplements and raw food 105
   12. Find out for yourself 106
   13. Supplements and healthy foods 106
   14. Finale 106

Part 4: Nutritional deficiencies and emotional disorders – The link 109
   Section A: The science of nutritional deficiency 109
      1. Introduction 109
      2. The science of nutritional deficiency 109
      3. Vitamin B3 deficiency and the disease of Pellagra 110
      4. Nutritional treatment of emotional problems 111
...continued...

Section B: The Minnesota Starvation Experiment 111
    1. Introduction 111
    2. Evidence from the Minnesota Starvation Experiments 112
    3. Summing up 113
Section C: The role of inflammation in emotional disturbance 113
    1. Introduction 113
    2. Depression is associated with inflammation 115
    3. The sources of inflammation 115

Part 5: Summing Up 119

Part 6: How to change for good 133
  Section 1: Introduction to habit change 133
    1. General theory 133
    2. The benefits of exercise and dietary self-management skills 133
    3. Our approach to behaviour change 134
    4. A personal example 134
    5. A second example: Using rewards and penalties 135
    6. The stages of change 136
    7. How to use this book to promote change 136
  Section 2 (of Part 6): How to change your negative habits 141
    1. The nature of habits 141
    2. The structure of a habit 141
    3. The importance of craving! 142
    4. Duhigg's own experiment 143
    5. The importance of substitution 144
    6. Stopping addictions 144
    7. The rewards of drinking 145
    8. The result of one experiment 145
    9. Analysing your own habits 146
    10. Creating 'keystone habits' 146
    11. Habit reversal 147
    12. Conclusion 148

References 149

Index 161

Endnotes 171

How to control your anger, anxiety and depression:

Preface

By Renata Taylor-Byrne

> *"Healthy food can have a powerful effect on mood".*
>
> Dr Michael Greger (2016)

~~~

> *"Thirty minutes of moderate-intensity exercise, five times a week, is associated with numerous health benefits. These range from improving mood and self-esteem to reducing the risk of cancer and heart disease".*
>
> Dr Mark Atkinson (2007)

~~~

Who is this book for?

We wrote this book with three audiences in mind:

1. Professional carers and helpers, like counsellors, psychologists, psychotherapists, social workers, health coaches, lifestyle coaches, nutritional advisers (who need to learn the linkages to emotions, and the role of exercise), personal trainers (who need to learn the role of diet and the link to emotions); plus psychiatrists, and others.

2. Students of the caring professions, including psychology and counselling in particular, but also nutritional science (for the link to emotional disturbances).

3. And self-help enthusiasts, who want to learn how to manage their emotions by taking more responsibility for their physical health, via diet and exercise approaches.

About the structure of this book

We live in a world of information overload. And yet we need to take account of those elements of information that are newly emergent, which could make a significant difference to the quality of our lives. For this reason, we have designed this book to minimize the information that you have to digest in order to get the essence of the revolutionary message of how to manage your emotions by managing your diet and exercise regimes. The four major subdivisions of the book are *summarized* in Part 5; and Part 6 is designed to help you to change negative habits as effectively as possible. So, if you are in a hurry, you can skip to Part 5, and get an overview of the books conclusions; and then go to Part 6 to get advice on how to implement our insights.

On the other hand, if you have a specific emotional problem that may be linked to your diet and exercise practices, you could jump to the relevant sections of Part 1 (diet) and/or Part 2 (exercise) to find out how to manage your particular emotional problem.

Next, we have expanded the index, so you can see the subsections of each of the parts of the book, and therefore you can go straight to the sections that interest you most.

We have also expended a lot of time and energy (or Jim has!) constructing a highly user-friendly index, so you can quickly find those pieces of information that are of most interest to you; and use this book as a handy resource, to be picked up as and when you have questions to answer about the linkages between diet and exercise, on the one hand, and anger, anxiety and depression on the other.

And finally, we want you to be able to learn and apply the ideas that you read about in this book as quickly and effectively as possible. So, as mentioned above, we have added Part 6, which deals with how to turn the information in this book into *durable habits* which support you in your daily life!

~~~

Where this book came from

We live in a "toxic food environment"[1], in a world of sedentary lifestyle; and standards of health are falling.

For more than thirty-five years, we have been studying the emerging research on a broad range of approaches to personal and professional development, including: counselling and psychotherapy systems; lifestyle coaching options; health and fitness; and some spiritual and wisdom traditions. We were consistent about applying our learning in our own lives, and also teaching our insights to our students and counselling clients.

In 1991, I (Renata) studied for a Diploma in Stress Management, with Mike Hoolihan, at the Manchester Institute for Stress Management. Among other things, this made me acutely aware that stress is not 'all in the mind'. It is a whole body-brain-mind response to external stressors.

Around the same time, I discovered some books on Rational Emotive Behaviour Therapy (REBT), which emphasises the 'belief system' of the individual, and claims that people are 'upset by their beliefs, and not by what happens to them'.

In 1992, Jim began to use REBT on himself, to cope with a serious career crisis; and he eventually trained to be a rational therapist. (After fifteen years of using that system, he then began to evolve a more humane, holistic system of his own, based on many of the lifestyle management systems that we had been learning together, plus his own research in psychology and philosophy).

In 1994, we both began to train in Chi Kung (Qigong), with Penny Ramsden – who had been trained as an instructor by Michael Tse. Again, it was obvious from this physical training that we could calm our minds by exercising our bodies with particular kinds of movements. And we have both been meditating together since 1980 (and Renata has been mediating since the early 1970's). We have also been using audio-based relaxation programs, for decades; and making sure we get adequate amounts of sleep each night.

Despite our learning about the body-mind connection, from stress management, Chi Kung, relaxation and meditation, we continued to be controlled by the dominant psychological and psychotherapeutic model (as expressed in rational and cognitive therapy, and all other systems of therapy), in which the mind and body have been pulled apart and treated as separate entities. And therefore we continued to believe it was possible to help individuals who had problems with depression and anxiety, simply by *talking* about their beliefs, perceptions, interpretations and attitudes – regardless of how they *managed* their bodies.

We both continued to have this schizophrenic attitude towards the body-mind – seeing them as *united* (for purposes of stress management), but strongly believing them to be *separate* (for purposes of psychology and psychotherapy).

This schizophrenic approach fell apart in 2007, when Jim began to 'add back the body' to his psychological and psychotherapeutic understanding of human disturbance. (See the Holistic SOR model, in Byrne 2016; and the body-connection, in Chapter 3 of Byrne 2017).

This present book came about because we wanted to *consolidate* our understanding of the part that nutrition and exercise play in the well-being of our coaching and counselling clients, so that we can help them as much as possible; and also to inform a wider audience of a range of helpful research studies. Our overall aim is to put an end to the false assumption that the body and mind are *separate* entities, which can be treated in isolation from each other (by medicine, on the one hand, and by psychotherapy on the other).

Human beings are very complex; indeed the most complex entities in the known universe. But that does not mean we cannot hope to come to understand ourselves better than we currently do.

There are, for example, some identifiable factors which contribute to the makeup of human personality; and there is now a good deal of research which needs to be added to the psychological model of the human being. We can learn to better understand our body-brain-mind interactions with our social environments, and this can enable us to understand ourselves and our clients, and to help them, and ourselves, more effectively.

For example: we are affected (emotionally and physically) by our diets; the amount of exercise we do; our self-talk (or 'inner dialogue'); our sleep patterns; our family of origin; and all the patterns of behaviour we observed and experienced in our development; plus our current relationships, and environmental circumstances: e.g. our housing accommodation; the educational opportunities we had; our social class position; and our opportunities for employment (or earning a living).

These key factors - (each and every one of them) - have a part to play in the holistic model of coaching and counselling which we have created: (Byrne 2016). However, the importance of nutrition and exercise in the treatment of a person, (when they have physical and/or emotional problems), has not been fully acknowledged by the people who shape policy and provision in the psychiatric and medical communities in the UK and US, and elsewhere. And the problem is no less extreme in the world of counselling and psychotherapy. The medical model emphasizes the body (and brain chemicals, and drugs), while the counselling and psychotherapy community tend to emphasize the mind (or psyche, or soul).

The medical model dominates the world of psychology, almost totally. How do we know this? An indication is contained in a news item which was published in January this year, (2017), when a national tabloid newspaper in the UK informed the general public that in January 2017 the number of prescriptions for anti-depressant drugs in the UK had reached *61 million!* This suggested to us that the findings of recent research into the role of gut bacteria and food, in the causation of depression, just wasn't getting through to people.

And we also realized that the amazing results from research studies - about how exercise greatly reduces the likelihood of feelings of anxiety, anger and/or depression, when adversities strike – were also largely being ignored!

How could it be that Hippocrates knew about the importance of diet and exercise to health promotion and maintenance, and the link between mind, body and spirit, and yet today this information has been lost? According to the authors of *The China Study* – T. Colin Campbell and Thomas M. Campbell – the culprits are money, ego, power and control:

> *"While it is unfair to generalize about individual doctors, it is safe to say that the system they work in, the system that currently takes responsibility for promoting the health of Americans (and the situation is almost as bad in the UK – Eds), is failing us. No one knows this better than the tiny minority of doctors who treat their patients from a nutritional perspective"*. (Page 321 of Campbell and Campbell, 2006).

This present book is our attempt to rethink the balance of body-brain-mind-environment, by presenting some of the latest and most useful research findings in just two areas – nutrition and exercise - which we hope will help the reader to see how powerful these factors are. (We are planning a separate book on sleep).

It will also help them to see that they can, *if they so wish*, quickly improve the quality and level of happiness in their lives by taking on board the findings of the specialists whose invaluable work we have summarised in these pages.

For example, in a paper from 2007, Fernando Gomez-Pinilla has posited a model to account for the effect of diet and exercise on mental health, as follows:

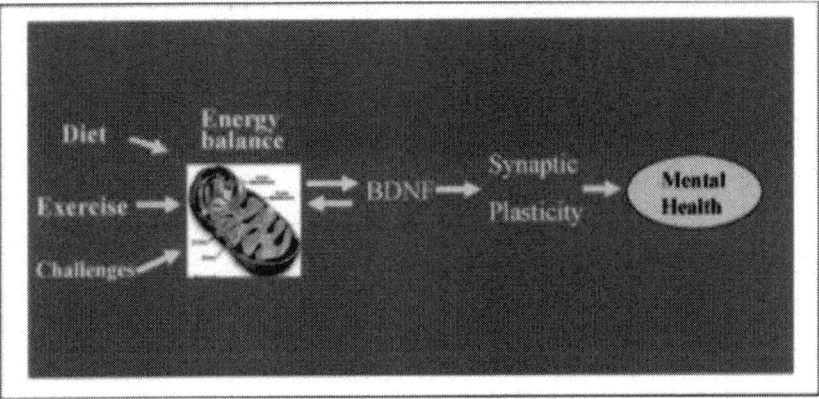

This is intended to illustrate a general mechanism by which diet, exercise, and other environmental challenges can affect mental health. It is postulated that "...control of cellular energy balance is a confluent point for the effects of environmental factors. Energy balance via interaction with BDNF[2], in conjunction with other factors, can modulate synaptic plasticity underlying cognitive processes". (Source: Gomez-Pinilla, 2007)[3].

In a nutshell, the quality of our diet, our level of physical exercise, and our general stress management approach, can and will impact the physical structures of the body-brain, altering the mind, mood control, emotion expression, and so on.

~~~

There are six parts to this book: The first part deals with diet and nutrition and how they influence anxiety, anger and depression.

The second part of the book deals with physical exercise and how it can affect these common emotional problems.

The third part is a description of a 'stress and anxiety reduction' diet and offers guidelines for understanding different types of diets and their effects.

The fourth part shows some of the key findings from the science of nutritional deficiency, and the role of inflammation in the creation of depression.

The fifth part is a summing up of the key findings of the book, so that you can spot the most useful material that you can use for yourself - or for your clients, if you are a health-care or psychotherapeutic practitioner, counsellor or psychologist.

And the sixth part is our attempt to coach you through the process of habit change; and to give you a map to guide you through the process of accessing, learning and applying the transformative information in this book.

It is one thing to read and understand this book, but it is quite another thing to bring about behaviour change in relation to your diet and exercise approaches; and part six will hopefully help you to bridge that gap between *understanding* and *doing*!

We hope you enjoy the journey through this learning experience.

Whether you are a professional practitioner, looking for help for your own clients; a self-help enthusiast, wanting to improve your own physical and mental health; or a student of any discipline related to helping and caring for others, there is something special for you in this book.

~~~

Renata Taylor-Byrne, Hebden Bridge, November 2017

~~~

Foreword

By Dr Jim Byrne

> *"Total health is the positive and vibrant state of physical, emotional, psychological and spiritual health that emerges from within when all major barriers to healing are overcome".*
>
> *Dr Mark Atkinson*[4]

~~~

Anger, anxiety and depression

Because this book is about how to control your anger, anxiety and depression, we must begin by understanding those phenomena. For Aristotle, in ancient Greece, body and mind were one thing: the body was seen as the 'substance' and the mind (or soul) was seen as the 'form' that it takes in the world. Thus a mind (or soul) should be expected to be a true expression of the state of the body, and its journey of experience through life. And this was certainly the view taken by Hippocrates.

But then, in 1639, Rene Descartes ripped the body and mind apart, and tried to suggest that they were connected through the pineal gland. Of course, the body-mind of every individual since 1639 continued to be *united*, like the form and content of a flowing stream; but the world now lived *in ignorance* of the connection; and treated the human body as one 'thing' (to be healed by various forms of medicine), and the soul (or mind) as another 'thing', to be healed by spiritual ministrations, religious rites, or, in the twentieth century, by counselling and psychotherapy – and, of course, by 'miracle drugs'.

Sigmund Freud was the first major theorist of the modern view of the 'mind' and emotions. Although he was originally trained as a neurologist, and his theory of personality development is based on the evolution of the individual body over time, he did not link this to how well that body is fed, rested or exercised. Fritz Perls, who created Gestalt Therapy, was aware of the way emotions were anchored in the body, but again, he failed to link this insight to diet, exercise, sleep, and so on. By the time Carl Rogers, Albert Ellis and Aaron Beck came along, the 'mind' had become completely detached from the body, in most of the major forms of counselling and psychotherapy: (See: Woolfe, Dryden and Strawbridge, 2003; McLeod, 2003; and Corey, 2001).

In 2016, we produced a new model of the human body-brain-mind-environment complexity. (See Byrne, 2016). It's called the Holistic SOR model, and this is how it looks:

The Holistic Stimulus-Organism-Response Model (H-SOR)		
Column 1	Column 2	Column 3
S = Stimulus	O = Organism	R = Response
When something significant happens, which is apprehended by the organism's (or person's) nervous system, the organism is activated or aroused (positively or negatively)	The organism responds, well or badly. The incoming stimulus may activate or interact with: (1) Innate needs and tendencies; (2) Family history and attachment style; (3) Recent personal history; (4) Emotive-cognitive schemas (as guides to action); (5) Narratives, stories, frames and other storied elements (which may be hyper-activating, hypo-activating, or affect regulating); (6) Character and temperament; (7) Need satisfaction; goals and values; (8) Diet and supplementation, medication, exercise regime, sleep and relaxation histories; (9) Ongoing environmental stressors, state of current relationship(s), and satisfaction with life stages, etc., etc.	The organism outputs a response, in the form of visible behaviour and inferable emotional reactions, like anger, anxiety, depression, embarrassment, etc.

You will see from the central column that a person may become angry, anxious or depressed for a wide variety of reasons, when the 'incoming stimulus' (or experience) in Column 1 interacts with any and all the elements of Column 2, which include diet, exercise, sleep, family history, ongoing environmental stressors, and so on.

Anger, anxiety and depression are based upon innate, inborn, 'affects', which have been 'selected' by nature to ensure our survival. Anger (properly controlled) protects us from oppressions of various kinds. Anxiety (properly controlled) keeps us 'on our toes' in terms of potential threats and dangers. And sadness/grief helps us to come to terms with losses and failures (but can turn into 'stuck depression' if we fail to *process* those losses and failures).

The content of Column 2 above is too complex to teach in one volume. (We know, because we tried to teach it all in Byrne, 2016!) So, therefore, in this volume, we are going to restrict our teaching to the role of diet and exercise in emotional problems.

One of the oversights in Column 2 is this: A person may present with anxiety or depression in a counselling context, and the cause may be largely (or to some significant degree) a result of an undiagnosed medical condition, like an autoimmune disease (like Celiac disease, or multiple sclerosis – [Personal communication from Julia Duffin]. And also see Footnote 10). So, as a general principle, every counsellor and psychotherapist should make sure their clients have been checked out for physical diseases before they conclude that the problem is purely psychological; or simply linked to diet, exercise and so on.

Poverty and mental illness

It would be so easy, and so wrong, to imply in this foreword that the dynamic relationships between diet and physical exercise, on the one hand, and both mental health and emotional wellbeing, on the other, can be addressed as a *technical problem*, related to *understanding* the scientific information available on this subject, and nothing else.

There is, after all, no longer any doubt that people who eat an unhealthy diet, and fail to get enough physical exercise, are in serious danger of developing not just physical diseases, but also mental health problems, and problems of emotional distress.

In his foreword to a recent book – by Dr Leslie Korn - on nutrition essentials for mental health, Dr James Lake wrote this:

> *"In the face of widespread and often inappropriate prescribing of powerful psychotropic medications, accumulating research evidence supports the use of a range of non-pharmacological approaches for the prevention and treatment of depressed mood, anxiety, dementia, substance abuse, and other common mental health problems. Diet, exercise, and stress management fall under the broad heading of 'lifestyle' changes and, among these, diet is certainly the most important."* (Page xi of Korn, 2016)[5].

What Dr Lake fails to say is this: We now know that drugs for depression and anxiety are no better than placebos; and that changes of diet offer a much better chance of helping a counselling or therapy client to regain positive mood and buoyant emotions. We know this because of the work of Dr Abram Hoffer, a Canadian psychiatrist who was one of the first to draw attention to the ways in which nutrient deficiencies make us emotionally unwell and potentially psychotic[6]. (See also Part 4 of this book, below, which looks at the most recent research on the link between nutrition and mental health, or emotional wellbeing).

Diet and stress affect the central nervous system via the guts, and via the bacteria that live and work in our guts (the 'microbiota')[7]: (Enders, 2015, page 3). Diet and exercise protocols can be used to reduce and control stress, and to improve the health of the microbiota, which directly affects mood and emotions: like anxiety, depression and rageful anger.

But because much of our modern food is low in nutritional content, and because very few people know what they would need to eat, on a daily basis, to achieve a 'balanced diet', Korn and Lake advocate the use of high-potency nutritional supplements; but also foods high in the B vitamins, which includes leafy green vegetables, and whole grains (like brown rice; plus amaranth, quinoa, buckwheat [which is not related to wheat!], teff, etc.) Beware of gluten which can cause inflammation, and a leaky gut, which negatively affects mental health! And avoid the use of oats because they contain avenin, which could (theoretically, at this stage!) cause neurological reactions (in at least some people), even if they do not affect your guts.

(Oats can cause allergic reactions, a whole range of them, including skin allergies; and thus we have to wonder if they can cause brain allergies [and mood problems] too?)

The full list of recommended gluten-free wholegrains is this: amaranth, millet, teff, buckwheat and quinoa.

We recommend that you avoid wheat, rye, oats and barley, in order to avoid gluten. (Even though it is possible to get *gluten-free oats* [which have not been cross-contaminated by wheat or rye], it is **not** possible to get avenin-free oats; and avenin "...has the same properties as gluten (it is the 'prolamine storage protein' of oat seeds, that helps protect the dormant seed and nourish it when it begins to grow)". (Source: Celiac.com. This article assumes that avenin is safe to consume, because it does not cause "histological (or cellular) gut damage".)[8]. But we now know that there are forms of gluten sensitivity that do not damage the guts, but do damage the brain. And we should be careful about avenin since this possibility has not been tested for (as far as we can tell at this stage); and certainly not eliminated.

Wholegrain rice is (probably) okay (for most people), in small portions: never more than a quarter of your dinner plate. (But you must test to see how you respond to eating it). See also the Mayo clinic's recommendations (Footnote 33 below).

Dr Michael Greger has challenged the idea that grains cause inflammation, and supported it to some extent, but he has, in the process, thrown the baby out with the bathwater, by refusing to take seriously the problem of gluten-induced leaky gut syndrome. Because this is such an important point, we have posted a footnote to consider the issues involved[9]. The bottom line is this: At least 26% of us are at risk of neurological damage and emotional distress from ingesting gluten: (Hadjivassiliou, 1996); and we don't know which 26%. (And it could be higher than 26%).

There is also research to support the idea that people who have a physical illness, specifically an autoimmune disease – like celiac disease, or MS, and twenty-eight others, are significantly more likely to present with problems of anxiety and depression[10].

~~~

Dr Lake ends by saying: "*Optimal nutrition and the strategic uses of supplements should be included as a necessary and central component of integrative treatment addressing depressed mood, anxiety, bipolar disorder, substance abuse, attention-deficit/ hyperactivity disorder, schizophrenia, cognitive decline, and dementia...*" (**Pages xiii-xiv**).

This approach is very much in line with the emerging field of *nutritional mental health* approaches, which use improved diet and nutritional supplements to reduce inflammation, and to eliminate symptoms of depression and anxiety[11].

The Enlightenment philosopher, Rene Descartes, was wrong to argue that body and mind are separate, and 'connected' via the pineal gland. Much modern scientific research, dating back to the 1970's, suggests that the body-brain-mind is a constant conversation, via biochemical substances called neuropeptides, and "...these neuropeptides are produced not only in response to emotions but also to the food we eat, the way we breathe, and even the way we move and hold our body". (Atkinson 2007, page 17).

And these neuropeptides carry signals from the guts to the brain-mind to determine mood, emotions and behaviours. Some elements of these ideas date back to ancient Greece, and probably beyond, into ancient India and China.

Modelling the body-brain-mind-environment interaction

In the Preface above, Renata Taylor-Byrne presented a little model by Fernando Gomez-Pinilla (2007), to account for the effect of diet and exercise on mental health. However, a similar kind of understanding actually dates back to ancient Greece, to 480 BCE, in the medical perspective of Hippocrates. As presented by Simopoulos (2004), Hippocrates believed that: "Positive health requires a knowledge of (man and woman's) primary constitution (which today we call genetics) and of the powers of various foods... But eating alone is not enough for health. There must also be exercise, of which the effects must likewise be known..." (From the Declaration of Olympia on Nutrition and Fitness, Ancient Olympia, Greece, May 28-29, 1996, reproduced in Simopoulos [2004], Page XXV).

According to Simopoulos, "The Concept of Positive Health may be represented by a triangle involving genetics, nutrition and physical activity that influence the spiritual, mental and physical aspects of health. (Fig 1):

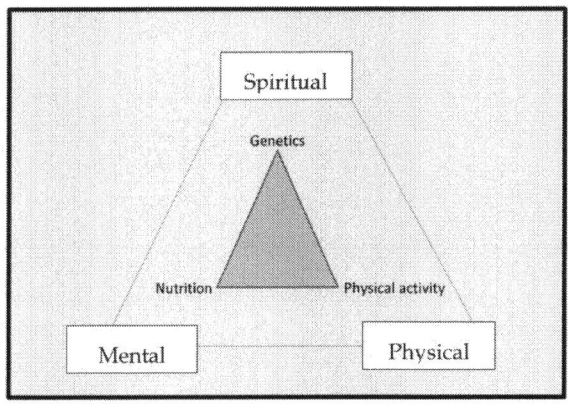

Who can afford to live well?

However, there is a serious problem with making use of this information. As I said in opening this foreword, it would be wrong to overlook the fact that a healthy diet and adequate supplementation involves considerable cost. And this is a big issue in the 'highly successful' capitalist economies of the UK and the USA at the moment, because substantial sections of our populations are unable to afford a decent standard of living, including adequate amounts of nourishing foods.

For example: *"One in eight workers (in the UK) are skipping meals to make ends meet because their wages have lagged behind inflation for a decade, the Trades Union Congress (TUC) claims"*. (From *'The I'* newspaper, Page 8, Thurs 7th September 2017).[12]

Furthermore, *"Almost half (of employed workers) are worried about affording basic expenses such as **food**, transport and energy..."*.

And, quite clearly, the problem of poverty-driven ill-health is much worse among the unemployed, the sick, the pensioners, and the disabled.

So, almost half of the working population in the UK is unable to afford the kind of diet and supplementation regime we will be recommending in this book. This is a scandal, which arose to a significant degree because of the promotion of neoliberal economic policies (or 'monetarism') by the Thatcher and Reagan governments in the 1980's, which produced greater inequality, the deregulation of markets, and the marginalization of working class power bases like the trades union movement; and these developments caused wages to stagnate and profits and managerial bonuses to soar.

Diet and supplementation are strongly affected by the ability to buy the right kinds of goods and services. And the ability to buy those goods and services are clearly dependent upon the ability to earn a living wage (and to defend a living pension beyond that point). And the ability to earn a living wage (and defend your pension, in real terms) clearly depends upon having an independent powerbase for working class people to negotiate with their employers and with the government.

The downward spiral in mental health on both sides of the Atlantic, and elsewhere, is clearly linked to, and affected by, the neoliberal economic policies pursued by British and American governments. (James (2007) and Pickett and Wilkinson (2010).) And this book – our present book - cannot directly affect those policies.

Unless and until we get governments on both sides of the Atlantic who promote greater equality, and viable living standards, we cannot look forward to any significant improvements in mental health across all social classes.

~~~

Multiple causes of emotional distress and mental health problems

It is also important to recognize that there are *several* obvious causes of emotional disturbance and mental health problems. Anger, anxiety and depression do not just result from poor diet and lack of physical exercise. The main causes seem to include:

1. Stress and trauma: (some of which comes from social policy and class stratification; insecure employment, and low wages)

2. Suboptimal diet: (suggested by nutritional epidemiology studies)

3. Sedentary behaviour: (little or no exercise!)

4. Obesity: (which is 'an inflammatory state')

5. Gut health! (Which can benefit from both nutrients and friendly bacteria, like lactobacillus supplements)

6. And perhaps other sources... (Such as family of origin problems; sleep problems; etc.)

Although improved diet and adequate exercise can have an effect upon stress levels, this is unrealistic in relation to psychological trauma[13]. Psychological trauma from past relationships can only realistically, or effectively, be tackled by talk therapy, especially therapies like Affect Regulation therapy and Attachment therapy, and more modern forms of psychoanalysis. So we are not talking about *replacing* talk therapies with dietary and exercise approaches, but rather of *adding* diet and exercise interventions to the toolkit of counsellors, psychotherapists and counselling psychologists.

When a client comes to see me, I recognize that different pathways may emerge:

1. It may be that talk therapy, like CBT and TA and Person-centred counselling - which mainly involves left-brain to left-brain communication, using language and concepts, about current realities – will prove to be sufficient.

2. Or, it may be that this kind of talk therapy will be *necessary*, but not *sufficient*. In some cases it will be the non-verbal, emotional, right-brain to right-brain communication that helps to build a potent relationship with the client, and help them to develop a secure attachment style, and to learn how to regulate their emotions (or 'affects') more successfully.

3. Or, it may be that those two processes – the left-brain and the right-brain communications – may be *necessary*, but not *sufficient*. In many cases, I may also have to review the client's approach to diet and nutrition; and/or their level of physical fitness, related to exercise and sedentary activity. Or some other aspects of their lifestyle.

~~~

But why, you might wonder, have you never heard of this before? According to Dr Giulia Enders (2015), this understanding of the link between the guts, on the one hand, and the brain-mind-emotions on the other, is *a brand new, but rapidly growing field of scientific research*[14]. And there is also some exciting new research on the subject of the impact of physical exercise upon the body-brain-mind and emotions.

~~~

Political integrity and social policy

Politics is also part of the current problem. Assuming we get decent governments in the UK and the US, in the next few years, and incomes increase, there is still the problem that junk food has been promoted as *desirable* through the 'black magic' of food technologists, backed up by huge marketing budgets, which have not been adequately supervised by democratic governments. And junk food also aims to outsell healthy food by 'selling on price': so it appeals more to those with limited budgets.

What hope is there that an ill-informed individual, with limited financial resources, will walk past a cheap burger bar, or low-cost chicken joint - where they can get a 'light meal' for between GBP £1.00 and £2.00 (or $1.50 to $3.00 US) - and on into the market area, where they can buy salad vegetables to take home, chop up, and eat raw; or vegetables and fruit to cook? (The 'devil', it seems, has all the best tunes, and all the best 'mouth-feel' effects - at the moment!)

Again, we need government intervention in this area. Food 'technologists' (or food *polluters* and *degraders*, to give them a more accurate, descriptive label) must be named and shamed. Government campaigns against junk food, and pre-packaged, *processed* foods, and in favour of healthy diets, must be initiated and promoted vigorously, if the physical and mental health of our nations are to be improved.

~~~

Getting the message out there

Then there is the problem of promoting public awareness through non-governmental channels. According to Brian Tracy, an American business coach, 80% of all the best books are bought by 20% of the population, and therefore, most of the people who *need* to read this book will never buy it. Consequently, we have to hope that it will be bought by opinion-shapers in the worlds of health promotion, politics, and the counselling psychology profession.

Counsellors and psychotherapists should take particular note of the fact that their clients can have *apparent* psychological problems - including anger, anxiety and depression - which are actually coming from a disrupted 'microbiome' (such as some form of *disbiosis* [or from too much caffeine, alcohol and or sugar!]) and not from psychological stress as such. Or, rather:

(1) Sometimes the problems will be coming from the client's environmental stressors,

(2) Sometimes from the client's (learned) inability to manage their affects (or emotions), and

(3) Sometimes from the client's guts, as a result of poor diet and inadequate supplementation. Or from sedentary lifestyle, causing a build-up of lymph in the system; a build-up of stress hormones which are not being removed by physical activity; and a lack of release of endorphins, which depend upon physical activity.

In this book, counsellors, lifestyle coaches, health coaches and others will find a good grounding in the theoretical understanding of the links between the body-brain-mind-environment in terms of diet, exercise and supplementation; and the specific links to problems of anger, anxiety and depression; plus guidelines on how to help individuals with those problems of anger, anxiety and depression, using specific dietary and exercise guidelines.

Some will be surprised to learn that about eighty percent of the serotonin in our bodies is manufactured in our guts; that our guts are in constant communication with our brains; and that research shows that much (though not all) emotional distress and mental health problems originate in the guts.

We need to develop a holistic approach to helping people to feel better by promoting better physical health.

And physical health can also be improved by talk therapy for emotional problems. It's very much a two-way street! We hope you enjoy exploring it.

~~~

Dr Jim Byrne, Hebden Bridge, October 2017

~~~

Part 1: Diet, nutrition and the implications for anger, anxiety and depression management

By Renata Taylor-Byrne

> *"Unfortunately, in my experience, most people do not have a clue about how their physical health affects their cognitive and mental health".*
>
> Dr Daniel Amen[15]

~~~

1. Introduction

What we eat has a very powerful effect on our bodies and minds. And knowing and understanding how our body-mind *reacts* to the substances we feed ourselves is a crucial part of self-care.

For instance: depression can be caused by psychological reactions to losses and failures. But it can also be caused by certain kinds of body-brain chemistry problems, some of which can begin in the guts, and be related to bad diet, and lack of physical exercise. For example:

> "If you are depressed while you suffer from regular yeast infections (like Candida Albicans), or athlete's foot, or have taken antibiotics recently, there is a connection. Our brains are inextricably tied to our gastrointestinal tract and our mental well-being is dependent on healthy intestines. Depression, bipolar disorder, anxiety, and a host of other mental illnesses from autism to ADHD can be caused by an imbalance of gut microbes like fungi, and 'bad' bacteria".
>
> (Source: Michael Edwards (2014))[16].

And when we take antibiotics, we kill off all of our friendly bacteria, and often what grows back first is the unfriendly stuff, like Candida Albicans, which can then cause depression, anxiety and other symptoms, as listed above.

Also, we can really benefit from knowing some of the latest ideas about where - (in our diets) - our depression, anxiety and anger can originate from; as provided by specialists who have devoted their lives to years of investigation into the workings of the human body and mind (or body-mind).

Firstly, then, in these pages, I will be defining nutrition, and what the constituents of a balanced diet are (in so far as that is possible), based on research evidence.

Secondly, the views of health professionals, including medical doctors, neuroscientists, psychiatrists and nutrition researchers will be reviewed, in relation to the effects of the following substances on the body-brain-mind: transfats; sugar; alcohol; caffeine; processed food (and junk food); and gluten.

Thirdly, I will look at the question: Do we need supplements? The reasons for their usage will be considered; and arguments, from a few experts, will be presented, showing that it's not possible to gain all the nutrition we need from our food (under modern conditions of food production).

Fourthly, I will look at the problematical experience and/ or expression of anxiety, anger and/or depression, and these emotional states (of over-arousal [as in anger and anxiety] and under-arousal [as in depression]) will be defined.

The ways in which our diets can precipitate and/or worsen our experiences of these exaggerated emotions, according to some of the latest research, will be examined.

Finally, which diet is best for physical and mental well-being?

And which lifestyle practices complement and enhance the value of a healthy diet? Some of the research findings, which answer these questions, will be reviewed; and the key ideas of doctors, and other specialists - who know the interconnectedness of our dietary and lifestyle practices, on the one hand, and our physical and emotional states, on the other - will be summarised.

~~~

> *"If you don't think your anxiety, depression, sadness and stress impact your physical health, think again. All of these emotions trigger chemical reactions in your body, which can lead to inflammation and a weakened immune system"*
>
> Kris Carr[17]
>
> The reverse is also true. As argued by Dr Kelly Brogan and many other theorists: *Our bodily health affects our moods and emotions.* [18], [19], [20].

2. Why is nutrition important to the body-brain-mind?

Before we get to the link between nutrition and the health of the body and emotional well-being, we must lay some groundwork.

Firstly, what is nutrition?

According to the Oxford English Dictionary (2012)[21] it is the process of taking in and absorbing nutrients. Nutrients are those substances which are essential for life and growth. These nutrients are used by the body to maintain the growth, upkeep and reproduction of the cells.

Nutrition is very important for the body because without the energy we get from food we would not be able to move our bodies, or take part in any work activities, search for food or communicate with other people. And we would quickly die, because we are not a result of our acts of will.

We are physical-social-animals, who are guided by innate emotions; who learn refined emotions from our family and schooling. We are body-mind-environment wholes, and we cannot think or feel independently of the use of brain food (like glucose, and essential fatty acids: [Footnote 214 below]), which comes from our diet; (plus oxygen which is optimized by our physical activity which promotes deep breathing).

Our full physical and mental development is dependent on the food that we eat. Without sufficient food we would not grow, our bodies would be stunted and our physical organs would be undeveloped; and the development of our brain would be irrevocably harmed.

We need high quality nutrition so that the body can repair itself, wounds can heal and cells can repair themselves as necessary. Our immune system needs a supply of high quality nutrients to keep it strong. In this way, viruses, infections and diseases can be kept out of the body.

There are many processes going on in the body and they need energy to work properly. Let's look at the example of the digestive system. Brewer (2013)[22] cites the amount of energy used up by the body when it is digesting food, which is 10% of the total energy gained from a meal. And our brains can use up to 40% of our consumed energy.

Nutrition is therefore crucial for the human body and brain. Without it, we could not survive or function in the world.

3. What would a *balanced diet* look like?

(And how do we know we are getting enough protein[23], carbohydrate[24], fats[25], and vitamins[26] & minerals[27]? [See Footnotes 23 to 27 for definitions]).

There are lots of different diets around today, recommended for physical health, weight loss, weight gain, lower cholesterol, and so on. And increasingly, attention is turning to the link between diet and mood.

There is no universal agreement about the precise kind of diet which will promote good physical health and/ or stable moods and emotions; though elements of potentially 'good practice' and 'bad' practices are beginning to emerge.

It would be impossible to list, and discuss, in a book of this scale, all of the diets which are represented in the popular bookshops today. However, there are some important diets that we must at least touch upon in this book.

So let us look at some of the most important types of diets; and then some general dietary guidelines which we have evolved:

(a) Types of diet

The UK National Food Guide: This is the 'official diet' of the UK, produced by the Food Standards Agency (FSA) in 2001. It is similar in essence to the US Food Guide pyramid. Governments around the world are in the habit of promulgating recommended diets for their citizens. However it is important to bear in mind that all governments are subjected to intense pressure by lobby groups. So let us critically review the UK national diet guidelines. (See Chapter 3 of Barasi, 2003).

The UK National Food Guide (UK NFG) is represented by a dinner plate, divided into sections, as follows:

Bread, other cereals and potatoes = 33%

Fruit and vegetables = 33%

And the final one-third (or approximately 34 percent) is divided up into three sub-groups, like this:

Meat, fish and alternatives = 12%

Milk and dairy foods = 15%

Fatty and sugary foods = 7%

Thinking about using those guidelines ourselves, we would want to adjust them as follows (as a provisional, and preliminary, and potential guide to action):

Vegetables (mainly) with some fruit =	40%
(Wholegrain) Bread, other (wholegrain) cereals and (sweet) potatoes =	20%
Nuts, seeds, beans, organic eggs, wild Alaskan salmon, sardines, and (very occasional) meat (like a weekly lamb steak; or twice or three times weekly if grass-fed) =	25%
Milk and dairy foods (or oat or nut or rice alternatives) =	10%
Sugary foods =	5%

> Avoid all transfats, and processed oils, and margarine. Minimal use of butter. Avoid all sugar and products with added sugar.
>
> Avoid 'fish and chips' (because of the transfats and acrylamides), crisps, sweets, cakes, biscuits, processed foods (in packets, jars and cans, from supermarkets, etc.) Avoid white sliced bread, and soft sliced bread, even if it has been dyed to look somewhat brown. Buy wholegrain breads from artisan bakers (if you can tolerate grains at all!), rather than highly processed breads. Avoid or minimize alcohol and caffeine, sugary drinks, diet sodas and pops, and processed foods of all kinds.

The different emphases between our (personal) selection and proportions, on the one hand, and those of the UK NFG, on the other, reflects our researches on the subject over a number of years, and the fact that we cannot be lobbied by commercial interests! However, our ideas come from the books we've studied, and the theorists by whom we have been influenced. And the rule – that there is no **universal** agreement about diet and nutrition – applies just as much to *our ideas* as to the ideas of anybody else!

Our ideas also come from our own experiments, in trying different combinations of food, or different diets, and monitoring the effects upon our skin, mood and energy levels. And recently, one of us has had to give up *virtually* all grains – with the exception of two or three gluten free pies each week – because he (Jim) was suffering bad skin allergies and linked mood problems.

So you have to make your own mind up, by research and experimentation, and with professional support from your medical advisor/ GP/ alternative practitioner (although, it seems from *some* [anecdotal] reports that *at least some* GPs will not advise you on diet unless you ask – as they prefer to prescribe 'high-tech solutions' [like drugs] to their patient's problems).

You need to find out: *What works for you? What keeps you healthy? What causes reactions, in terms of energy or mood, or skin allergies, or digestive distress?*

And you need to face up to the fact that 'pills' cannot cure diseases which are caused by lifestyle 'sins', like eating junk foods and avoiding physical activity.

You might find some of the ideas in the following diets useful, interesting or helpful. From these, and other ideas in this book, you should try to craft your own *personalized diet* (which is discussed at the end of the section).

~~~

The Anti-Candida diet: Candida overgrowth in the large intestine has been linked to symptoms of depression and anxiety. The main components of this kind of diet involves the exclusion of sugary and yeasty foods. Junk foods and all forms of processed food should also be eliminated. Avoid bread and cheese, and all forms of fermented foods, including vinegar, beer, mushrooms. Also avoid foods which are loaded with antibiotics, like pig meats, factory-farmed chicken, non-organic eggs, and some others. Low carbohydrate foods are favoured, plus complex carbohydrates (like fresh vegetables, or gluten-free wholegrains); so using some elements of the Atkins or Paleo diets (below), *for a period of some weeks*, may often be indicated. But check with a qualified and recommended nutritional therapist, and avoid long-term use in case you suffer from nutritional deficiencies.

~~~

The Atkins diet: This diet is a high-protein, high-fat, and very low-carbohydrate approach. It emphasizes meat, cheese, and eggs, butter, oil, poultry, fish, and cream. (The best fish to eat are herring, mackerel, wild salmon or fresh sardines, two or three times each week [Holford, 2010]). The daily amount of complex carbohydrates allowed equals about three cups of salad vegetables, such as lettuce, cucumber, and/or celery. The Atkins diet discourages foods such as bread, pasta, fruit, and sugar. It is a form of Ketogenic (or 'fat-burning') diet. There seems to be a positive effect upon mood and emotions, as we will see later: but this may come from the elimination of junk foods, processed foods, and sugary foods in general. And, we have to warn you, the authors of the China Study warn against eating animal-based foods: "*People who ate the most animal-based foods got the most chronic disease. People who ate the most plant-based foods were the healthiest*". Campbell and Campbell (2006).

And Dr Michael Greger (2016) would support this China Study conclusion, on the basis of his argument that eating a high meat and (non-organic) eggs diet will put too much *arachidonic acid* – which is a form of omega-6 fatty acid - into your system, causing inflammation, which is linked to depression, and most likely to other emotional and physical health problems. But you probably should eat some eggs, preferably free-range and organic. (Do not go for 'omega-3 fortified' eggs, as they cost as much as organic! And the type of omega-3 in fortified eggs is probably ALA instead of EPA or DHA, which occur naturally in the eggs of grass fed [organic] chicken)[28]. (Also, organic eggs do *not* contain antibiotics. This is important because antibiotics kill off your friendly bacteria, and potentially allow unfriendly bacteria, like Candida Albicans, to take over your guts, triggering depression and anxiety, as well as skin allergies, and other problems).

~~~

The 'FodMaps' diet: Most people are aware that sugars occur naturally in fruits, and that too much fruit can be bad for your blood-glucose level, triggering problems that could promote diabetes, plus fluctuating moods (as in manic depression). And sugar can also increase stress levels. But most people are probably unaware that many *vegetables* contain high levels of various kinds of sugars, which have been shown to be implicated in the causation of irritable bowel syndrome (IBS). This is where the 'FodMaps' diet can be helpful. FODMAP is the rather clumsy acronym for Fermentable Oligosaccharides, Disaccharides, Monosaccharides, and Polyols, which can be found in a range of vegetables. You can find lists of foods to exclude on a low-FodMaps diet in specialist books and on Internet blogs. Those kinds of low-FodMap diets have now been shown, scientifically[29], to control IBS symptoms, and some people have found them helpful for controlling Candida Albicans (which thrives on sugars of all kinds) - and of course, there is a link from Candida to depression, and so the low-FodMap diet can help to reduce and/or eliminate depression by reducing sugars and inflammation.

But make sure you get most of your nutrients (70% or more) from vegetables (40+%) and wholegrains (20% - if you can tolerate them); and try to get some nutritional expertise to support you, to avoid nutritional deficiencies. (One of us [Jim] has found he can no longer tolerate grains, because they cause him to have very sore and painful allergic reactions; and there is now evidence that allergic skin reactions can precipitate emotional/psychological problems; or rather, that the allergen provokes both skin reactions and mood reactions [See King, 1981]).

~~~

The Hay diet: This diet was developed by Dr William Howard Hay, beginning in 1904, as a way to cure himself from 'Bright's Disease' (which included high blood pressure, kidney disease, and a dilated heart), at a time when he had been told he would die from his condition. He saved his own life (and lost 50 pounds in weight, in just three months) by exploring the idea that some foods fight with other foods, and thus slow down the digestive process, allowing toxic waste products to linger much longer in the colon[30]. For example, he would argue that, if it takes a slice of bread X hours to travel from mouth to anus, and it takes a lamb chop 2X hours to make the same journey, then combining the bread and lamb will take 8X hours, or more. (In actuality: *"Gut transit time is only 36 hours for vegetarians compared with 72 hours for meat eaters"*. [Collings, 1993: page 29]. But Grant and Joice, 1984, would argue that those times could be significantly reduced by changing some of the food combinations eaten by both vegetarians and meat eaters!)

More generally, according to the Hay diet, if we combine starches and proteins in the same meal, then we slow down the digestive system to dangerous levels. Dr Hay's idea was that rapid elimination of waste products from the digestive system leads to a healthy body, while slow and sluggish elimination leads to ill health. There is no scientific evidence that this diet works, but there is anecdotal evidence. The authors of this present book have both used the Hay Diet, on and off, to varying degrees, for decades, and found it helpful in promoting efficient digestion.

(Efficient digestion is also taken up by Enders 2015. Dr Enders emphasizes chewing each mouthful of food at least 50 times, and using a squat toilet [or simulating a squat toilet], to promote efficient 'in and out' processes! To simulate a squat toilet, if you do not have one, simply put a foot stool, of say 6-9 inches in height, in front of your toilet; sit on the seat, and place your feet on the stool. It certainly accelerates the process!)

One website blog suggests that the Hay diet may be able to help with "*depression, schizophrenic and aggressive behaviours*"[31]. However, like the other diets in this book, you should not engage with this diet without the support of a qualified nutritionist, as nutritional deficiencies and insufficiencies may result from uninformed or ill-informed changes.

Because you can eat almost anything (apart from peanuts and margarine – and junk foods) on the Hay diet, so long as you combine them properly, there is less concern about the possibility of nutritional deficiencies.

~~~

Mediterranean diet: This diet, or versions of this diet, are eaten in many Mediterranean countries (such as Spain and Italy and parts of Greece) – and followers of the Mediterranean lifestyle also emphasize the importance of appropriate levels of physical exercise, and family mealtimes. According to some authors, the Mediterranean diet consists mainly of cereals, grains, vegetables, beans, fruits, and nuts, combined with moderate amounts of fish, cheese, olive oil; plus wine and a small amount of red meat (grass fed!) So it seems, on this basis, to be a high carbohydrate, low protein diet. However, we were unhappy with the looseness of this definition, and so we searched further, and found this: *"The Mediterranean diet is **a way of eating** rather than a formal diet plan. It features foods eaten in Greece, Spain, southern Italy and France, and other countries that border the Mediterranean Sea"*: (WebMD, 2017).

There are some studies which suggest that the Mediterranean diet can be helpful in managing moods and emotions, and especially in eliminating or preventing depression: (for example, Rahe, Unrath, and Berger, 2014).

The WebMD blog goes on to list typical components of the Mediterranean diet, as follows: "*The Mediterranean diet emphasizes eating foods like fish, fruits, vegetables, beans, high-fibre breads and whole grains, nuts, and olive oil. Meat, cheese, and sweets are very limited. The recommended foods are rich with monounsaturated fats, fibre, and omega-3 fatty acids.*"

The proportions are not mentioned, but it is precisely the proportions which matter here. Too much bread and whole grains, and not enough fish, and depression is the result! Similarly with too much meat and cheese, and not enough vegetables and fruits.

Omega-3 and omega-6 (unsaturated) fatty acids are essential for physical and mental health, and have to be obtained from our diet. The omega-6s are *more than adequately represented* in most modern diets. The omega-3s can be obtained from eating oily fish

– like salmon, mackerel, sardines, and also from nuts and seeds. (The best seeds are flax, hemp, pumpkin, sunflower and sesame [Holford, 2010]). And/or you can supplement omega-3 from krill oil or cod liver oil. (See footnotes 25, 45, 65, 104, 174, and 214).

The evidence for the efficacy of omega-3 fatty acids in combatting heart disease, cancer and other physical diseases is patchy and conflictual (according to Greger, 2016; Campbell and Campbell, 2006); but the research evidence for the human need for omega-3 for brain health, and for mood and emotion regulation, is much more robust (Greger, 2016; Barasi, 2003; Perlmutter, 2015; Holford, 2010; Logan, 2004; Ross, 2003 [See quote in footnote][32]; Kiecolt-Glaser et al, 2011; Simopoulos, 2002; Schoenthaler, 1983a, 1983b; and Gesch et al, 2002). So make sure you get a good daily intake of omega-3 fatty acids, from food or supplements, or preferably both; and make sure you get more omega-3 than omega-6, by eating lots of oily fish, and minimizing your grain-fed meat consumption.

We recommend that you avoid grains that contain gluten. See the Mayo Clinic blog on alternative whole grains[33].

The Mediterranean diet is a good basis for beginning to develop your own personalized diet. But we will show later that the Nordic diet might have more to recommend it, because it contains more fish. (See Brewer, 2013, on the role of fish in preventing and/ or curing depression).

~~~

Metabolic typing diet: We discovered the 'metabolic typing' diet from Dr Mark Atkinson, in his book titled *The Mind Body Bible*, (2008). Dr Atkinson writes:

> *"Metabolic typing is an accurate and precise way of creating a customised diet and nutritional programme. Rather than guessing which foods are best for you, it uses a questionnaire to identify your particular metabolic type: carb-type, mixed-type or protein-type. Each 'type' reflects a dominant pattern of metabolic processing, which in turn determines how food is dealt with by the body..."* (Page 50).

If you go to the website of the author of the leading book on the metabolic typing diet, William L. Wolcott, you will find this description:

> *"When you identify your metabolic type and fine-tune your diet, you'll learn two primary things:*
>
> *"1) exactly what foods are compatible with your body chemistry*
>
> *"2) how to combine proteins, carbohydrates and fats in a ratio that is just right for you*
>
> *"In The Metabolic Typing Diet you'll find very comprehensive lists of foods that are compatible with your metabolic type - including specific types of meat, poultry, fish, dairy products, grains, legumes, vegetables, fruits and nuts."*[34]

According to Christian Bates: "*You really don't need to understand all of the science behind metabolic typing in order to reap the health benefits for yourself. These include an increase in energy and mental clarity, freedom from cravings and hunger between meals, improved digestion and immunity, excellence in athletics, a decrease in fatigue, anxiety and even depression.*"[35]

I (Jim Byrne) completed the questionnaire, found out my 'type', and experimented with the relevant dietary advice. But it did not work for me, and I found it too complex and difficult to work with. However, it clearly has worked for others. And Dr Leslie Korn has presented a scientific thesis regarding why it makes sense:

"What foods/fuel mix we require is determined by our genetics, just like the colour of our eyes, our height and our blood type. We are a product of our parents' rates of oxidation, also called metabolism (or how we burn our internal fuel – Eds). If we are eating food that does not burn efficiently based on the need of our engine, then we will not function optimally and this also underlies not only physical but mental health problems/illness". (Pages 8-9; Korn, 2016).

So you could try the Metabolic diet for yourself, and see how well it works for you. And, if necessary you can work with a nutritional therapist, and keep a food diary to track the effects of particular foods on your moods and energy levels.

~~~

The Nordic/Scandinavian diet: The Nordic diet, which is eaten in Norway, Sweden, Finland and Denmark, is similar to the Mediterranean diet, in that it is about eating local, seasonal foods. It involves eating less meat than the traditional British or American diets, and instead eating lots of fish. Portions are relatively small, so they do not overindulge. And they eat home-cooked food, in a relaxed, family environment.

According to one blog: "*The Nordic Diet encourages an all-round healthy lifestyle including exercise, avoiding junk food, upping your fruit and veg intake and reducing the dairy and fat in your diet.*"[36]

According to a new book, by Trina Hahnemann, on the Nordic diet:

"*The Nordic Diet isn't a prescriptive weight-loss plan. It's about getting back to basics so that you can make a real difference to your health, waistline and happiness. But that does mean making a few changes to the way we eat now:*

"Meals must be balanced with a focus on whole grains and seasonal produce. (But, firstly: choose gluten free whole grains. See the Mayo Clinic guidelines in footnote 33 at the end of this book. And, secondly: watch out. High carb diets, of big portions, can build blood sugar levels to dangerous degrees, precipitating stress, mood fluctuations, and even type-2 diabetes! So, thirdly: we would prefer to focus on the fish, vegetables and fruit in this diet, and keep the grains low [if you can tolerate them at all]!)

"Cooking from scratch is a must, including baking your own bread.

"Eat less often, avoid sugar, too much salt and junk food and exercise for at least thirty minutes every day.

"Up your fruit and vegetables - aim for six portions a day.

"Eat veggie meals and fish twice a week at least; limit meat to three meals a week and cut back on dairy. (We think this point should be number 1, and not number 5! And fish three times per week would be better!)

"Enjoy cooking and eating! The kitchen should be the centre-point of your house and mealtimes should be shared with friends and family as much as possible.

"Take time over your food. Lay the table even if you're eating alone, sit down and eat slowly - a meal should take 30 minutes to eat.

"Food should be naturally healthy so you don't have to count calories".[37]

But will this help with your emotional self-management?

The *Sydney Morning Herald* (online) carries a report about new guidelines produced by the International Society for Nutritional Psychiatry Research which validates three standard diets which may help to alleviate or prevent depression: the Mediterranean, **Norwegian** or Japanese diets![38] And oily fish, high in omega-3 fatty acids are a big part of the Nordic diet (as we interpret it!), and this is good for brain health and mood control.

On the other hand, the Nordic diet may contain a little too much meat; and they favour grains over vegetables. We think you should reverse that priority. In general, we have detected some agreement around the following ideas:

The Nordic diet probably has a better balance of omega-3/omega-6 than the Mediterranean diet, and that is an advantage. We should aim to balance our omega-3 and omega-6 intake, so that it is close to 1:1. It could be a little higher, 2:1, or even 3:1. But lower is probably better. (For more on omega-3 and omega-6, please see footnotes 25, 45, 65, 104, 174, and 214).

It is, however, very difficult to *calculate* how much of each of these essential fatty acids we are consuming, so a general guideline might be this: Keep your meat consumption super−low (below the Nordic level, and even possibly below the Mediterranean level [say one meat-based meal per 7-10 days {unless it's grass-fed, in which case two or three meals per week might be okay, according to the Nordic diet guidelines]); and keep your fish consumption (including oily fish) quite high (at about the Nordic level [of, say, two to three fish-based meals per week]).

(Another kind of fat – apart from omega-3 - which is important for cognitive and emotive functioning – including major depression, schizophrenia and bipolar disorder - is called 'phospholipids', which are used in building brain cell walls, and in promoting communication between brain cells[39]. The most important of these is probably phosphatidylserine. "It's manufactured by the body but can also be obtained through dietary sources such as meat, fish, white beans, barley, and soy lecithin. Notably, mackerel and cod, contain significant levels of phosphatidylserine")[40].

~~~

The Okinawa diet: This 'Japanese island' diet is described in a book by Willcox, Willcox and Suzuki (2001), based on a twenty-five year study, as part of a lifestyle approach, as follows: *"...the general principles of living the Okinawa way are not foreign. Indeed, they are highly accessible to everyone and quite consistent with the latest medical research on healthy lifestyles and healthy aging. They include getting lifelong, regular physical activity, eating a mostly plant-based diet that includes fish and soy foods with a great variety of vegetables and moderate amounts of the right kinds of fat, and enjoying strong social and community support as well as a sense of independence and self-responsibility for health"*. (Page xii).

(Watch the soy! Processed soy products are probably very much less acceptable than unprocessed edamame beans! [Edamame are young, soft, fresh, green soy beans]).

The Okinawa diet differs from the Japanese by including much less rice; about 30% yellow and green vegetables; plus purple-fleshed Okinawan sweet potato. And the overall sugar content is much lower than the traditional Japanese diet. They eat three servings of fish each week, and lots of whole grains, vegetables and soy products.

According to Willcox, Willcox and Suzuki (2001): *"...the Okinawa diet – high in complex carbohydrates, rich in whole grains, legumes, fresh vegetables, and fruits – can benefit our physical health, but it's also extremely beneficial to our mental and emotional health"*. *(Page 269)*. The main reasons they give for these conclusions are that whole grains promote the production of serotonin, and are rich in B vitamins, which *"are essential for dealing with stress"*.

However, one British professor, John Mather, thinks the scientific evidence is stronger for the Mediterranean diet; with the Nordic diet in runner-up position. (See Michael Booth's *Guardian* article from 2013).

~~~

The Paleo diet: This diet emerged in 1975, and splintered into various forms, known as the *caveman* diet, or *hunter-gatherer* diet, or the *Paleo* diet. There are many versions in existence today; and the three main theorists leading the field are Dr Loren Cordain, Mark Sisson and Robb Wolf.

This is a low-carb, high protein, high fat diet, which is assumed to be more in line with how our pre-agricultural ancestors lived and ate. The Paleo guidelines, in general, and most often, reject dairy foods, cereal grains, starchy vegetables and sugar. However, some of the schools of 'caveman-thought' allow low fat dairy, and small amounts of certain grains. But in general, they are in favour of wild, lean animal foods, non-starchy fruit and vegetables and honey. Some advocate a lot of fruit, and some a little. Healthy fats are encouraged such as the unsaturated varieties and specifically oils like olive, flax, walnut and avocado.

The Paleo diet may go too far in rejecting all grains. (Although there is no doubt that some people cannot tolerate grains without experiencing symptoms of allergic skin rashes and mood problems: [Myhill, 2015]). A better guideline (at least initially) would be to avoid those grains that contain gluten. We therefore recommend that you avoid wheat, rye, oats and barley. (Most oats are cross-contaminated by grains that contain gluten, but it is possible to get gluten-free oats [but not avenin-free oats!]). And wholegrain brown rice may be okay (for many people), or wild rice, *in small portions* (meaning, less than a quarter of your dinner plate!)

Additionally, there are other wholegrains which are naturally gluten free. For example, the Mayo Clinic has posted a blog about gluten-free grains, which describes five grains, or pseudo-grains, that we can eat to get our wholegrain nutrients, without the gluten. They also describe the process for cooking each of these grains.

These recommended grains are: amaranth, millet, teff, buckwheat and quinoa. See the Mayo Clinic blog extract. [33 above.]

You could try experimenting with those wholegrain, gluten-free grains, or grain substitutes, and see if they suit your body-brain-mind, in terms of mood, skin allergy, and energy level.

Lindeberg, Jönsson, Granfeldt (2007) conducted a small scale comparison study of two groups of people: one on a Paleo diet, compared with another on a 'Mediterranean-like diet' (called a 'Consensus' diet), and found that blood glucose levels fell by 26% in the Paleo group, as compared with the 'consensus' group. This is not surprising, on the basis of a 'Glucose in – glucose out' model, (and the tested Paleo diet *was* low in glucose). However, these results do not help us to make any overall assessment of the desirability of one of these diets over the other. There are, of course, lots of personal testimonials about the benefits of the Paleo diet, available online.

The main foods excluded by most of the Paleo diets include: legumes[41], potatoes, and refined sugar, cereal grains, dairy, salt, root vegetables and processed foods.

Some of the main benefits of the Paleo diet may be that it necessarily reduces our dependence on *refined carbs* and *simple sugars*. But the various Paleo diets allow lots of meat, which may invite an imbalance in omega-6 to omega-3 fatty acids (when the meat is grain-fed), which will probably cause lots of inflammation, which can trigger depression as well as physical diseases. (Greger, 2016).

Some criticisms of the Paleo approach include the following, by BBC Health Editor, Roxanne Fisher: *"What our ancestors ate would have been dependent on where they lived in the world, making avocadoes an unlikely dietary staple for us Brits. The Paleo diet also ignores the health benefits of consuming whole-grains as well as beans, legumes and starchy veg. Numerous studies have reported a reduced incidence of heart disease in those who regularly consume three servings of whole-grains a day*[42]*. The low GI (Glycaemic index)*[43] *properties of beans and legumes make them especially useful for those with blood sugar issues and starchy veg are a great source of nutrient-dense energy. All of those foods supply B vitamins, which among other things help us to unlock the energy in our food. Finally, omitting dairy has received much criticism in that it may limit the intake of minerals like calcium"*. (Fisher, 2016).

On the other hand, if you have emotional problems which cannot be accounted for by psychological stressors, then you might want to experiment with eliminating grains for a few days, keeping a food diary in which you note any changes in energy level, mood, stomach and gut responses, skin reactions, and so on. Then you could begin to reintroduce grains, one type at a time, and monitoring the effects on mood and energy. In this way, you can find out for yourself if you have a problem with grains, and what to do about it. (In this process, you might want to have a registered dietician, or nutritional therapist, support you, to ensure you do not experience nutritional deficiencies or insufficiencies! If you can afford it!)

~~~

Vegetarian diet: Dr Michael Greger (2016: ix) presents evidence from his personal life - (in the case of his grandmother's health problems) - that giving up the meat-heavy, Standard American Diet (SAD), and adopting a vegetarian diet, combined with exercise, was able to transform her health and mobility. On the other hand there is at least one scientific study which suggests there is no solid evidence that a vegetarian diet is either better or worse for mental health (according to Michalak, Zhang and Jacobi, 2012)[44]. Then again, the China Study, a respectable 25-years study of the eating habits of thousands of people in China, suggested that animal-based foods are not necessary, while *"people who ate the most plant based foods were the healthiest"*. (Campbell and Campbell, 2006).

And the China study seems to be supported by Beezhold, Johnson and Daigle (2010) – cited in Greger (2016), page 201 - who conducted a study with Seventh Day Adventists which seems to support the view that *"eating less meat isn't just good for us physically; it's good for us emotionally too"*. (Greger, 2016, page 201). One way to interpret the results was to assume that eating less meat reduced the amount of arachidonic acid[45] (which is an omega-6 fatty acid) in the body, thus *reducing* inflammation in general, including brain-based neuro-inflammation). (This is important because there are some studies which suggest that depression, and perhaps the other major emotional disorders, are linked to inflammation).

We could also use this research to justify a *low-meat diet*, rather than a completely vegetarian diet. (But there is no evidence that a completely vegetarian diet will worsen emotional states, provided B12 and omega-3 are acquired via supplements).

(But remember, with regard to vegetables, that the low-FodMaps diet suggests that some vegetables are too high in sugars, [for some people, {some of the time?}]; so we may have to be selective in the vegetables we eat if we are highly sensitive to sugars).

~~~

Personalized diet: The safest way to follow healthy diets seems to us to be this: Get a couple of good recipe books which emphasize the kinds of foods found in elements of the Mediterranean, Nordic, and Vegetarian diets; and Chapter 11 of the China Study, which emphasizes eight principles of food and health. And, if you can afford it, consult a good nutritional therapist.

According to Leslie Korn:

"No single diet is right for everyone. Each person has a different cultural-genetic heritage and therefore a different metabolism. Some people like the Inuit require mostly meat and fish, whereas people from India do well on a predominance of legumes, vegetables, fruits, and grains. Most people require a mix. However, that mix of food can vary greatly. Know your ancestral and genetic heritage and try to eat for your individual metabolic type". (Page 14, Korn, 2016).

But one thing we can safely predict, based upon scientific studies which are cited in this book: No race of people will ever exist who can, for long, remain physically and mentally healthy on a junk food diet; or an inadequate diet in terms of nutrients![46] and [47].

Invest time and effort in shopping for raw ingredients, and spend time in the kitchen engaging in food preparation.

Make more than fifty percent of your meals raw salads, combined with nuts, seeds and fruits. Eat lots of plant based proteins: [such as, vegetables (avocado, broccoli, spinach, kale, peas, and sweet potato), legumes (such as lentils and beans), nuts and seeds (including sesame, sunflower, almonds, walnuts, and hazelnuts), non-dairy milk (almond, coconut, and/or oat milk), gluten-free grains (quinoa, amaranth, and buckwheat [if you can tolerate them]). And take Spirulina and Chlorella for their nutrient and protein content.]. Supplement with: Vitamins B, C and E (at the very least!); plus omega-3 fatty acids (as in fish oils), Co-enzyme-Q10 (Footnote[48]), and live acidophilus and other live bacteria[49]. Use some fermented foods, like Miso and sauerkraut. Chew your food well, and use a squat-toilet (if at all possible) to optimize elimination. (And if you don't have a squat toilet, use a foot stool – sit on the toilet with your feet on the stool [of 9-12 inches in height] - to simulate that squatting position). Drink eight glasses of filter water per day. Do the reading, and find out for yourself. Monitor the effects of dietary changes on your moods, emotions and energy levels, and adjust accordingly.

The best way to do that is to keep a food diary for a few weeks, and record everything you eat and drink. And also record your exercise and sleep patterns. And check each day to see how you feel: *Is your energy up or down since yesterday? Is your mood up or down since yesterday? Do you feel physically better or worse than yesterday? Any sign of skin allergies?* And if any of those indicators is negative, that should be linked back to what you ate 24 to 30 hours earlier [approximately]. Plus what has been happening during those 24 to 30 hours: like sleep disturbance; lack of physical exercise; increased stress from any source; the emergence of a problem that you feel you cannot handle; and so on. (If you can't track it back on your own, see a professional helper to support you).

And consult a suitable nutritionist, medical expert or health coach, when and if necessary.

~~~

(b) Some general dietary guidelines

If we can generalize at all, it is advisable to eat lots of fresh vegetables and fruit: seven or eight portions per day (mainly vegetables, and much less fruit [because fruit contains fruit sugars, which can raise your blood glucose levels to problematical levels]!)

Many experts recommend the ***Mediterranean diet***. Some recommend the ***Okinawa diet***. Or the ***Nordic*** diet. And some the ***Paleo diet,*** though we have reservations about the Paleo/ Atkins/ Ketogenic diets, which will be discussed later.

The safest way to ***begin*** is probably to follow the UK National Food Guide (or the US equivalent 'food pyramid'), or our variation on that set of guidelines. (See the start of section 3(a) of Part 1, above).

Eating organic wholefoods is one way of minimizing the chemical pollutants that get into our bodies and impair our ability to function healthily in the face of the pressures and strains of daily life, according to Bart Cunningham, PhD.[50] Patrick Holford (2010) recommends that we eat (gluten-free) wholegrains, lentils, beans, nuts, seeds, fresh fruit and vegetables, and avoid refined, white and overcooked foods. (But we think he should have emphasised fish and vegetables before grains, lentils and beans. [Fish twice per week is probably optimal for most people. Some might be able to handle three times. But others need to be careful they do not provoke an allergic reaction to fish!]).

There is also recent research which suggests a link between trans-fats (including hydrogenated fats in processed foods) and aggression, irritability and impatience.[51]

But which fruits and vegetables should we eat? Patrick Holford (2010) recommends dark green, leafy and root vegetables. He lists spinach, carrots, broccoli, sweet potatoes, green beans, and Brussels sprouts. He favours eating (as much as possible) raw or lightly cooked. Salad vegetables make an energizing breakfast. Holford suggests, also, that we choose berries, apples, melon, pears, or citrus fruits. He suggests moderation in the consumption of bananas, because of the high sugar content. For this reason, we should also limit out consumption of dried fruits (to something like 6-10 raisins or sultanas, etc., per meal). Kiwis and blueberries are low GI (Glycaemic index, or sugar content). Variety is the key. Keep the sugar content low, especially if you are particularly sensitive to fruit and vegetable sugars. (See the FodMaps diet, and the Anti-Candida diet).

The Stress Management Society gives the following advice: "*If you want a strong nervous system, boost your intake of vitamins B, C and E, together with minerals magnesium and zinc. The best source of these nutrients is from food, rather than supplements. So eat a balanced diet of meat, nuts, seeds, fresh fruit and vegetables and oily fish. If you need to snack during the day, try pumpkin or sunflower seeds and fruit, particularly bananas. Fresh organic food is the best source. If you can't get fresh, frozen vegetables are a reasonable alternative as much of their nutritional content is retained.*" [52] (However, it may be that a low-meat, high vegetable, moderate carbohydrate diet is best: Greger (2016), page 67 and 201-203).

We suggest you follow most of the advice of the Stress Management Society, except for the supplementation of vitamins and minerals; and it's probably best to *keep your meat consumption low*. Unless you are on a wholly organic diet, your food will be largely denatured and devoid of much nutritional value; therefore you need to use vitamin and mineral supplements of a good, natural-source quality.

It seems to be important to keep your meat consumption low – not just for red meat, but also for white meats. Meats seem to increase the omega-6 fatty acids (including arachidonic acid) in the body (perhaps because they are mostly grain fed, instead of grass fed). Dr Michael Greger writes that: "*...Maybe the pro-inflammatory compound arachidonic acid found in animal products can 'adversely impact mental health via a cascade of neuro-inflammation'.*"[53]

And Greger also states that (non-organic) chicken and eggs are also a problem because of their omega-6 (arachidonic acid) content! So perhaps you should eat those foods in moderation. (And only the organic variety, because grass-fed animals are high in omega-3 fatty acids, while grain fed animals are high in omega-6).

~~~

Some theorists believe that combining complex carbohydrates with a protein can reduce stress and provide a solid fuel for daily energy requirements (Holford, 2010). This, however, contradicts the **Hay diet**, which recommends keeping carbohydrates and proteins separate, in meals separated by at least four hours! (You could experiment with the Hay diet to see if it works for you). Others argue that too much carbohydrate could cause stress – and it is reliably established that refined carbohydrates ('junk foods' – like white bread, processed cereals, sugar, sugary drinks, etc.,) do cause stress and other problems in the body. (See the section on 'sugar' below).

On the other hand, oily fish - like salmon, mackerel and sardines - with green vegetables and complex carbohydrate (like whole grains [which are gluten free]) - are believed to be particularly beneficial.

Patrick Holford recommends five servings of fruits and vegetables per day; and four or more servings of wholegrains. (A serving, roughly, is half a cup of cooked green vegetables, or one whole apple or banana, or one slice of bread. For more precise guidelines, you can search online for a definition of a "serving").

There are scientific studies to support the claims about the impact of oily fish (which contain essential fatty acids [especially omega-3's]) on the reduction of panic attacks, for example. (Perretta, 2001, page 90)[54]. So eating oily fish at least twice each week seems to be a sensible step for good brain health.

~~~

Back to the Paleo diet argument: Our ancient ancestors in the Stone Age (or Palaeolithic era) were hunter-gatherers, and their diet helped them survive and evolve. So what was the earliest diet like? Their diet probably consisted of mostly protein from fish, game birds and animals, and there were relatively few carbohydrates. Brewer (2013) described purslane, berries and low-glycaemic wild grains as being the carbohydrates they would have consumed. The fats in the Palaeolithic diet were mostly polyunsaturated omega 3's plus other unsaturated fats.

Because we still have Palaeolithic genes (according to some theorists), and our way of life is estimated to be more than 60% sedentary, compared to our highly active ancestors, we have problems with our health arising out of inactivity and poor diet. These problems include: diabetes, high blood pressure, obesity and coronary heart disease. Plus diet-related *emotional* problems.

Therefore a diet related more closely to our Stone Age ancestors has been advocated by many (Paleo-influenced) nutritionists. This means that the diet would have balanced amounts of food from all the food groups, with vegetables, whole grains (gluten free!), and (*small* amounts of) fat-free or low fat milk and milk products (Brown, 2017). Some theorists advocate avoiding dairy and grains completely[55]. But we prefer to try to keep some gluten-free grains, and dairy substitutes (with a small amount of occasional dairy), in our diets – if at all possible. Although, recently one of us (Jim) has had to abandon almost all grains, because of negative skin and mood reactions.

The amount of total fat intake would need to be 20–25% of calories, with most of it obtained from fish, nuts, seeds and vegetable oils (polyunsaturated and monounsaturated fatty acids).

(There is also a new coconut diet, which advocates consuming raw coconut oil as a main ingredient of the diet, instead of vegetable oils. Again, we have tried this one without any success!)[56]

The Paleo theorists advocate eating high quality protein - from seeds, nuts, fish, lean (grass fed) meat and whole grains (which are gluten free) - and this element would need to make up about 20% of our food intake. There would also need to be plenty of fluids – ideally mostly water and juices (but not too much fruit sugar). And the water should be either filtered, or mineral water bought in glass bottles. Filtering tap water is the most cost-effective option.

However, a pure Paleo diet would not allow the consumption of any grains. Most Paleo theorists probably believe that "we haven't adapted to eating grains and their gluten, lectins and phytates, and therefore they always and inevitably cause inflammation; and so should be avoided"[57]. As we have already argued, there is *no universal agreement* about diet and nutrition. And the debate about the value, or evil, of grains is no exception to that rule. Here is one summary of the debate:

"This discussion is one of the great nutrition debates of our time... In one camp are vegans, vegetarians, and macrobiotic dieters, who eat a ton of whole grains. They say grains will help them live longer and healthier, free of chronic disease. Indeed, recent news seized on a Harvard study connecting grains with lower risk of death... In the opposing camp, you've got the Paleo, Whole30[58], and Atkins advocates, who strictly limit or even completely avoid grains. They say not eating grains will help them live longer and healthier, free of chronic disease. They dominate plenty of news, too". (Source: Brian St. Pierre at Precision Nutrition).[59]

Overall, St Pierre (2017) finds the case against *whole grains* unsupported by the research studies *he has read*; though there is a strong case to be made against *refined* carbohydrates, or *processed grains.* He cites a long list of references in support of his conclusion. (This does not prove that the Paleo theorists could not construct an equally long list of respectable research studies).

A middle way compromise might be to keep a food diary, and follow the Paleo guidance, *some but not all of the time*; and monitor any mental or physical symptoms you notice about twenty-four to thirty-six hours after the consumption of each (grain free) meal. Then switch to a more conventional diet, and monitor any mental or physical symptoms you notice, twenty-four to thirty-six hours following the consumption of any whole grain foods. This would help you to build up a relatively scientific body of knowledge about food and your body's response to it.

Also, if you can afford it, check this process out with a nutritional therapist, who can support you with your experiments.

Our own belief is this: The Paleo diet probably goes too far in rejecting all grains (for people who seem to be able to tolerate them, with no physical or mental symptoms), and in promoting the consumption of too much meat. A better guideline would be to make sure you avoid those grains that contain gluten. We therefore recommend that you avoid wheat, rye, oats and barley. (Most oats are cross-contaminated by grains that contain gluten). And wholegrain brown rice is probably okay, or wild rice, in small portions (never more than 25% of your dinner plate!). There are other wholegrains which are naturally gluten free. For example, the Mayo Clinic has posted a blog about gluten-free grains, which describes five grains, or pseudo-grains, that we can eat to get our wholegrain nutrients, without the gluten. They also describe the process for cooking each of these grains.

These recommended grains are: amaranth, millet, teff, buckwheat and quinoa. See the Mayo Clinic blog extract [33 above].

But if you notice any fall in your energy level, or skin allergies, or serious mood fluctuations, about twenty-four to thirty-six hours after eating any wholegrains, then you probably need to exclude them, at least temporarily. (And you should consult a registered nutritional therapist for support with this process).

~~~

Some people are fructose intolerant – including people who suffer from Candida Albicans[60], or IBS).

~~~

The Stress Management Society, in the UK, emphasizes the importance of drinking lots of water over the course of the day: *"If you want to deal with stress, drink water"*, they write. *"It hydrates every part of the body and brain and helps you to better cope with stressful situations. A good rule is to take a few sips every 15 minutes. The best source is room-temperature still water bought in glass bottles (some plastic bottles can leach chemicals into the water inside) or use a jug filter system that you fill from the tap."* (Stress Management Society, 2012/2016)[61].

~~~

4. What kinds of foods should we avoid for the sake of our physical, mental, and emotional health and wellbeing?

> *"The food you eat can be either the safest, most powerful form of medicine or the slowest form of poison"* Ann Wigmore[62]

We should avoid food that has been _processed_, including processed meats, trans-fats (or hydrogenated super-heated oils), fried foods, sugar and sugary refined grains, and alcohol; and we should minimise our intake of saturated fat from meat and dairy products (Holford, 2010). We also need to avoid gluten and excess caffeine. All of these food stuffs cause problems for our bodies (or body-brain-minds). Each of these foods will be described next, and the effects on the body-brain-mind will be outlined.

(a) Trans-fats:

> *"Trans fat is lethal"*. Stanfield (2008)[63]

Trans-fats are vegetable oils (which, in their original form, are healthy) but they are *industrially processed*. The industrial process adds hydrogen to vegetable oil, which causes the oil to become solid at room temperature. And the process of hydrogenating these vegetable oils results in unsaturated fatty acids, which are 'rogue' fat molecules: (Stanfield, 2008).

What happens is as follows: The industrial process consists of boiling the vegetable oils at a temperature above 260 degrees centigrade. Because of the intense heat, the atomic structure of the oil is altered, the reason being that the molecules in the oil have been vibrated so much. This means that, when they are consumed by a human, the trans-fatty acids raise serum levels of LDL-cholesterol (or "bad" cholesterol), and reduces levels of HDL-cholesterol, (or "good" cholesterol), and can promote inflammation[64] in the body. This can cause endothelial dysfunction, and influence other risk factors for cardiovascular diseases.

The motivation of 'food technologists' for damaging oil in this way is this: The partially hydrogenated oil is less likely to spoil, so foods cooked or mixed with trans-fats have a longer shelf life. Some restaurants use partially hydrogenated vegetable oil in their deep fryers, because it doesn't have to be changed as often as do other oils. So convenience is traded for health!

In bakeries, trans-fats are used as a cheaper alternative to butter, so we find these fats in bakery goods such as cakes, biscuits, snack bars (including 'healthy' energy cereal bars). It is also found in takeaway food: *"Sometimes as much as 40% of their overall fat content can be trans fats"*. (Stanfield, 2008).

The effects of trans-fats on the body-brain-mind are wide-ranging. These completely unnatural, man-made fats, cause *chaos* in your body-brain on a cellular level and stop natural biological processes taking place. Studies have linked trans-fats to cancer because they interfere with enzymes your body uses to fight cancer. And there is at least one major study linking trans-fats to angry outburst and problems with rage[65].

These fats can cause diabetes because they interfere with the insulin receptors in your cell membranes; and they cause obesity. And trans-fats can cause major clogging of your arteries. (Among women with underlying coronary heart disease, eating trans-fats increases the risk of a sudden heart attack, **threefold**).

Maggie Stanfield stated in her book that: *"Just one doughnut a day that contains trans-fats could be increasing your risk of heart disease fivefold"*.

Trans-fats even interfere with your body's use of beneficial omega-3 fats, (which are essential for maintaining your brain!) and have been linked to an increase in asthma. (Dr Mercola, 2010)[66]. And anything that reduces the beneficial effects of omega-3 fats, also invite the development of depression and anxiety in the consumer.

Eating diets rich in omega-3 fatty acids, as in oily fish, like salmon and sardines, and taking omega-3 supplements, like cod liver oil, or krill oil, can improve physical health and emotional stability.

See the section on 'Fats and oils', in Part 3, below, for advice on how to choose and use healthy oils in the kitchen.

~~~

(b) Sugar

> *"Avoid any form of sugar, and foods with added sugar"*. Holford (2010, Page 428).

Julia Ross, a psychotherapist based in California, wrote a very useful book titled 'The Mood Cure'[67]. This was based on her research findings into natural nutritional solutions to emotional problems, implemented at her clinic. She found that sugar was a big part of the mood problems her clients encountered. She writes: *"Many of our clinic's clients have been freed from the moodiness they've endured for years, simply by dropping sugar and refined white flour starches from their menus. No supplements, no other changes, dietary or otherwise, were required"*. (Page 122, Ross, 2002)

Sugar is described as one of the most addictive substances on the planet, and it was imported into Europe in the 1100's as a prized drug. It was considered so valuable that apothecaries kept it under lock and key, and the slave trade was created in order that there could be cheaper and quicker ways of gaining access to this highly addictive substance.

Dr Daniel Amen (2012)[68] describes sugar as: *"Toxic calories"*. But why? Here are some of the reasons:

Firstly, sugar is a ***refined***[69] carbohydrate. There are different types of sugars: white and brown sugar, honey, (raw and processed) molasses, cane sugar, many artificial sugars, fruit drinks and natural fruit juices without the fibre.

Sugar is *eight* times more addictive than cocaine. It creates fat around our organs, and contributes towards premature ageing.

It takes the body a long time to get rid of sugar from the immune system. For as long as 4-6 hours after eating sugar, your immune system will still be damped down and recovering, because sugar and the immune system are enemies.

Sugar doesn't just reduce immune function but is also likely to cause diabetes and lead to obesity, both of which conditions will lower your mood. It increases inflammation in the body; causes brain cells to fire erratically, and can send blood sugar levels *"on a roller-coaster ride"* (Amen, 2012).

Many scientists believe that if you have very high insulin levels, as a result of consuming sugar, then this can contribute to cancer. (Boyd, 2003)[70]. Sugar affects our digestion in negative ways, leading to bloating, cramps, sluggishness and headaches. And it destroys ***collagen***[71], which is one of the most important building blocks of the human body.

All types of sugars are 'fast releasing' which means that they deliver a high glycaemic load which stimulates a rise in blood sugar levels. And high blood sugar leads to a stress response, including anger and/or anxiety.

Why is this bad for the body-brain-mind? What happens is that the body-mind responds to this sudden increase in sugar in the bloodstream by releasing insulin, which then propels the sugar into the cells. This can overload the cells, so if there is too much sugar, this is transformed into a substance called glycogen, which is stored in the liver and muscles.

When that storage capacity has been reached, the rest is stored as fat. In addition, as suggested earlier, white sugar has had about 90% of its vitamins and minerals removed. Too much sugar increases adrenaline[72] - (the stress hormone – known in the US as 'epinephrine') - to a great extent, which negatively impacts our moods and emotions.

Here is an example of what happens: Researchers at Yale University in the US gave 25 healthy children a drink which had the equivalent amount of energy that was in a popular soft drink.

The next thing that happened is called the *'Rebound blood sugar drop'*. When there is a fast increase in the amount of sugar in the blood, then insulin overcompensates for this by taking too much sugar out of circulation. This results in a compensatory increase in the children's adrenaline to over five times its normal level, for up to five hours after taking in the sugar. And if there is too much adrenaline in the bloodstream this results in irritability and anxiety, and the children also had difficulty concentrating: (Holford, 2007)[73].

Finally, sugar is very bad for our teeth, because the bacteria in our mouths are fed by sugar. And poor dental and gum health are now linked to Alzheimer's disease and heart disease.[74] Because the brain is so close to the gums and teeth, dental health is closely linked to brain-mind health.

~~~

(c) Alcohol

> *"Alcohol acts just like sugar, biochemically, only more so. It contains more calories per gram and gets into your bloodstream faster"*. (Ross, 2002)
>
> ~~~
>
> *"As soon as you start to get drunk, you are damaging your brain"*. (Holford, 2010)
>
> ~~~

Alcohol is defined by the Oxford English dictionary as: '*A colourless, volatile flammable liquid which is produced by the natural fermentation of sugars and is the intoxicating constituent of wine, beer, spirits, and other drinks, and is also used as an industrial solvent and as fuel'*.

What is the effect on the body? The physical effects of alcohol are as follows: Firstly, 20% of it goes straight into our bloodstream, and what is left is taken in all over the body. It can permeate almost every biological structure of the body because cell membranes are extremely permeable to alcohol.

Alcohol dissolves (essential) fatty acids *inside* the brain. Then it replaces helpful omega-3 DHA, (which is docosahexaenoic acid, a long chain omega-3 fatty acid). This elimination of omega-3 DHA is very bad for us, because this substance provides cardiovascular health benefits, supports visual performance and enhances brain health, including memory. DHA represents up to 97% of the omega-3 fats in the brain.

Alcohol *replaces* DHA with docosapentanoic acid, which is a less valuable form of omega-3, and it also stops the process of fats being converted into DHA and prostaglandins. This is the reason why the memory is affected by alcohol.

The body's reflexes are slowed down by alcohol, there is reduced co-ordination, impaired thinking, poor judgement, depression, impaired memory and a reduced ability to control motor functions. And alcohol, because it is a disinhibitor, allows angry outbursts which would normally be controlled.

Patrick Holford (2010) describes alcohol as the brain's worst enemy, because when the liver is unable to detoxify any more alcohol, then *it attacks the brain*. As a result, the communication systems within the brain are thrown into disarray and it affects our memory – so we forget our problems.

Dr Perricone (2002) recommends drinking a small amount of wine with a meal. To drink any more is to invite a very quick increase in blood sugar in your body, resulting in a strong inflammatory response in every part of the body[75].

Pure spirits are even worse. Because the alcohol content of hard liquor is extremely high, there is considerable harm to cell plasma membrane (or the structure of our cell walls); and to the interior of the cells; as well as triggering the inflammatory response – which seems to be implicated in the causation of most major diseases, including major depression and anxiety.

Alcohol also affects our ability to get a sound night's sleep: Drinking alcohol in the evening can make us feel drowsy but then afterwards it triggers an influx of adrenaline in our body systems. Adrenaline is a hormone which is released as a reaction to excitement or stress, and it makes us wake up, hours later, usually in the early hours of the morning. And high adrenaline levels can make us feel anxious and panicked.

Alcohol extracts water from our cells, and dehydrates every cell in the body, accelerating the ageing process. It also generates huge amounts of free radicals, (which are unstable molecules that can damage the cells in the body). This increases the drinker's risk of hormonal cancers, particularly breast cancer.

It places an enormous strain on the liver, which then has a reduced ability to detoxify the body. And fatigue, dehydration, weight gain and late-onset diabetes, mood swings, and poor eyesight are also some of the consequences.

Its effects on the mind are as follows: it initially increases feelings of relaxation and happiness and sociability, but this can develop into more negative feelings and behaviours, including depression.

According to the NHS in Scotland, more than half of people who ended up in hospital because they'd deliberately injured themselves, said they'd drunk alcohol immediately before or while doing it. And 27% of men and 19% of women gave alcohol as the reason for self-harming.[76]

Finally, if you drink alcohol regularly, the level of serotonin in your brain is lowered, and (according to one dominant theory) as this controls your moods, feelings of depression are more likely to take place. (However, this theory of low serotonin being linked to high depression has never been demonstrated in practice; and there are serious counter arguments). So, it may be that drinking alcohol regularly causes depression via *some other biochemical route* altogether, such as through inflammation affecting mitochondrial functioning!

~~~

(d) Caffeine

The Oxford dictionary's definition of **caffeine** is:

'An **alkaloid**[77] *compound which is found especially in tea and coffee plants and is a stimulant of the central nervous system'*. (Waite, 2012).

Caffeine is also found in cocoa and cola drinks and in some drug preparations as a preventative for migraines.

Julia Ross, in her book titled *'The Mood Cure'*, describes caffeine as one of serotonin's number 1 enemies, along with diet pills, ephedra, ma huang[78] and cocaine (Page 29, Ross 2002). Since serotonin is widely seen as underpinning our positive moods, this is said to be not good. (However, since it now seems that the serotonin-depression link is highly contested, it may be that caffeine operates in a different way to lower mood)[79].

Research findings indicate that the people who drink the most coffee suffer chronic depression as well.[80] But caffeine also depletes potassium, calcium, and zinc, vitamin C, and the B vitamins. It also weakens and overstimulates the kidneys, pancreas, liver, stomach, intestines, heart, nervous system and adrenal glands and over-acidifies the 'ph' (the balance of acidity and alkalinity levels in the stomach and body generally), causing premature ageing, and compromising health and well-being. (And we do not currently know *how* it might cause or worsen depressive symptoms).

Also, caffeine has a negative effect on the quantity and the quality of our sleep, and can make us tired and irritable; and anxiety can be increased by the use of caffeine.

Caffeine can also affect academic skills: A study published in the *American Journal of Psychiatry* studied 1,500 psychology students and divided them into four categories, depending on their coffee intake: Abstainers; Low consumers (one cup or equivalent a day); Moderate (1-5 cups a day); and High (5 or more cups a day).

The Moderate and High consumers were found to have higher levels of anxiety and depression than the Abstainers; and the High consumers had the greatest incidence of stress-related medical problems, as well as a lower academic performance. (Gilliland and Andress, 1981, pp. 512-4).[81]

Holford (2010) has explained that, with increases in your consumption of caffeine, there is a corresponding insensitivity, within the brain, to the body's own natural stimulants of dopamine and adrenaline.

So then more stimulants are needed to feel normal, and these push the body to produce more adrenaline and dopamine. These result in adrenal exhaustion, and so the result is less motivation and less energy in the body. Indifference and apathy can follow. For some people, the effects of caffeine can result in them being diagnosed with schizophrenia or mania.

Patrick Holford stated that: *"As a nutritionist, I have seen many people cleared of minor health problems such as tiredness and headaches just from cutting out their two or three coffees a day"*. (Holford, 2010: page 93).

~~~

(e) Processed food (or 'Junk food')[82]

> *"Junk moods come from junk foods. Junk foods are addictive and lead to overeating. Overeating leads to overweight"*. (Ross 2002)

Processed or 'junk food' is food that has been transformed from its raw, natural state by chemical or physical means. The food has been altered from its natural state so that it can be packaged in cans, boxes or bags. Or it has been pre-cooked in a fast-food take-away restaurant, using high calorie, low nutrient constituents; or with high trans-fat and sugar ingredients.

And it can come from a variety of sources. Felicity Lawrence, in her book titled *'Not on the Label'* (2004)[83] explains how a ready-made lasagne: *"…can have about 20 different ingredients which could have originated from all over the world, according to Tara Garnett of the Sustainable Transport Trust, Transport 2000."*

This type of food can cause real problems for your body, for the following reasons:

Firstly, the food can be high in bad fat and/or sugar and can have very few nutrients, and lots of calories (or simple sugars). In fact, the food company, Mars Food, which makes Dolmio and Uncle Ben sauces, has recently announced that it will put a health warning on these and other products, to say that *they shouldn't be eaten more than once a week*. This is because their food sauces are so high in salt, sugar and fat. (*Daily Mail*, 2016)[84].

Secondly, with processed food there can be a health risk from excessive sodium (which is salt). Bearing in mind the welfare of our hearts, Melodie Ann Coffman at the 'Healthy Eating' website, in an article entitled, 'The Disadvantages of Junk Food'[85], considers that we should not eat more than 1,500 milligrams of sodium each day (which is three quarters of a teaspoon). (A single take away meal can contain more salt than a whole day's allowance). Too much sodium in our diets can increase blood pressure, so steering clear of processed food can help us to avoid getting high blood pressure.

The processed foods that contain the most sodium include delicatessen meats, hot dog sausages, and microwave dinners. The sodium comes from salt and other sodium compounds which are used to give the food more flavour and make it last. But too much sodium can disrupt the potassium-sodium balance.

It may be that a high sodium-potassium ratio results in stress and anxiety; while a too-low ratio results in depression and fatigue. But the kind of salt you need to avoid depression is iodized salt (enriched with iodine), and this is not normally the kind of salt used in junk foods and processed foods in general. (You can get your iodine needs met by taking a kelp supplement).

Also related to the sodium levels, there is the risk of stroke. The more chips, French fries and pepperoni pizzas which are eaten, the higher the risk of stroke becomes.

There is very little fibre in processed junk food, and fibre is essential to keep our bowels moving.

Otherwise, we can become constipated, and it can become painful for us when we eventually pass faeces; and regular bowel movements reduce toxicity in the body.

And anything which improves bowel function tends to support optimum emotional functioning

~~~

(f) Gluten

Cereal flours (mainly wheat flours, but also rye and barley) contain proteins called gliadins and glutenins, which become glutinous when the cereal flours are mixed with water.

These substances (gliadins plus glutenins) are called, (when combined), gluten; and they can inflame and cause breaks in the lining of the digestive tract. This can lead to food particles escaping through the gut wall into the bloodstream, causing inflammation.

(In the case of oats, this grain contains *avenin*, which could cause inflammation in some individuals. And oats also tend to be contaminated by other grains during the growing or processing or packing processes).

Sensitivity to gluten is called gluten intolerance, and the main form is called coeliac disease. However, we also are now aware of non-celiac gluten sensitivity (NCGS); and to non-gut-based neurological disturbances caused by gluten. (Sources: Perlmutter, 2014 [who cites twenty sources, including eight from academic journals, with two from *The Lancet*]; Ross, 2003 [who cites six sources, including four from academic journals, like the *New England Journal of Medicine*]; Hadjivassiliou, 1996 [who discovered the 'gluten syndrome']; plus 16 other sources from academic journals)[86].

The latest thinking in the world of neurological medicine is that gluten affects the gut, **and** it affects the brain. It is no longer "...*regarded as principally a disease of the small bowel*". (Hadjivassiliou, in Perlmutter, 2014: page 53). Sometimes it affects the brain **because** it has affected the gut; and sometimes it affects the brain, **without** showing any obvious evidence of a negative impact on the gut! This is known as 'the gluten syndrome': Ford (2009). And there are blood markers (antibodies) of its presence in the body-brain, even in the absence of intestinal damage. See Footnote 86.

According to Hadjivassiliou (1996): "*Our data suggest that gluten sensitivity is common in patients with neurological disease of unknown cause and may have aetiological* (or causative – Eds) *significance*".

How does gluten affect the gut? Gliadin, within gluten, pulls apart the **tight junctions** that exist between the cells in our guts. The space between the cells start to widen, and the result is that toxins and larger molecules of food (that normally pass through the intestine and are eliminated in bowel movements), begin to leak into the blood circulation system of our bodies. This is called 'leaky gut syndrome'.

As a result, you get increased inflammation in your body when your intestinal barrier is compromised. This means that you are susceptible to health challenges such as rheumatoid arthritis, food allergies, asthma, eczema, coeliac disease, inflammatory bowel disease, HIV, cystic fibrosis, diabetes, autism, Alzheimer's and Parkinson's.

What happens is that the blood-brain barrier (which has been thought of as a "highly protective, fortified portal keeping bad things out of the brain") is weakened if the gut is leaky, and this lets in molecules that are really bad for the brain, including bacteria, viruses and proteins that would normally have been prevented from crossing the blood/brain barrier[87].

According to Julia Ross (2003), thousands of people are affected by gluten, and there are many studies which validate the theory that depression can be caused by gluten intolerance. She describes the symptom of depression disappearing when wheat and other grains are removed from the diet.

Here is Julie Ross (2002) describing her experience of the effects of gluten:

"People with gluten intolerance have low levels of the antidepressant, anti-anxiety brain chemical serotonin, and gluten has been implicated in mental illness since at least 1979". (Page 126).

The fact that gluten is implicated in mental illness, or emotional disturbances, like anxiety and depression, does not prove that the link is via serotonin. This proposed link is heavily contested. (See later). But there is undoubtedly a link *of some kind* – see Footnote 87 – and gluten therefore has to be taken seriously as a risk factor in the causation of neurological and emotional problems of unknown origin. Dr Michael Greger has argued against such a stance, but we have dismantled his argument in Footnote 9).

~~~

Some people have a formal diagnosis of Celiac disease, and those individuals should stay well clear of gluten-containing foods, to avoid damaging their intestinal tracts further.

Some people have a formal diagnosis of Non-Celiac Gluten Sensitivity (NCGS), linked to a neurological problems or disorders, with biomarkers for gluten antibodies in the blood. And those individuals have to remain gluten-free for life.

And, it seems, some people *self-report* that they have all the symptoms of gluten sensitivity, and their symptoms do improve when they *exclude* gluten-containing foods.

However, that third category of non-diagnosed, self-reporting gluten sensitivity individuals ***may be*** *misdiagnosing* the source of their own problem. According to a recent study, involving 59 individuals on a self-instituted gluten-free diet, for whom celiac disease had been excluded, the real source of their problems was Fructans (which are a form of sugar found in vegetables and grains). (Source: Skodje, G.I. et al., 2017, in press).

As a precautionary approach, nobody should assume that they are Fructan sensitive rather than gluten sensitive, unless and until they get themselves tested - not just for Celiac disease, but also for Non-Celiac Gluten Sensitivity (with biomarkers for gluten antibodies).

~~~

Apparently, in the US, according to Kelly Brogan, the wheat crop is composed of varieties of grains which have been modified so that more gluten is produced, because food technologists believe this will improve the composition of baked goods, creating more "puff" in them. (Michael Greger, 2016, argues against this point. However, a blog by the Agricultural Marketing Resource Centre seems to support Kelly Brogan's argument rather than Michael Greger's)[88].

Brogan also states that gluten is one of the most notable food items that is known to make a dramatic difference to the brain, as it raises the production of endorphins.

"The gluten in these grains affects the brain like an opiate......that's why you may love or feel comforted by your bread or pasta – your brain gets a drug-like rush every time you eat those foods." (Page 126)

Some other ailments that have been linked to gluten include: bowel problems, headaches, diabetes, chronic exhaustion, bad moods, depression and severe anxiety.

~~~

5. What kinds of regular supplements (of vitamins, minerals, etc.) should we take to support our physical health and emotional wellbeing?

Do we need to take supplements? Here are several different views on the type of daily supplements that we need to take. In this process, I will summarise some of the main views of a variety of specialists in the field of nutrition, and other health researchers:

(a) The British National Health Service (NHS) view

The NHS Choices website[89] considers that "*most people can get all the vitamins and minerals they need by getting a healthy, balanced diet*". However, they accept that people do take vitamin and mineral supplements, and they warn that they need to make sure that they are not taking higher amounts than they need.

They quote the guidelines of the National Institute for Health and Care excellence (NICE) which considers that some members of the population could be at risk of getting insufficient nutrients. They refer to pregnant women, as well as those contemplating having a baby, as being in need of a folic acid supplement to prevent neural tube defects. (However, they seem to overlook the fact that most people – who cannot afford high quality foods, including organic foods – are eating denatured foods which have few if any nutrients [e.g. junk foods]. That some people are skipping meals to make ends meet. That many people skip breakfast because of poor time management. And they also overlook the fact that most people do not know which foods deliver which vitamins, so that it is often more convenient, and optimizing of health, to simply take a strong multivitamin and mineral supplement every day, plus a B complex preparation; plus a couple of grams of vitamin C, as a minimum!)

NHS Choices also mention that vitamin D supplements should be taken by all pregnant and breastfeeding women. Also children between the ages of 6 months and 5 years should take them, and people who are 65 or over. (They fail to mention that there is a definite link between vitamin D deficiency and depression. Dr Mercola emphasizes that we should get our daily need for vitamin D from direct sunlight, for which purpose we would have to stop using sunscreen creams, or use very weak barriers![90] And neither NHS choices nor Dr Mercola take account of the fact that many of us live in parts of the world where it is difficult to get adequate amounts of vitamin D from sunlight all year round!)

NHS Choices acknowledge that children between the ages of 6 months and 5 years old need to take supplements containing vitamins A, C and D because there may be a lack of variety in their diets.

A medical doctor (GP) might recommend vitamin supplements, the NHS Direct website states, if you had a medical condition; and they cite the example of iron supplements being recommended when someone has iron deficiency anaemia.

~~~

(b) A Nutritional Therapist's perspective

Julia Ross (2003), who is the Executive Director of the Nutritional Therapy Institute Clinic in Mill Valley, California has a different approach towards the use of supplements. She is a psychotherapist and, since 1986, she has been using a combination of nutritional therapy and holistic medical care, with conventional counselling, at the Nutritional Therapy centre which is in the San Francisco Bay area in America.

She has created a 'Master Supplement Plan' which is a basic list of supplements that she recommends for everyone, for the long term, regardless of any conditions such as anxiety or depression that they may have.

She recommends elements that occur naturally in foods and that have a consensus of opinion on their wholesomeness. The nutrients she includes are intended to rebalance and restore the level of nutrients in the body.

She has pointed out to the readers of her book - *'The Mood Cure'*, (2003) - that there are certain factors that stop us achieving a full level of nutrition from food alone and she mentions the following: the amount of light and/or heat to which foods are exposed; the age of the food; inadequate soil used; and the effect that processing has on the food.

Because modern methods of agriculture have resulted in reduced levels of nutrition in our foods, and many of these foods are further denatured by the food processing industry, you are strongly advised to take a good quality multivitamin and mineral supplement, plus a full spectrum B-complex, including B9 (folate); plus magnesium and calcium. You will also benefit from extra vitamin C (at least one gram per day, and perhaps more). Perretta (2001) recommends the following foods in particular: avocado; mushrooms; spring greens and spinach; liver; millet; guava and papaya. Green vegetables are recommended by many nutritionists. And don't forget the oily fish (which contain lots of essential fatty acids [especially omega-

3's])! It aids all brain functions, including managing stress. (Best oily fish: Wild Alaskan salmon, which is available fresh or in tins at Marks and Spencer [UK]; tinned sardines, which can be with tomato sauce for taste purposes; grilled fresh mackerel; or trout).

Ross (2003) also points out that that nutritional needs can vary from person to person, and describes factors which can cause an increased demand for nutrients in the body, such as: levels of stress; undetected illnesses which could have affected someone's level of health; genetic factors; and their level of physical exercise.

Furthermore, the National Diet and Nutrition Survey, by the Food Standards Agency (2004) found that only 14 percent of respondents are eating the recommended five portions of fruit and vegetables every day; and the majority are not getting their full recommended daily allowance (or Reference Nutrient Intake [RNI]) of essential nutrients[91]. This points to a clear need to promote nutritional supplementation alongside a better diet.

(c) A dissenting voice

However, in contrast, a professor at the Yale School of Public Health's Division of Chronic Disease Epidemiology, Susan Taylor-Maine, is of the opinion that supplements are not appropriate, because they "*deliver vitamins out of context.*" (Ballantyne, 2007).[92] There are thousands of phytochemicals, which are protective against chronic ailments such as Alzheimer's disease, cancer, cardio-vascular disease, which are available in vegetables and fruit and other foods, according to Taylor-Maine. She cites the example of isothiocyanates in cabbage and broccoli, carotenoids in carrots and tomatoes, and flavonoids in red wine, soy and cocoa.

She considers that this fusion of the phytochemicals and vitamins has much more impact on the body than if a nutrient was taken on its own. The example cited is lypocene, which is the carotenoid responsible for the red colour of tomatoes.

Because it has been associated with a lower risk for prostate cancer, there has been a lot of supplement manufacturers who have created supplements of lypocene.

However, in Taylor-Maine's opinion, the research suggests that the chemical composition of the food is more beneficial, so that eating tomatoes or tomato products like pasta sauce and ketchup would contain all the varied nutrients inherent in the food. (What she ignores is that this is not an either/or problem. Most people who take vitamin and mineral supplements also try to eat a balanced diet, so that, in addition to getting a reliable source of nutrients [from the supplements], they may also get the range of phytonutrients that she mentions, [assuming those phytonutrients are not also depleted by modern methods of food production!] And you will see, below, when we come to look at research on the provision of vitamin and mineral and omega-3 supplementation of the diets of violent prisoners, in the UK, that *the supplements alone* helped to reduce anger and violence, without any change to the *actual foods* consumed! So, quite clearly, ***supplementation works*** to help with mood management! This is empirical proof, as against Taylor-Maine's non-empirical theorizing.)

(d) In favour of supplements

In contrast with Taylor-Maine, Patrick Holford states - in his book titled *'Optimum Nutrition for the Mind' (2010)* - that he considers supplements to be essential. He considers that nutrition holds the key to optimising mental health, and reducing mental health problems.

He cites evidence of the effectiveness of supplements in a research project conducted by Gwillym Roberts and David Benton in 1988[93]. They ran a randomised, double-blind, placebo-controlled trial. Sixty children were involved in the research study. Thirty of them were put on a special multivitamin and mineral supplement which was created to make sure they had an ideal intake of key nutrients.

The other thirty children were on an identical looking placebo. The children's IQ scores were measured at the start of the trial, and again after 8 months.

After the 8 months of taking the supplements, there was an increase of over 10 points in the non-verbal IQ of the children. Also some children were getting more than a 20 point improvement in their IQ.

No changes were observed in those on the placebos, or a control group of students who hadn't taken any supplements or placebos.

Holford stated: *"The study was published in the Lancet medical journal and was the subject of a BBC Horizon TV documentary, the day after which every single children's multivitamin in Britain sold out."*(Page 121)

He also recommends essential fat supplements, because they promote brain function and health; as well as supplementing with amino acids[94], in particular for people suffering with depression or neurotransmitter deficiencies.

(e) A critique of Holford´s position

Ben Goldacre has criticised Patrick Holford's views on the need for supplements in our diet, and considers that, as Holford sells supplements with his own brand name on them, then by implication there are commercial interests at work in his promotion of the need for supplements.[95] However, this would only be a valid criticism if there was *no evidence* - from reliable research sources - for claims of efficacy by vitamin pill manufacturers. But that evidence does exist!

Ben Goldacre describes Patrick Holford as a *"man who sells pills"*. Goldacre ("a man who sells books castigating others") also describes himself as being very critical of the *"whole phenomenon of pill dependence"*, and thinks that commercial interests are trying to persuade people that all our problems of lack of sleep, headaches, lack of sexual appetite, and heart disease **can be cured by biological means**. He considers that these afflictions are as a result of our lifestyle and social behaviour, and are not easily cured. (It is quite wrong to imply that Patrick Holford believes that all health problems can be cured by vitamin supplements, and supplements alone!)

We totally agree with Goldacre's claim that it is impossible to solve *a lifestyle imbalance* by working on any **one** aspect of that imbalance (such as supplementing vitamins and minerals). But Goldacre is *disingenuous* in presenting his argument in this way. *Almost nobody in the field of lifestyle medicine* is suggesting that people should "**just** take supplements"! This, apparently, includes Patrick Holford. See for example the three video testimonials on Holford's website - here: https://www.patrickholford.com/health-club. These video testimonials are not "all about Holford's supplements". These three individuals, who have recovered from various diseases or health conditions with the help of Patrick Holford's 'lifestyle management' approach, mention: **Diet** (including the glycaemic load diet) ... **supplements** ... **mental attitude** ... and **physical exercise**. So it is not all about supplements by any means.

The fact that Goldacre focuses on the 'commercial interest' that Holford has in promoting supplements is a sign of how *shallow* his critique is. He does not mention any *weakness* in the idea that supplements can be *helpful* (alongside diet and exercise approaches) for people who want to take responsibility for managing their own health and wellbeing. People in glasshouses should not throw stones. Ben Goldacre has a 'commercial interest' in "debunking" Holford and others. Ben Goldacre, it seems, is a 'professional debunker of apparently *scientific efforts* (as well as *pseudoscience*)'. He gains money from *selling books that castigate other people's efforts*.

In Goldacre (2012), he makes the following opening statement, with which we heartily agree:

"*Medicine is broken. And I genuinely believe that if patients and the public ever fully understand what has been done to them – what doctors, academics and regulators have permitted – they will be angry*". (Goldacre, 2012. Page ix)[96].

This statement, logically, should put Goldacre in the same camp as Holford and others who are leading a movement towards 'lifestyle medicine', where individuals *take personal responsibility* for their own health, through diet, exercise, mind management, stress management, vitamin and mineral supplementation, and so on.

This author (Renata Taylor-Byrne) has used multivitamin and mineral supplementation for years – alongside organic food, balanced diet, adequate water consumption (which means at least six glasses per day), elimination of sugar, alcohol, tobacco, (most) grains, and other sources of inflammation – to maintain her own physical health and emotional well-being.

My co-author of this book (Jim Byrne) has used a similar strategy of balanced and healthy diet, supplementation, exercise, meditation, relaxation, and so on, to manage his own health and well-being.

We do, of course, accept that any particular brand of vitamin pill, or any type of pill, could have negative side effects, and consumers should monitor how they feel 24 to 36 hours after taking a new vitamin pill, to see how ti affects their energy, mood and skin response (if any). And if problems build up over time, not only should they experiment with the elimination of particular foods, but also particular vitamin pills, to see what might be causing the problem.

But to advocate the elimination of all vitamin supplements because the 'Little Pharma' industry promotes its own products is not a sensible response. There is, as yet, no evidence (that we know of) that 'Little Pharma' engages in the kind of dirty tricks that characterizes Big Pharma!

(f) Additional forms of dietary supplementation

Dr David Perlmutter (2015)[97] recommends, for optimum brain health, that people supplement with probiotics[98]. This is to ensure that there are more good gut bacteria in the body than bad, and that there is enough to strengthen the lining of the intestines, reduce gut permeability, and any inflammatory molecules, and increase BDNF[99], which is the brain's growth hormone.

In his book titled *'Brain Maker' (2015),* he describes the views of the biologist and Nobel laureate Elie Mechnikov who observed that for humans to live a long life, a healthy balance of bacteria in the gut was essential. He considered that the good bacteria must outnumber the bad, and Dr Perlmutter states that since Mechnikov put forward this thesis, more and more scientific research is confirming the idea that... *"Up to 90% of all known human illness can be traced back to an unhealthy gut".* (Page 7).

That deserves to be repeated. It seems, from scientific studies, that: ***Up to 90% of all known human illness can be traced back to an unhealthy gut. And this, by implication, may also refer to all emotional disturbances which are not based on social-psychological sources that can be identified – such as external stressors, loss, failure, frustration, or interpersonal conflict.***

This idea is certainly supported by scientific evidence cited by Enders (2015, pages 114-133).

Perlmutter approves of supplementation with live bacteria and considers that five core probiotic species are the best ones for supporting brain health. These are: *Lactobacillus plantarum, Lactobacillus Acidophilus, Lactobacillus brevis, Bifidobacterium lactis,* and *Bifido-bacterium longum.*

He also recommends five supplements that will encourage and preserve an equilibrium of healthy bacteria in the gut: DHA, turmeric, coconut oil, alpha-lipoic acid and vitamin D.

~~~

Of course, if you cannot afford to buy probiotic supplements, you can try to consume pre-biotic foods, which manufacture probiotics in your gut. As a general rule, high fibre foods promote the growth of friendly bacteria. One of us (Jim) supplements with psyllium husk for this purpose – though we both eat high fibre diets.

A local life coach in Hebden Bridge – Max Kohanzad - has written about prebiotics:

"There is a way to fix the gut and replenish your gut with good powerful healthy gut bacteria. Firstly stop eating wheat, alcohol, cheese, milk and sugar. If you can, don't eat any grains or pulses for about two weeks (think Atkins diet with organic meats and wild fish) so that your gut wall has a chance to heal.

"You can eat most vegetables, but do aim to mainly feed your good bacteria by eating lots of asparagus, green bananas, parsnips, leeks, onions, garlic, endives, cold potato and or cold rice.

Secondly invest in the best pre- and probiotics you can afford.

...

"This small article is not intended to replace medical advice".[100].

~~~

Much of this advice will be helpful to many people. There are, as always, exceptions to be considered:

Caveat 1: If you are suffering from IBS, you would be advised not to eat the pre-biotic foods listed above, since many of them may be high in FodMaps (fructans, oligosaccharides, disaccharides, and polyols). Indeed, when one of us (Jim Byrne) changed to a largely low-FodMaps diet, his symptoms of Candida Albicans (including physical tiredness and itchiness, plus lowered mood) quickly improved!

Caveat 2: To resolve any outstanding questions you might have regarding whether or not to supplement with multivitamins and minerals, friendly bacteria, or other nutrients, please talk to a good, personally recommended, lifestyle health professional, or a nutritional therapist. (If you are over the age of forty years, they might also recommend that you supplement with digestive enzymes).

And when you make dietary changes, keep a food diary or journal, and monitor the effects of those changes on your mood, energy level, and skin condition.

~~~

6. How good is the evidence that anxiety, anger and depression can be created by the wrong kind of food and drink?

CBT and REBT theorists take the view that most human disturbance is caused by the *beliefs* and *attitudes* of the client; their 'negative automatic thoughts'; or 'irrational beliefs'. In E-CENT counselling and therapy, we take the view that emotions are innate (as 'affects'), including a capacity for anger/rage, grief/sadness/depression, and anxiety/fear/concern. But it often takes particular kinds of environmental triggers to precipitate strong feelings of anger, anxiety or depression – such as losses, failures, threats, dangers, and so on. But the list of factors that can contribute to emotional problems is very long indeed. (See Byrne, 2016)[101].

On the other hand, we also emphasize that the state of the human organism, in terms of stress, relaxation, health, nourishment, and so on, has a lot to do with how environmental stressors are experienced.

For example, in our experience, a *substantial minority* of clients present with emotional disturbances which cannot be linked – or *entirely* linked, or satisfactorily linked – to their beliefs, attitudes, or even their life challenges. Amongst these cases are:

(a) People who have symptoms of **depression** because of their sugary diets, which sugars cause an overgrowth of 'unfriendly bacteria' in their guts (especially Candida Albicans. See Part 3 for more on this subject). And they are too physically drained to do any exercise.

(b) People who are wrecking their relationships, at home and in work, because of **angry** and **rageful** outbursts, which seem to be largely (or significantly) caused by their overconsumption of junk food (containing lots of trans-fats and sugars). And:

(c) People who are **anxious** and **panicked** because of over-consumption of caffeine, sugar, alcohol, recreational drugs and other stimulants; and who are failing to exercise.

There are many different views on how effective changes in diet can mitigate the problems which are created by harmful diets and I will give you a summary of these views, firstly in relation to the experience of anxiety.

(a) Anxiety and nutrition

Before we look at the role of diet in causing and curing anxiety, we had better define what we mean by anxiety.

(i) What is anxiety?

The *Oxford English Dictionary* (Waite, 2012) defines anxiety as a *"feeling or state of unease or concern"*. And Nicky Hayes (1994)[102] describes it as a state of emotional arousal which persists.

She gives the example of being anxious about paying bills. This can be a *constant worry*, and not just a passing concern. She describes it as *an unpleasant emotion*, and it is a state of physical arousal, and is also described as stress.

Anxiety (in the present moment) is built upon our innate sense of fear of threats and dangers (which seem to be just up ahead, in the immediate future). Of course, our *innate* sense of fear, with which we are born, is socialized by our family of origin, and our schooling, so that it takes forms which are historically dictated.

Back to Nicky Hayes' example: Worrying about paying bills, for example, if prolonged, can interfere with our physical health. This can result in our immune system lacking sufficient strength to fight off colds, infections and serious illnesses. So anxiety can lead to physical illness, and not taking care of our physical body can also lead to anxiety.

Many people who experience regular feelings of anxiety either "self- medicate" or go to the doctor, who then prescribes tranquilisers (or, even worse, antidepressants). Here is an interesting statistic quoted by Patrick Holford (2010).

"In one week in Britain, we pop 10 million tranquilisers, puff 10 million cannabis joints and drink 120 million alcoholic drinks" (page 174). And much of this seems to be directed at reducing our feelings of anxiety.

Dale Pinnock (2015)[103] describes anxiety as one of the most common mental health disorders in the UK, and affecting more women than men; and mainly people in the 35-59 age group.

He considers anxiety to be a valuable constituent of our survival skills, and *only* becomes a problem for people when there is a build-up of anxiety. It is very practical to be apprehensive about a challenge to our skills or self-concept, and it makes us want to take measures to improve the stressful situation we are in. But if nothing is done about it, it can develop into a general anxiety disorder. This means that people suffer from anxiety continually, and even when the obvious anxiety-arousing situations are eliminated, the anxiety doesn't go away. It simply moves onto another problem. It has become a generalized state of arousal, looking for things to worry about.

(ii) Nutrition for anxiety

So how can nutrition help in relation to these high levels of anxiety? There are certain substances which the body needs which will reduce anxiety levels. And one such substance which has a powerful effect on the nervous system is omega-3 fatty acid, which is present in fish oils, plus plant and nut oils. (Common sources of omega-3 fatty acids include cod liver oil, and krill oil).

Pinnock (2015) cites evidence of the benefits that were derived by 68 students who took part in a 2011 double-blind, crossover trial or research experiment. (Kiecolt-Glaser, and colleagues, 2011)[104]. This research was considered to be the first double-blind trial to conclude that there could be anxiety-reducing benefits in omega-3 fatty acids. And there are earlier scientific studies to support the claim that oily fish can be helpful in the reduction of panic attacks (which are a result of anxiety about anxiety about anxiety). (See Perretta, 2001, page 90)[105].

However, as there were no participants in the Kiecolt-Glaser (2011) study who were diagnosed (officially) as having a specific anxiety disorder, at the time of the research, this fact has to be taken into account.

But this is balanced out by the fact that "...*there are literally hundreds of anecdotal reports of omega-3 offering benefits to patients with anxiety issues. Reports abound from practitioners, on patient forums, and so on*". (Pinnock, 2015).

Pinnock (2015) also considers that magnesium, glutamine, and blood sugar management play key roles in the reduction and management of anxiety.

Magnesium is very important for the body in terms of ensuring relaxation in the muscles, reducing nervous tension, and helping the mind to slow down. It is involved in over 1,000 biochemical reactions in the body, and is described by Pinnock as *"one of the most deficient minerals in the modern diet"*. So he encourages people to consume seeds and nuts, dark green leafy vegetable like spinach and kale, and fruit: e.g. bananas.

Magnesium is also recommended for anxiety by Linda Lazarides, who "...has worked as a pioneering alternative health professional in a GP practice", in the UK, "treating hundreds of people referred to her by a doctor"[106]. She mentions the following food sources of magnesium: "Bitter chocolate, leafy green vegetables, nuts, sunflower and sesame seeds, soya beans, whole grains (particularly [gluten free] oats." (Page 281).

She also recommends "standardized extracts" of the "power mushroom", Reishi. (Page 290).

Glutamine is a constituent of the neurotransmitter, GABA (gamma-amino-butyric acid). GABA has a calming effect on adrenaline and noradrenaline, and serotonin. If there is a low level of GABA in our brains we can experience tension and anxiety (and depression and insomnia).

Glutamine isn't available in the UK as it has been classified by the European Union as a medicine. It isn't found in food but its constituents are, and one of these is the amino acid glucosamine. The food sources of this nutrient are obtained from spinach, walnuts, broccoli, brown rice, almonds and bananas.

Another important factor in the management of anxiety involves regulating our blood sugar levels[107]. Dale Pinnock considers this to be a simple skill to master, "...*but the impact it can have on your mind **and** mood is quite staggering.*" (Page 36)

Why can it make such a difference? The reason is because the sugar that we get in our bodies from processed foods such as white bread, white rice, white pasta, chocolates and fizzy drinks (to name a few junk foods) is immediately available, and immediately affects us. The body doesn't have to work hard to digest the food and extract the nutrients.

As a result, blood sugar rises rapidly and we can feel full of energy as a consequence. But this reaction is very bad for our body, which handles this sudden influx of sugar by releasing the hormone *insulin*. This informs our cells to mop up excess sugar very quickly.

As a result of this activity by our insulin secretions, our blood sugar then drops, but it goes *too low*. Because of this drop, the hormone adrenaline is released. This is to initiate the unleashing of *stored* glucose, and then the experience of adrenaline is felt by the body. And "*...adrenaline is to anxiety what petrol is to a bonfire*": (Pinnock). You will then experience a change in your breathing rate; your heartbeat gets faster and faster; and your mind starts to race. These symptoms can be very unpleasant if you are already prone to experiencing anxiety.

Pinnock (2015) recommends always combining protein in a meal with unrefined carbohydrates[108], so that the digestion of a meal takes longer and releases energy for the body in small increments, rather than as a sudden onslaught with the corresponding release of adrenaline. This is said to be a good mood and energy level stabiliser. (However, this contradicts the Hay diet, which suggests not combining protein and carbohydrates, because a sluggish digestion can promote a toxic gut and promote inflammation and disease!)

A better strategy, and one that many theorists advocate, is to avoid refined carbohydrate[109] and simple sugars; to mostly eat vegetables, to reduce meat[110]; to eat lots of oily fish, like salmon and sardines; and to eat seeds, nuts and fruits (to the degree that you can tolerate them).

Dale Pinnock thinks that our diet can be a very useful tool for improving our health, because like a drug, food affects the internal environment of the body. In his view: "*To dismiss nutrition within the healthcare picture is at best irresponsible, at worst insane*".

~~~

(iii) Gut bacteria and anxiety

Dr Perlmutter (2015), who is a neurologist, describes anxiety disorders as affecting more than 40 million Americans, and he considers, on the basis of the research he has been doing, **that anxiety is strongly related to a state of disturbance in the gut bacteria.** When people experience unrelenting anxiety, then this means that they may be experiencing what is described by some theorists as an anxiety disorder. This includes panic disorder, obsessive-compulsive disorder, and social phobia and generalised anxiety disorder.

Perlmutter considers that anxiety disorders are caused by a combination of factors which include the condition and processing ability of the gut, and the bacteria which inhabits it. Dr Perlmutter states: "*When the balance of gut bacteria isn't right, other biological pathways – be they hormonal, immunological or neuronal, aren't right either. And the brain's processing centres, such as those that handle emotions, aren't right either.....I've found that patients report never feeling anxious or depressed until they start having problems with their guts. Coincidence? I think not*" (Page 87).

He quotes two significant experiments to substantiate his argument: In a 2011 study published in the Proceedings of the National Academy of Sciences, mice fed probiotics had significantly lower levels of the stress hormone corticosterone, than mice fed plain broth. (J.A. Bravo *and colleagues*, 2011).[111]

The second study he describes was conducted at Oxford University. Neurobiologists found that giving people prebiotics (which is food for the promotion of good bacteria in the gut), resulted in positive psychological effects. It was conducted by K Schmidt *et al.*, (2014)[112]

Forty-five adults between the ages of eighteen and forty-five took either a prebiotic or a placebo every day for three weeks. The participants were then tested so that their ability to process emotional information could be ascertained.

The underlying theory was that if the participants had a high level of anxiety to start with, then they would be more sensitive to and react more quickly to evidence of negativity. The types of negativity shown were negative words and images.

What was observed by the Oxford researchers was that, compared to the placebo group, the individuals who had taken the prebiotics paid more attention to positive information, and less attention to the negative information.

This effect, which has been noticed with individuals on antidepressants or anti-anxiety medication, indicated that the prebiotic group experienced less anxiety when faced with the negative stimuli.

Also, the researchers discovered that the people who took the prebiotics had lower levels of cortisol, when measured via their saliva samples, which were taken in the morning, when cortisol levels are at their highest.

Dr Perlmutter considers that these examples are relevant to the growing evidence of research studies that show a connection between mental health and gut bacteria, in particular in relation to anxiety.

On page 88 of *Brain Maker*, Perlmutter describes a client called Martina, 56, who came to him because she was suffering from anxiety and depression. She had been taking anti-depressants and non-steroid inflammatory drugs (NSAIDs) for 10 years. He immediately ordered laboratory tests which revealed that she was particularly sensitive to gluten and had low levels of vitamin D.

She also had a very high level of LPS. LPS stands for "lipopolysaccharide". This is an endotoxin, which means it's a toxin which comes from within the bacteria in the intestines. When this toxin gets into the bloodstream it triggers an intense inflammatory response in the body. (Normally this endotoxin is blocked from getting into the bloodstream by the *tight junctions* that are present between the cells lining the intestines, which are loosened by gluten and NSAIDs [See footnote 113]).

But when there is damage to the junctions (as can happen with gluten and NSAIDs) then the lining becomes leaky and permeable[113]. Then LPS goes into the blood circulation and can inflict damage on the body. So the level of LPS in the blood indicates that there is leakiness in the gut and of the presence of inflammation in the body in general.

Dr Perlmutter explained to the client that he needed to return her gut to full health. He recommended a gluten-free diet, an oral probiotic program, with probiotic foods and vitamin supplementation.

He also recommended other changes in her lifestyle, such as aerobic exercise and more hours of sleep. Then he asked to see the client again in six weeks.

He describes her as being *"transformed...she looked radiant"*. He and his colleagues at his clinic in Florida always take a picture of their clients at their first session and at the end of the treatment, and he has posted the "before" and "after" pictures of Martina on his website at: www.DrPerlmutter.com.

Her chronic anxiety had vanished and she was now off all medications (although Dr Perlmutter points out that he did not recommend that she stopped her medication. Apparently she had stopped taking her antidepressant four weeks prior to the first appointment with him).

"I feel like the fog has finally lifted", she said to the doctor, and reported that she was sleeping well, enjoying her exercise and for the first time in decades was having regular bowel movements.

Dr Perlmutter has found reports by researchers whose experiments have been printed in the Journal of Applied Microbiology, who have described the potential of specific types of *lactobacillus* and *bifidobacterium*, in probiotic form, to reduce anxiety, and restore the gut to normal functioning and intestinal health.

Jenny Sansouci, who wrote a research paper on 'Nutritional approaches to anxiety' in 2002[114], summarised some of the key points of her nutritional research in her internet blog. She described the fact that millions of Americans take anti-anxiety medication, with the side effects of *"...slurred speech, tiredness, mental confusion, memory loss and delirium"*.

She has found that people's diets play a very big role in reducing anxiety, and that medicinal drugs are unnecessary as a form of treatment. She considers the top offenders for the creation of anxiety in the human body are as follows: caffeine, sugar, artificial sweeteners and alcohol. She cites an example of the Starbucks "Grande-sized" coffee, which contains 330 mg of caffeine. And if a dose of caffeine is 300 mg or above, then this causes a very strong, sudden increase in tension and anxiety. This response has been corroborated in one research study.

She states that when we consume sugar, it has the effect of causing our blood sugar to drop, resulting in an increase in anxiety, light-headedness, irritability and feelings of weakness. She also mentions artificial sweeteners, which are composed of chemical elements which reduce the level of serotonin in the brain, with the result that stress, anxiety and depression are experienced. (Again, the link is most likely not via serotonin, but some other, as yet undiscovered, route).

The bottom line seems to be this: Avoid caffeine, or keep your consumption low, because caffeine can simulate anxious arousal in the guts and chest, causing the mind to panic. Keep blood glucose levels even, by consuming slow-burning foods, and avoiding sugary and starchy foods, process foods, junk foods of all kinds. Keep your magnesium and GABA levels high, by eating dark green leafy vegetables (like spinach and kale); nuts (walnuts and almonds); and seeds; fruit (e.g. bananas); and gluten-free oats (if you can tolerate them), and others. Take probiotics for gut health, and eat lots of fibre (including supplementing with psyllium husk) to serve as prebiotics, which encourage the growth friendly bacteria. Avoid gluten, sugar and artificial sweeteners and alcohol. Consume calming foods: Drink camomile tea and eat lots of salads with lettuce, which has a calming effect. Finally, eat lots of oily fish, and take omega-3 fatty acid supplements, like cod liver oil and/or krill oil.

~~~

(b) Anger and nutrition

Now the experience of anger will be examined to see if its emergence is at all engendered, or brought about by, nutritional factors. But first we need to define anger.

(i) What is anger?

Anger is defined as: *"A strong feeling of extreme displeasure"* by the Oxford English Dictionary (Waite, 2012). It can have a negative effect on the person experiencing it, and their relationships with others, at home and at work. The E-CENT theory of anger says that anger is one of our basic emotions. It's innate. It's the emotion that drives the 'fight response' (just as anxiety drives the 'flight response'). It was selected by nature for its survival value. We would not survive for long without an innate sense of angering in response to abuse or neglect. We also would not survive for long if we did not quickly learn how to *moderate* our anger as young children. My anger is a two-edged sword. It can help to protect me, and it can attract hostile reactions from others.

When we are stressed, we may over-react and behave in angry and aggressive ways, which we later regret. Sometimes this loss of control may result from inadequate sleep, or lack of physical exercise, use of alcohol and other recreational drugs – but it can also result from certain approaches to diet and nutrition, as well as powerful negative attitudes towards frustrations of any kind, or insults of any kind.

(ii) Nutrition and anger

Julia Ross (2003) - a psychotherapist who runs an addiction, mood and eating problems centre in California - is of the opinion that if we have low levels of serotonin in our bodies then this causes feelings of "irritability, edginess and impatience": (Page 37)[115]. (There is a lot of controversy around the idea of a link between serotonin levels and depression; but there has been at least one recent study linking serotonin to anger control)[116]. Ross (2003) gives the example in her book, *'The Mood Cure'*, of the difference which was observed in the serotonin levels of violent and non-violent criminals. Apparently violent criminals have much lower levels of serotonin than non-violent criminals. She hypothesises that there is a relationship between the expression of angry feelings and low levels of serotonin.

Very low levels of serotonin can damage relationships, in her experience. Many of her clients have dramatically improved their marriages, by raising serotonin levels, as they have subsequently become less angry and judgmental with their partners. So she concludes that a low levels of serotonin is the trigger for angry behaviours and states. From this she concludes that, if people understand the brain chemistry of anger, then this will help them, because:

"Understanding the brain chemistry of anger can be a powerful force for healing old family wounds and putting an end to the wounding pattern..." (Page 37).

Presumably, once you realize that anger can be driven by 'bad chemicals' it become easier to forgive others for their former angry outbursts.

She also describes being *"intimidated"* by her own angry clients and describes one sixteen year old teenager who was brought to her consulting room by his frightened but loving mother.

It emerged very slowly from their conversation that he was suffering from long-standing irritability, insomnia and depression and a low sense of self-worth.

After consulting a nutritionist at the clinic, Ross gave the boy two capsules of 5-HTP. After ten minutes had passed, there was a visible change in his behaviour from sullen and moody withdrawal, to behaviour which was open and friendly towards the therapist and he actually gave unrequested information to her. (Of course, there could have been a placebo effect here; and his attachment system may have been differently affected by Ross's behaviour before and after the administration of the pills!)

The client's mother was very moved to observe this change in her son's behaviour and was very grateful to see him returning to the happy boy that she knew he was (or had been).

Ross also states that variations in the minerals copper, manganese or other nutrients in the body can bring about very angry behaviour.

We also know of research findings, reported by Patrick Holford in his book, *'Optimum Nutrition for the Mind'* (2010), include a description of a study which was conducted with sixty nine repeatedly violent offenders. The research was conducted by Dr Matti Virkkunen in Finland[117]. Here is a summary:

(iii) Blood sugar levels and transfats affect anger levels

The glucose balance of these sixty nine violent offenders was investigated and revealed that each one of them had *reactive hypoglycaemia* **(defined in footnote)**[118]. And a later study conducted with the same type of repeat offenders replicated the findings of this earlier study by Vikkunen.

In another research project, this time conducted by Professor Stephen Schoenthaler (1983)[119] of California State University, three thousand inmates of a prison were placed on a strict diet. The diet contained a marked reduction in sugary and refined foods. The results of this dietary restriction were as follows: There was a 25% reduction in assaults at the prison, a 21% reduction in anti-social behaviour, a *75% reduction in the use of restraints and a 100% reduction in suicides!*

A later study affirmed the validity of the results of Schoenthaler's research. In 1983, in a double-blind study of 1,382 detained juvenile offenders on a sugar-restricted diet, the effects of this restricted diet were as follows: the anti-social behaviour dropped by 44% with the most outstanding reductions happening to the most serious offenders (Schoenthaler 1983)[120].

There is also research which suggests a link between trans-fats (including hydrogenated fats in processed foods), on the one hand, and aggression, irritability and impatience, on the other.[121]

And, there have been several follow-up studies which have replicated and extended Schoenthaler's (1983) results, demonstrating a strong link between healthy diet and more pro-social behaviour indicative of better mood management and emotional control[122]. Of particular note is the finding that keeping the poor quality diet of prisoners, but adding vitamin and mineral supplements, plus fish oil supplements, will normally reduce anti-social behaviour, as levels of anger decline. (This shows that *supplements can improve diets which are nutrient deficient!)*[123]

And in the UK, between 1995 and 1997, at Aylesbury Young Offenders Institution, a placebo-controlled, randomised trial, was conducted by Dr Bernard Gesch (2002), in which young offenders were given food supplements (including vitamins, minerals and essential fatty acids), and it was found that they committed 37% fewer violent offences, while the inmates who received the placebo showed no such reduction; thus demonstrating that improved nutrition reduces angry outbursts (which were being fuelled by vitamin and mineral and fatty acid deficiencies).

The whole range of research studies, described above, point out the relationship between the body and its reaction to:

(1) Toxins in the diet - like alcohol, caffeine and trans-fats – and also:

(2) The negative effects of nutritional deficiencies (such as lack of omega-3 fatty acids), and/or:

(3) Blood-sugar regulation...

...in these cases resulting in anger and anti-social behaviour; but also potentially playing a role in anxiety and depression.

~~~

(c) Investigating links between diet and depression

Before we look at the links between diet and depression, we need to consider what we mean by depression.

(i) *What is depression?*

The Oxford English Dictionary (Waite, 2012) defines depression as: "*a mental state in which a person has feelings of great unhappiness and hopelessness*".

More specifically, the Oxford Dictionary of Psychology defines it as: "*a mood state of sadness, gloom and pessimistic ideation, with loss of interest or pleasure in normally enjoyable activities, accompanied in severe cases by anorexia and consequent weight loss, insomnia, feelings of worthlessness and guilt, diminished ability to concentrate, or recurrent thoughts of death or suicide...*". *(*Colman 2002)[124].

One of the difficulties of defining depression is that it can easily be confused with grief. Feelings of grief, sadness and loss at the death of someone or some animal that we loved - or if we have lost a job or career, or a love partner (through divorce, for example) - are perfectly natural. There is a therapeutic healing process that we all go through as we come to terms with our loss. It has survival value, helping us to slowly rebuild our map of reality, and adjust ourselves to the new world, of which our loved person, or other treasured object, is no longer a part.

We need to go through that natural process, crying and completing our acceptance of the loss, so that we slowly heal. Grief is transient (though it can go on for a year or more, and often eighteen months or more – *gradually* diminishing).

If someone is *still* experiencing deep pain and feelings of loss after about eighteen months, and the feelings of grief and hopelessness persist, then this is what we properly call **depression**, or **stuck-depression**.

The NHS Choices web-blog (2016) states that there is no single factor which brings about depression. You can develop it for different reasons and it has many different triggers; and some of the triggers they mention are: bereavement, divorce, redundancy, illness, and worries about job security and/or money. It is also considered to be brought on if you have a life-threatening or chronic illness. Additional causes they mention include your personality, family history, giving birth, loneliness or taking drugs.

In CBT/REBT, depression is normally thought to result from loss or failure, and our *demanding attitudes* towards loss and failure. But for the Buddhists, it is enough to desire something which you cannot have, and depression can result. Furthermore, the CBT perspective overlooks those cases where depression is triggered by *gut disbiosis*, Candida Albicans, or sedentary lifestyle; or unhealthy diet and inadequate nutrition. And it also excludes natural and normal grief.

~~~

(ii) Treating depression

There are many different views about how to treat depression, and here is a summary of some of the most recent explanations of what is happening to us when we are depressed.

Firstly, the views of Dr Kelly Brogan will be summarised, as she has a unique explanation, which she has described in her recent book, titled *'A Mind of Your Own'* (2016)[125]. She is a practising psychiatrist in America, with training as a medical doctor, and a degree in cognitive neuroscience, including clinical training from the NYU School of Medicine. She uses holistic methods of treating her patients and describes her work as 'lifestyle medicine'. In this approach, she uses the techniques of meditation, nutrition and physical activity as crucial daily habits with which to treat her depressed patients (and this approach overlaps, but is not co-extensive with, *the E-CENT approach* [Byrne, 2016]).

Dr Brogan's view is that depression is a symptom or sign: *"...that something is off-balance or ill in the body that needs to be remedied"*.

She considers that mental illness symptoms aren't entirely psychological or solely neurochemical. And she points out in her book that there is no single study which has produced evidence that depression is caused by a lack of chemical equilibrium in the brain.

She considers depression to be a grossly misidentified state and in particular for women who, in the US, are being medicated at the rate of one in seven. Also, one in four women in their 40's and fifties use psychiatric drugs.

She states: *"We owe most of our mental illnesses – including their kissing cousins such as chronic worry, fogginess and crankiness – to **lifestyle factors** and undiagnosed **physiological** conditions that develop in places far away from the brain, such as the gut and the thyroid"*, and she goes on to state that:

*"You might owe your gloominess and unremitting unease to an imbalance that is only **indirectly** related to your brain's internal chemistry. Indeed, what you eat for breakfast … and how you deal with that high cholesterol and afternoon headache (think Lipitor[126] and Advil[127]) could have **everything** to do with the causes and symptoms of depression."*

Her opinion of the foolishness of applying chemical solutions to people's problems is very clear. In her view: *"… if you think a chemical pill can save, cure or 'correct' you, you're dead wrong. That is about as misguided as taking aspirin for a nail stuck in your foot."*

Her approach is to get a medical and personal history of her clients, their manner of birth (natural or section), whether breast fed or not; and she orders lab tests to ascertain the whole picture of their biological make-up.

She focusses on the information from their cellular analysis and the workings of the immune system, and points out to the reader of her book that, over the last twenty years, medical research has identified *the significant part that* **inflammation** *plays in the creation of mental illness.*

She also focuses on the client's lifestyle, dietary habits e.g. sugar consumption, the condition of their guts, and microbe balance (in their guts), hormone levels - e.g. thyroid and cortisol - and genetic variations in their DNA, which could affect their susceptibility to depression. And finally, their beliefs about their own health can also play a role, she says.

So Dr Kelly Brogan shares the same conviction as Dr Perlmutter (2015): *that the state of our guts is a very important determinant of our emotional well-being.*

Dr Perlmutter (2015) states: "*Depression can no longer be viewed as a disorder rooted solely in the brain. Some of the studies have been downright eye-opening. For example when scientists give people with no signs of depression an infusion of a substance to trigger inflammation (in the body), classic depression symptoms develop almost instantly*". (Page 76)

Perlmutter is a board-certified neurologist and Fellow of the American College of Nutrition. He is also president of the Perlmutter Health Centre in Naples, Florida. Dr Perlmutter considers that our mental health and physical wellness are *totally affected* by the internal systems of bacteria that operate in the gut.

But what exactly is going on in our guts? Apparently, we've all got millions of microbes in our body and most of them live in our digestive tract (10,000 species!). And each of the microbes have their own DNA, and that means that for every human gene in our body, there are at least 360 microbial genes. These organisms include fungi, bacteria and viruses. In a healthy gut, most of these microorganisms are 'friendly', with a few 'bad' bacteria which are controlled by the 'good' stuff.

These tiny microbes: (1) strongly influence our immune system; (2) affect absorption of nutrients; (3) signal to us whether our stomach is empty or full; (4) and determine our level of inflammation and/or detoxification (which are directly related to disease and health). They also affect our moods.

Apparently our guts contain 70-80% of our immune system, and so our gut bacteria participate in maintaining our immunity.

They can also keep cortisol and adrenaline in check. These are the two major hormones of the stress response, which can cause havoc in the body when they are continually triggered and flowing.

And our gut microbes influence whether we get any or all of the following conditions: Allergies, ADHD, asthma, dementia, cancer and diabetes, a good night's sleep; or whether we quickly fall prey to disease-causing germs. And there is increasing evidence of a link to anxiety and depression.

Dr Perlmutter makes recommendations for changes in people's diet which he says will:

(1) treat and prevent brain disorders;

(2) alleviate moodiness, anxiety and depression;

(3) bolster the immune system and reduce autoimmunity problems; and

(4) improve metabolic disorders, including diabetes and obesity, which are all linked to overall brain and body health.

He makes recommendations which are very practical, including the following six essential keys:

(1) Only eat gluten-free foods;

(2) Consume healthy fats;

(3) Take prebiotics (which are functional foods, high in fibre, that stimulate the growth of healthy bacteria, helping produce digestive enzymes);

(4) Take probiotics (like *Acidophilus*), which stimulate the growth of micro-organisms, especially those with beneficial properties (which are the 'friendly' intestinal flora);

(5) Eat fermented foods (like sauerkraut); and low-carb foods (such as: meat, fish, [organic] eggs, vegetables, fruit, nuts, seeds, high-fat dairy, fats, healthy oils and maybe even some tubers and non-gluten grains).

What's wrong with gluten? As was described earlier in the book (in Part 1, Section 4(f)), gluten is a protein found in wheat, rye and barley and (by cross-contamination, in oats – unless they are declared to be gluten-free). Gluten damages the lining of our guts, because it causes the release of a protein called gliadin, which damages the tight junctions, allowing toxins to enter the blood stream, and on into the brain.

To recap on what gliadin does, it pulls apart the tight junctions that exist between the cells in our guts. The space between the cells start to widen, and the result is that toxins and larger molecules of food (which normally pass through the intestine and are eliminated), begin to leak into the blood circulation system of our bodies.

As a result, you get increased inflammation when your intestinal barrier is compromised. If we have a 'leaky gut' then the blood/brain barrier's integrity is also threatened. The blood-brain barrier (which has been thought of as a "highly protective, fortified portal keeping bad things out of the brain") is weakened if the gut is leaky, and this lets in molecules that could be really bad for the body, including bacteria, viruses and proteins that would normally have been prevented from crossing the blood/brain barrier.

Dr Perlmutter illustrates in his book how eating gluten harms the gut wall and causes all sorts of problems for the body and brain. The effects on our mental life of a change of diet is clear to see in the experiments Dr Perlmutter describes, especially in relation to children who have autism.

As I have mentioned previously in this part, Dr Perlmutter has a lot of case studies on his website (www.DrPermutter.com) and he presents a picture of one of his clients, Martina, who came to him for anxiety and depression. He advised Martina to change her diet (gluten-free, prebiotics, probiotics, etc.), and he has presented a "before" and "after" picture of her on his website. The contrast is dramatic. If you go on his website, and click on "Success" and then go to "Older posts", which is right down at the bottom of the page, at the left hand side, you will see a picture of Martina before and after treatment from Dr Perlmutter. This is dramatic evidence that Dr Perlmutter's theory of gut-brain linkages is valid and helpful. *You can cure depression by healing your guts!*

Patrick Holford (2010) states that depression is the result of various factors, and there is also never one single cure.

"One of the greatest unrecognised truths is that ensuring optimum nutrition for your mind not only improves mood but gives you the energy and motivation to make changes in your life".

"Few psychotherapists recognise how much better their results would be if they helped their clients tune up their brain chemistry". (Page 145)

He considers that a lot of people taking anti-depressants have something in their life which is not working, and he gives the examples of jobs, or relationships, or unrealised dreams that are affecting a person. Unexpressed anger ("anger without enthusiasm") could be the problem, when it is being bottled up inside.

He also considers that people can suffer from depression: *"because they are betraying themselves"*, and he encourages his readers to ask themselves: *"In what way am I betraying myself, not living my life true to who I am or could be?"* And if there is any resonance within the reader as they read this question, then he recommends that they would get a lot of value from seeing a counsellor or psychotherapist.

However, he considers that *"as a general rule"* you need to make sure that there is equilibrium in your neurotransmitters, which are chemicals that are discharged from nerve cells. Each neurotransmitter passes on an impulse from one nerve cell to another nerve, or to a muscle, organ, or other part of the body. They are messengers of neurologic information, from one cell to another. And the composition of the neurotransmitters is of importance.

However, we must bear in mind that the serotonin-depression link has never been decisively proven, and there are lots of arguments against this theory[128].

In conventional medicine: Low levels of serotonin (which are related to depression) and dopamine, adrenaline and noradrenaline (which are related to motivation and drive) are assumed to be remedied by the use of prescription drugs, which have different kinds of side effects. *But there is no evidence that serotonin directly underpins happiness*[129].

Holford (2010) recommends supplementation of natural herbs, minerals and other chemicals to balance the neurotransmitters instead, and considers that the way forward for the treatment of depression is by the use of nutritional strategies. (Logically, he should also have added physical exercise, and perhaps meditation, and other lifestyle factors [and, indeed, elsewhere, he does just that!]).

His opinion (about the healing effect of dietary changes upon emotional states} is confirmed by evidence cited by Dr Sarah Brewer (2013) who describes the phenomenon of populations who rarely eat fish and have higher levels of depression when compared with frequent fish-eaters. The adding of fish oils – which contain essential fatty acids - (at the rate of 2 grams per day) to the standard drug treatment for depression, were shown to improve the symptoms of depression within *two weeks*, compared with the placebo. (This supports the theory that it is **new brain cell genesis** which clears up depression in some clients, and not the serotonin – since omega-3 fatty acids are involved in the building of brain cell membranes).

Robert Redfern (2016) - who is a nutritionist, author and broadcaster - describes the findings from research conducted at the University of Eastern Finland[130]. The researchers did a follow-up study of 2,000 men and found that a healthy diet can reduce the risk of severe depression. When the study participants ate a healthy diet free from processed foods, researchers observed fewer depressive symptoms and a lower risk of depression overall.

Apparently, the researchers identified that a crucial nutrient which benefitted mental health was increased by the healthy research diets - folate (vitamin B9)[131]. Also in the study researchers found that the eating of junk food, and processed meat and sugars brought about an increase in the symptoms of depression. According to Redfern:

"Depression levels spiked amongst the participants when they were eating an unhealthy diet, with foods like sugary desserts and snacks, sugary drinks, processed meats, sausages, manufactured foods, breads and baked or processed potatoes."

In conclusion: Depression, as shown in the different views of the researchers and writers quoted above, is a very complex topic; different solutions have been described, acknowledging the well-proven part that nutrition plays in reducing depression. What has also been mentioned is the value of investigating the reasons for its presence in someone's life which could be based on very difficult, unpleasant life circumstances, like losses and failures, which have not been dealt with or processed. But if we want to be optimally helpful to people who are depressed, we should look at their diet and exercise regimes, in addition to looking at their conditions of existence.

7. Diet and good mental and physical health in general

Research results on the effectiveness of the Mediterranean diet, and diets from Scandinavia and Japan, are beginning to be taken seriously by psychiatrists, and a new field of medicine, called nutritional psychiatry, is emerging out of the insights from recently published research findings.

For example, the diet which has the *strongest* evidence of its effectiveness is the Mediterranean diet, followed in Italy, Spain and Greece. This diet consists of vegetables, fruits, nuts, fish, whole grains, a small amount of lean meats, olive oil and small amounts of wine. The value of this diet as a preventative against depression was examined in a 2011 study of 12,000 healthy Spaniards over the course of a median period of 6 years[132]. The study was conducted by Almudena Sanchez-Villegas, who is a public health expert of the University of Las Palmas de Gran Canaria, and her colleagues.

The research showed that compared with people who *didn't* consume a Mediterranean diet, those people who did were much less likely to experience depression. Also for those participants who adhered to the diet most conscientiously, the risk dropped by a significant 30%!

Another research project led by Sanchez-Villegas - called PREDIMED (Prevention with Mediterranean Diet study); a multicentre research project - evaluated nearly 7,500 women and men in Spain. They were initially investigating whether the Mediterranean diet prevents heart disease, which was confirmed as true.

However Villegas and her colleagues then investigated the information relating to rates of depression in the PREDIMED participants. Compared to subjects who eat a general low-fat diet, those who stuck to the "nut-enriched Mediterranean diet" had a lower incidence of depression.

This was especially apparent with people who had diabetes. Their risk of experiencing depression reduced by 40%. (Sanchez-Villegas *et al.*, 2013).

As Robert Redfern (2016) points out, anything that promotes good physical health is most likely to help with high levels of emotional well-being. This is obvious, when we consider that we are body-minds, and not *separate* bodies with minds loosely attached.

Therefore, as a general rule, a good diet for physical and mental health, based on the most credible expert advice available, would include: Lots of vegetables; lots of salads; oily fish; nuts and seeds; supplements that may feed neurotransmitters (related to anger control); foods that feed and promote healthy gut bacteria (which are linked to mood control); plus seaweed (iodine, etc.) for thyroid function. And the main things to avoid would include: all forms of junk food, processed foods, high sugar, salt and trans-fat diets; and gluten. Also, reduce caffeine and alcohol. And avoid processed grains. But keep up the (gluten free) wholegrains: like millet, quinoa, teff, buckwheat, and brown rice (unless you establish that you are negatively affected by them, in practice). And keep meat consumption low, and oily fish consumption high.

Finally, there are research findings to show the wisdom behind the injunction to eat seven portions of fruit and vegetables every day. In an Online article entitled: "7 a day for Happiness and Mental health"[133], research undertaken by staff members at Warwick University examined the eating habits of 80,000 people in Britain. They found a correlation between the number of daily portions of vegetables and fruit, and the level of mental well-being. They found that the level of well-being reached its height at seven portions a day. This research was completed in May 2016 and is due to be published in the 'Social Indicators Research Journal'.

Professor Sarah Stewart-Brown, the study's co-author[134] and professor of Public Health at Warwick Medical School, said:

"The statistical power of fruit and vegetables was a surprise. Diet has traditionally been ignored by well-being researchers."

It is increasingly apparent that diet is crucial for physical and emotional well-being. Some doctors and researchers are increasingly aware that diet is inextricably bound up with a lifestyle which acknowledges the integration of mind and body.

For a healthy mind in a healthy body, we also need to ensure that we have sufficient sleep and regular exercise. Dr Kelly Brogan (2016) describes exercise as *"Nature's anti-depressant"*. And finally, we need the benefits to our body of daily meditation. This mindful process activates the "rest and digest" part of our autonomic nervous system. The result of this practice is that it helps to return the body to an anti-inflammatory state.

Dr Kelly Brogan states: *"...As I've been emphasising over and over again, the interconnectedness of your gut, brain, hormonal and immune systems is impossible to unwind. Until we begin to appreciate this complex system, we will not be able to prevent or intervene effectively in depression.*

"For true healing and meaningful prevention, take steps every day towards sending your body the message that it is not being attacked, it is not in danger, and it is well-nourished, supported and calm." (Page 170)

Of course, it is not just about 'sending messages'. It requires self-discipline to make sure we get to bed at a reasonable time, get enough sleep, arise in a timely manner for the day ahead, eat a healthy breakfast, exercise, meditate, and leave adequate time to get to our place of work/study, without putting our body-brain-mind under unnecessary stress.

There do appear to be significant links between diet, exercise, self-talk, and other lifestyle factors, on the one hand, and overly upset emotions of anger, anxiety and depression, on the other.

Finally, based on the findings described in this part of the book (and in the references which you can research for more information), it will be necessary for you to do a lot of *experimenting for yourself*, to see what works for *you*.

For example, some people cannot tolerate fructose; some can. Some people seem to be able to tolerate some gluten, and most others can't. (But gluten does seem to be a general problem, not specific to particular groups). Most people would be well advised to take their nutritional needs, and those of their family members, very seriously indeed; and to make sure those nutrients come from health-inducing sources.

In this section you have seen evidence of the power of different types of food to affect you physically and mentally. And, in addition, the lack of water in the diet, or the presence of alcohol and other drinks, can have a profound impact on well-being.

Make sure you consult your own nutritionist - (and/or your GP, or alternative health practitioner) - before you make *any* radical changes to your diet. But, also remember the Buddha's guideline: *"Find out for yourself!"*

~~~

Part 2: Physical exercise and common emotional problems

By Renata Taylor-Byrne, and Jim Byrne

~~~

1. Introduction

> *"Exercise strengthens the entire human machine — the heart, the brain, the blood vessels, the bones, the muscles. The most important thing you can do for your long-term health is lead an active life."*
>
> Dr Timothy Church (2013)[135].

~~~

Exercise is good for your body-brain-mind, boosting health and strength and emotional buoyancy. According to Dr Mark Atkinson (2007): *"Thirty minutes of moderate-intensity exercise, five times a week, is associated with numerous health benefits. These range from improving mood and self-esteem to reducing the risk of cancer and heart disease"*[136].

In the western tradition of physical exercise, three forms of exercise are recommended:

1. **Aerobic training**, which includes brisk walking, jogging, cycling, swimming, etc. (We [Renata and Jim] enjoy brisk walking, and dancing vigorously to pop music). Thirty minutes of brisk walking per day is sufficient to lift depression and reduce anxiety. And : *"Swimming for just half an hour three times a week can lower stress levels, raise mood, lower incidences of depression and anxiety and improve sleep patterns"*. (Source: Just Swim)[137]. Furthermore, running for just thirty minutes per time, three times per week can also lift mood and reduce depression by 16% (according to a recent study by the University of London)[138].

2. **Weight training**, which includes press-ups, sit-backs, climbing stairs, cycling, dumbbells, barbells, kettlebells, etc. (We [the authors] use press-ups and sit-backs; the 'Plank' position from Pilates; carrying some weight from the shops on a regular basis; and the 'PowerSpin' rotator). Weight training, or resistance training, is also good for improving mental health and emotional wellbeing. According to a meta-analysis of several studies, *"...resistance training (or weight training) is a meaningful intervention for people suffering from anxiety"* (O'Connor and colleagues, 2010). And: *"Four studies have investigated the effect of resistance training with clinically diagnosed depressed adults. The results are unanimous; large reductions in depression from resistance training participation"*. (O'Connor and colleagues, 2010)[139].

3. **Flexibility and stretching exercises**, which includes yoga and Chi Kung (Qigong, from Tai Chi), both of which are introduced and described, and extensively explored, below.

~~~

There is lots of evidence that physical exercise reduces all forms of stress. This includes:

> (1) *Transitory stress*, which crops up when we run into a threatening or dangerous situation, or we experience a momentary loss. And:

> (2) *Continuous stress*, arising out of nagging overloads of work and difficult life challenges.

The main forms in which stress manifests are: anger and anxiety.

Depression is not normally conceptualized as being a feature of the stress model, but rather to grief. Stress is a response to a pressure bearing down on an individual, when this pressure is greater than their coping resources.

When the pressure is too great for their coping resources, the individual may respond with either explosive or implosive anger – as in either rage outbursts or silent sulking – or with acute or chronic anxiety – as in generalized anxiety disorder, social anxiety, or panic.

Depression is related to *the grief response*, and is normally about loss or failure, whether real or symbolic. A person may become depressed after losing a job, a loved one, or losing face, social status, etc.

However, physical exercise helps to reduce all of these emotional states:

> - anger,

> - anxiety

> - and depression.

This part of the book will explain why exercise is so effective with these conditions and will describe evidence from researchers who have conducted experiments to prove the power of exercise to reduce anxiety, anger, stress and depression.

Then the views of the NHS and the Mayo Clinic will be described, and some Indian and Chinese forms of exercise will be explained and evaluated.

Finally, a recommended regular exercise structure will be described.

~~~

2. Anxiety disorders and the benefits of exercise

According to Dr Perlmutter (2015)[140], forty million Americans are affected by anxiety disorders. And in a survey conducted by the Office for National Statistics (ONS) covering Great Britain, 1-in-6 adults had experienced some form of 'neurotic health problem' in the previous week.[141] The most common neurotic disorders were anxiety and depressive disorders.

Anxiety is defined by the NHS (UK)[142] as a feeling of unease, such as worry or fear, which can be mild or very strong. All humans have feelings of anxiety at some point in their life, and it can be in response to a threatening challenge like a sudden natural disaster, family health problems, job interview, or exams, etc. But this NHS view ignores the fact that caffeine, or high sugar consumption, or lack of physical exercise, can all lead to feelings of anxiety and even panic. However, as we will see later, the NHS does acknowledge that exercise can help with anxiety and depression.

A stressful event, either real or imagined, is likely to switch on our *sympathetic nervous system*[143], and we then experience our heart beating faster, which may cause us to shake physically. When the stressful event has passed, we normally calm down, as our *parasympathetic nervous system* kicks in. (For definitions, see Endnote 143).

An anxiety disorder, on the other hand, is more severe, and normally continues long after any threat or danger to us (physically or emotionally) has passed. It can remain in the background as a constant sense of unease or apprehension.

Anxiety and physical exercise

Here is how Joshua Broman-Fulks, a researcher from the University of Southern Mississippi, discovered the power of exercise to help people suffering from anxiety: His research experiment - cited in John Ratey and Eric Hagerman's 2009) book, titled *Spark: The revolutionary new science of exercise and the brain'*[144] - took place in 2004.

Broman-Fulks took a group of 54 students and split them into two sub-groups. Both groups of students had high levels of anxiety and had generalised anxiety disorder, and they also exercised less than once a week.

Each of the two groups had six exercise sessions of twenty minutes duration, which were spread out over two weeks.

The first group ran on treadmills at an intensity level of 60-90% of their maximum heart rates.

The second group walked on their tread mills at a speed of one mile an hour, and this was approximately equal to 50% of their maximum heart rates.

The result of these exercise sessions was that *both sets of students became less sensitive to anxiety*, but the interesting result was that the more physically demanding exercises produced beneficial results *in a shorter space of time*.

Why was this? The reason given by Broman-Fulks is as follows:

If (during this kind of exercise session) you experience your heart beating rapidly, and you're breathing very quickly, you know exactly why it's happening. It's because you're exercising. And you also have the experience of your body *handling* the sensations of a rapidly-beating heart and rapid breathing. *Therefore* it doesn't lead to an anxiety attack as a result.

The students had got used to their body being in a state of high arousal, and had the knowledge that it had not resulted in anything particularly unpleasant.

Ratey and Hagerman (2009) state that if you exercise regularly and vigorously, your body goes through these experiences of physical arousal repeatedly – and nothing significantly unpleasant follows. Then, in the future, when you are presented with a challenge which creates anxiety in your body, you know that this will not necessarily harm you in any way, and that it is *merely* an *interpretation* (accurate or inaccurate) *of an event* which is causing the anxiety reaction.

And as your body has dealt successfully, over and over again, in exercise sessions, with bodily arousal, rapid breathing and fast-beating heart, then you learn the following:

"Over time you teach the brain that the symptoms don't always spell doom and that you can survive."

With this sense of security, you are able to see when your mind is distorting reality for some reason, or in the words of Ratey and Hagerman (2009): *"You're reprogramming the cognitive distortion."*

Apparently it has been known for a very long time that *exercise reduces anxiety*, but the way that exercise works in the body has only become apparent in the last few years.

What exercise, or strenuous exercise does, is to reduce the tension level in the muscles. This stops the "anxiety feedback loop" going to the brain, and if the body is relaxed then the brain doesn't worry.

And exercise itself produces relaxing chemical alterations in the body: as our muscles start moving, the body starts to break down fat molecules to release energy for the increased demand on the body. This releases fatty acids into the bloodstream and the levels of tryptophan (an amino acid) and then serotonin (a neurotransmitter) increases as a result of this exercise. Serotonin then calms us down and increases our feelings of safety. (We do not currently fully understand the role of these neurotransmitters).

Soon after the terrorist attacks in New York that took place on September 11th 2001, Joseph LeDoux and Jack Gorman wrote an article in the American Journal of Psychiatry.[145] The article was called: *A call to action: Overcoming anxiety through active coping.* In the article, LeDoux and Gorman explained that when we make a decision in the face of anxiety, there is *an alteration in the direction of the flow* of outside information.

Usually the information coming in from the outside world, goes straight to the amygdala. The amygdala - (described by Ratey and Hagerman [2009] as "*the brain's panic button*") - is an almond-shaped brain structure responsible for dealing with the emotions. There is one in each cerebral hemisphere of the brain, specifically attuned to possible threats or dangers in the environment. It registers an immediate fear response to a threatening situation, and instigates the switching on of the autonomic nervous system's response of 'fight or flight').

But when we make a *decision* in the face of an anxiety-arousing situation, then the flow of information, instead of going to the amygdala, goes to the basal nucleus. (This part of the brain is a cluster of brain cells at the base of the brain that helps humans perform practiced movements, because it is connected to the body's motor circuits).

So if we (1) make a decision, or (2) take action, in the face of an anxiety-arousing situation, we're *re-routing* the brain activity away from the amygdala (the fear-memory centre that controls the 'fight or flight response').

Ratey and Hagerman (2009) state: *"The basal nucleus is the action pathway, and we can even spark it with thought. For one of my patients, who was traumatized by losing both his job and his girlfriend at the same time, I suggested he start each day by getting to the gym, to keep from stewing in the trauma."*

"He could also shift the flow from fear to his action circuits by making a list of potential employers to call – a more classic example of coping – but it wouldn't affect the brain as broadly."

"By doing something other than sitting and worrying, we re-route the thought processes around the passive response centre and dilute the fear, while optimizing the brain to learn a new scenario.

"Everyone's instinctive response in the face of danger is to avoid the situation, like a rat that freezes in its cage. But, doing just the opposite, (or getting in action! Ed) we engage in cognitive restructuring, using our bodies to cure our brains." (Ratey and Hargerman 2009: Page 105).

There are several reasons which are given by Ratey and Hagerman as to why exercise is a very constructive way to reduce anxiety feelings and anxiety disorders.

Firstly, as has just been described, it provides a *diversion* from a current stressor by immediately investing your mental functioning into physical activity rather than emotional arousal.

Secondly, it lowers muscle tension and *"…serves as a circuit-breaker…interrupting the negative feedback loop from the body to the brain that heightens anxiety"*. (Page 106)

In 1982 a researcher called Herbert de Vries conducted a research study that revealed that people who experienced anxiety had *"overactive electrical patterns in their muscle spindles"* and exercise reduced that tension[146]. This led the researcher to coin the phrase: *"the tranquilizing effects of exercise."*

Thirdly, it increases the level of serotonin in the body, which (according to *some* theorists!) helps to control messages from the brain stem, and helps the prefrontal cortex minimize the fear response, which quietens down the amygdala.

Fourthly, as you experience your heart rate and breathing increasing with anxiety, this is the same experience as you have when doing vigorous exercise.

These two experiences, with practice, become connected, or associated with each other.

And as the exercise is self-initiated and can be controlled, this generalizes to the anxiety inducing experience. Thereafter, the fear response (when it is related to past experiences, not present threats or dangers) slowly fades.

According to Ratey and Hagerman (2009) exercise *"also increases resilience"*. This is developed because you learn the skill of effectively controlling your bodily responses and managing anxiety without allowing it to turn into panic. This is how they describe it:

> *"The psychological term is self-mastery, and developing it is a powerful prophylactic (therapeutic technique) against anxiety sensitivity and depression, which can develop from anxiety. In consciously doing something for yourself, you realize that you can do something for yourself."* Ratey and Hagerman (2009: Page 108).

~~~

3. Exercise and its effect on depression

> *"It's largely through depression research that we know as much as we do about what exercise does for the brain. It counteracts depression at almost every level".*
>
> Ratey and Hagerman (2009: Page 104).

In 1999, researchers at Duke University did a landmark study into the effects of exercise on depression. The study was called SMILE (Standard Medical Intervention and Long Term Exercise) and was led by James Blumenthal and his colleagues.[147]

Their goal was to compare the effectiveness of exercise and sertraline (sold as Lustral in the UK and Zoloft in the US), which is an antidepressant. (It is one of a group of drugs called selective serotonin reuptake inhibitors [SSRI's]).

This drug is *assumed* to affect chemicals in the brain that may be unbalanced in people with depression, panic, anxiety, or obsessive-compulsive symptoms. But there is not one single study which supports this theory).

So, 156 patients were randomly divided into three groups, as follows:

Group 1: Got Zoloft;

Group 2: Got physical exercise;

Group 3: Got a combination of the two.

The exercise group was given supervised jogging and walking exercise at 70-80% of their aerobic capacity. The session lasted 30 minutes (not including a 10 minute warm-up and five minute cool-down). This took place three times per week.

The results were as follows: all of the three groups showed a marked reduction in depression, and roughly half of each group had recovered from their depression by the end of the research. That is to say, they were in remission. Another 13% had reduced symptoms of depression, but didn't completely recover.

From the findings, Blumenthal *et al.* (1999, [and later, 2012]) judged that **exercise was as effective as medication**. And it led Ratey and Hagerman (2009) to make the following statement:

"This (Blumenthal, 1999) is the study I photocopy for patients who are sceptical of the idea that exercise changes their brain chemistry enough to help their depression, because it puts the issue in terms that are as black and white as psychiatry can hope to deliver, at least for now.

"The results should be taught in medical school and driven home with health insurance companies and posted on the bulletin boards of every nursing home in the country, where nearly a fifth of the residents have depression." (Ratey and Hagerman, 2009: Page 122).

Six months after the study, Blumenthal and his fellow researchers examined the patients to see how they were faring and found that *exercise surpassed medicine over the long haul*: 30% of the exercise group remained depressed, as opposed to 52% on medication, and 55% of those in the combined treatment group.

When the participants of the second SMILE study were reassessed a year later – by Hoffman and colleagues (2011) - irrespective of which initial treatment group they had been in, those participants who described doing regular exercise after the research project had ended, were the *least likely* to be depressed a year later.[148] And, as indicated by Hoffman and colleagues, this is about Major Depression, and not just mild depression.

~~~

Exercise is so well supported as a means of reducing depression (and anxiety, and anger) that it is now recommended by mainstream health organizations. For examples:

The British National Health Service (NHS) supports the view that exercise is good for mood disorders, like anxiety and depression. Here's their comment specifically on depression:

Exercise for depression

"Being depressed can leave you feeling low in energy, which might put you off being more active.

"*Regular exercise can boost your mood if you have depression, and it's especially useful for people with mild to moderate depression."*

(Please don't overlook the switch here! Blumenthal's research proved that exercise could eliminate *major depression* - not mild to moderate depression!)

"*'Any type of exercise is useful, as long as it suits you and you do enough of it,'* says Dr Alan Cohen, a GP with a special interest in mental health. *'Exercise should be something you enjoy; otherwise, it will be hard to find the motivation to do it regularly'*. And he considers that:

"*To stay healthy, adults should do 150 minutes of moderate-intensity activity every week."*[149]

~~~

The Mayo Clinic also recommends any form of physical exercise for stress and anxiety. This is their advice:

Exercise and stress: Get moving to manage stress

"Exercise in almost any form can act as a stress reliever. Being active can boost your feel-good endorphins and distract you from daily worries.

"You know that exercise does your body good, but you're too busy and stressed to fit it into your routine. Hold on a second — there's good news when it comes to exercise and stress.

"Virtually any form of exercise, from aerobics to yoga, can act as a stress reliever. If you're not an athlete or even if you're out of shape, you can still make a little exercise go a long way toward stress management. Discover the connection between exercise and stress relief — and why exercise should be part of your stress management plan."[150]

The Mayo Clinic article goes on to say:

"Regular exercise can increase self-confidence, it can relax you, and it can lower the symptoms associated with mild depression and anxiety. Exercise can also improve your sleep, which is often disrupted by stress, depression and anxiety. All of these exercise benefits can ease your stress levels and give you a sense of command over your body and your life."

Once again, please note the *switching* of 'mild depression' for 'major depression', which was what was investigated by Blumenthal and Hoffman and associates!

And elsewhere, the Mayo clinic acknowledges that exercise can remove major depression. The opening of that article acknowledges that:

"Depression symptoms often improve with exercise. Here are some realistic tips to help you get started and stay motivated."[151]

~~~

4. Exercise and anger

Exercise has a valuable role to perform in the management of anger, according to various credible sources. For example, according to the British National Health Service (NHS) website[152], they consider that *exercise will reduce the intensity of anger*, and they recommend specific forms of exercise, including walking, swimming, and yoga. (They also recommend the use of meditation and relaxation exercises. This is not surprising since virtually all emotional states are *produced by multiple causes*, and often need *several strategies* to sort them out!)

An anger management specialist, Isabel Clarke, is quoted on the NHS website as saying she considers that: *"You can control your anger and you have a responsibility to do so"*. She also advises people to *use exercise* as a constructive strategy to eliminate annoyance and anger.

Her views are similar to those expressed by the Mayo clinic.[153] They consider that there is a relationship between stress levels and the expression of anger – the higher the level of stress someone is experiencing, the more likely they are to have high levels of anger. This anger can be *diminished to a large extent* by taking active measures like going for an energetic walk, or trying other pleasurable forms of exercise.

But what scientific evidence do we have of this connection between the expression of anger, on the one hand, and physical exercise, on the other? A fascinating study - which was described in the *New York Times Sunday Magazine,* in an article entitled, *'Phys Ed – Can Exercise Moderate Anger?'* - outlined the attempts that researchers had been making to become clearer about the biochemical and physiological origins of anger.[154]

The study, which was presented at the annual conference of the American College of Sports Medicine, specifically set out to select 16 young men who had a high level of anger, from hundreds of undergraduates at the University of Georgia.

These 16 participants were selected on the basis of their responses to a questionnaire on their moods, and these revealed that they were regularly hypersensitive and easily enraged. They were shown a series of slides (designed to be angering or enraging), at two separate time intervals.

Results:

Interval 1. No exercise: When the participants hadn't done any exercising, it was very apparent in their behaviour after viewing the slides for a second time, because *they became angry.*

Interval 2. With exercise: But when the students, who *had* exercised, viewed the two slide shows, their level of arousal and annoyance stayed constant and *they did not have an increase in their level of anger.*

The lead researcher, Nathaniel Thom (a stress physiologist) stated that the message from this research experiment was as follows:

"Exercise, even a single bout of it, can have a robust, prophylactic (therapeutic) effect against the build-up of anger... It's like taking aspirin to combat heart disease. You reduce your risk".

He emphasized that, when the participants in the study didn't exercise, then they showed weakness in the face of emotional provocations, and were unable to manage their anger.

However, after they had exercised, they were able to show composure and self-assurance when managing their emotions. (Reynolds, 2010)[155].

~~~

5. Indian and Chinese exercises for health

Yoga

There is lots of evidence that *yoga* can help with the symptoms of depression and anxiety, with childhood autism, and even with schizophrenia and psychosis.[156] Some of this evidence is weak, and additional studies are needed.

There is also evidence that yoga can calm down angry, reactive people:

'...with a growing body of research backing yoga's effectiveness as an anger "defuser," physiologist Ralph LaForge regularly advises physicians to recommend yoga to their hostility-prone cardiac patients. LaForge is managing director of the Lipid Disorder Training Program at Duke University Medical Centre's Endocrine Division in Durham, North Carolina, where ground-breaking research has taken place on *"hot reactive" personality types – that is, people who react to anger more explosively than most... Yoga, particularly therapeutic forms like restorative yoga*[157]*,"* says LaForge, *"has proven to be a valuable method of cooling hot-reactives down."* (Alan Reder, 2007)[158].

Alan Reder continues like this: 'Stephen Cope suggests that asanas (or hatha yoga postures – of which there are between 32 and 84 - Eds) may be in fact the best yogic antidote for anger *"because asanas allow you to move the energy."* He cautions against meditation (or sitting still - Eds) for folks in an explosive state because meditative awareness just feeds the flames once the temperature has reached a certain point.'

Reder makes a very important point when he says that not everyone should use the same anger management strategy. Specifically, he writes that: *'Cope's observations underscore the fact that anger manifests differently in each person, and must be treated differently as well.*

'Some of us get so revved up by our catecholamines (or stress chemicals) that we can't think straight. In those cases, experts have found that methods such as deep breathing, moderate exercise, or walking away from a provocative situation are the best way to lower the arousal level.

But for those who are milder by nature, <u>awareness</u> can accelerate anger's rush through, and out of, the body. "Yoga helps people stay with the wave of anger all the way to the other end," explains Cope.'

So <u>focus your awareness</u> on your anger to dissipate it, *if you are mild mannered by nature;*

But <u>move your body</u> in some form of moderate exercise, and do some deep breathing, *if you tend to be more hot-tempered.*

Reder (2007) continues: '*Besides asanas (or yoga poses), Cope touts a yoga-based technique taught at the Kripalu Centre for Yoga & Health in Lenox, Massachusetts, for integrating emotional experiences. The technique, called "riding the wave," employs five sequential steps: Breathe, Relax, Feel, Watch, Allow.*'

Clearly, based on what has been said above, this process should only be used by people of mild manner, and not hot tempered individuals.

This is the process:

1. **Breathe** 'into' your belly (by lowering your diaphragm and expanding your belly). Do not allow your upper chest to rise; or gradually reduce the extent of the rise of your upper chest.

2. **Relax** your entire body. (It helps if you have previously done conscious relaxation exercises to appreciate how this feels, and how to do it. You could buy a relaxation audio program, for this purpose).

3. **Feel** whatever sensations are coursing through your body. (Do not try to suppress any angry feelings. But also do not indulge them. Just *feel* them).

4. **Watch** your mind. (Whatever arises in your mind, should be allowed to arise so long as you have been training yourself to feel compassion for those people who frustrate and thwart you!)

5. **Allow** things in your body and mind to be the way they are – and the anger will gradually burn itself out through awareness.

And repeat steps 1-5 again, and again, until the anger has fully passed.

~~~

More generally: According to Johnna Medina, in an article titled, '*How yoga is similar to existing mental health therapies*':

'*The ancient Eastern practice of yoga combines mindfulness training with exercise (hence the term, "mind-body"). For years, practitioners all over the world have reported receiving mental and physical health benefits from yoga.*'[159]

You could attend a class in which you practice yoga, and then continue to do the exercises at home when the class has ended; or, if you are good at learning from books and/or videos, you could study those kinds of resources.

~~~

Chinese exercise systems

Does the Chinese system of Qigong (or Chi Kung) – which is related to Tai Chi - have a similar effect on anxiety, depression and anger?

Marcus James Santer reflects on his own experience of using Qigong/Chi Kung to cure his own depression - and get off anti-depressants. His reflective study begins like this:

"In this post I'd like to look at what it is that makes Qigong/Chi Kung such a powerful tool for overcoming depression, anxiety, worry, fear and for raising self-esteem and resistance to stress.

"I know from my own personal experience of using Qigong to get off anti-depressants ...

"You can think of Qigong as a tool for increasing your emotional immune system."

...

He ends with this conclusion:

"Qigong is a powerful tool for overcoming mild to moderate depression, for overcoming anxiety, worry and fear. It is a potent way to raise self-esteem and increase your resistance to the stresses and strains of modern living.

"These 'illnesses' are known as empty illnesses because we don't know the cause of the symptoms and/or the location of the illness is not known. Western medicine does not have a brilliant track record at treating such empty illnesses, often resorting to the prescription of drugs to treat the symptoms whilst the root cause is untreated.

"I must point out that in cases of severe and long standing emotional problems, Qigong alone may not be enough and you may need the help and support of a skilled counsellor or psychotherapist." [160]

~~~

Michael Tse (pronounced Shay) is a Qigong master who has a large international following, and who practices in Harley Street, London and St. John's Street, Manchester, in the UK; and also overseas. He has made the study of Qigong his life's work, and in his book *'Qigong for Health and Vitality'* (1995)[161], he outlines what the benefits are of practicing this exercise method.

In terms of stress prevention, he considers that if you have a healthy body you will have a healthy mind, due to the inseparable connection between the body and the mind. As people do these slow, gentle, traditional Chinese exercises, their energy level increases, as does their skill at assessing their own body's state and whether or not they are over-working themselves. He states:

"When you lose the ability to judge your body's condition, you can easily become ill or suffer from chronic conditions like ME, heart disease and even cancer". (Page 37)

Tse considers *daily practice* of Qigong to be essential in order to reap the benefits, and he explains that, as a result of daily practice, our brains perform better, improving our memory and attention to detail. Also, in terms of handling anger or other aspects of living, he states that Qigong will enable people to become: calmer; more accepting of the flow of life; and physically relaxed.

To reduce depression, he recommends specific exercises (Page 39) and states:

"Qigong brings us back to nature, enabling us to stay away from what is artificial and letting the natural senses return".

~~~

A preliminary study by Linder and colleagues shows that Qigong may be beneficial for relieving stress, although more study is warranted in this area[162]. A much later comprehensive review by Jahnke and colleagues (2012) produces compelling evidence that Tai Chi and Chi Kung can help with depression, anxiety and self-efficacy. This is what they concluded:

"Conclusion: A compelling body of research emerges when Tai Chi studies and the growing body of Qigong studies are combined. The evidence suggests that a wide range of health benefits accrue in response to these meditative movement forms, some consistently so, and some with limitations in the findings thus far. This review has identified numerous outcomes with varying levels of evidence for the efficacy for Qigong and Tai Chi, including bone health, cardiopulmonary fitness and related biomarkers, physical function, falls prevention and balance, general quality of life and patient reported outcomes, immunity, and psychological factors such as anxiety, depression and self-efficacy. A substantial number of RCTs (Randomized Control Trials) have demonstrated consistent, positive results especially when the studies are designed with limited activity for controls. When both Tai Chi and Qigong are investigated together, as two approaches to a single category of practice, meditative movement, the magnitude of the body of research is quite impressive."[163]

In Jahnke *et al* (2010) you will find this statement:

"A substantial body of published research has examined the health benefits of Tai Chi (also called Taiji) a traditional Chinese wellness practice. In addition, a strong body of research is also emerging for Qigong, an even more ancient traditional Chinese wellness practice that has similar characteristics to Tai Chi. Qigong and Tai Chi have been proposed, along with Yoga and Pranayama from India, to constitute a unique category or type of exercise referred to currently as meditative movement.[164] These two forms of meditative movement, Qigong and Tai Chi, are close relatives having shared theoretical roots, common operational components, and similar links to the wellness and health promoting aspects of traditional Chinese medicine. They are nearly identical in practical application in the health

enhancement context, and share much overlap in what traditional Chinese medicine describes as the 'three regulations': body focus (posture and movement), breath focus, and mind focus (meditative components)".[165]

~~~

It may be that Qigong can help with anger, in particular with a belly-breathing exercise which is assumed to heal the liver. But since we can teach belly breathing as a way of calming down the body, we will stick to that approach in this book. Any deep breathing techniques that you study within Tai Chi or Qigong are likely to be helpful in controlling your anger. But remember, with hot-headed individuals, *movement* is most important.

~~~

6. Exercise and the brain-mind

Here's a short extract from a paper which we (Renata and Jim) wrote in 2011, which was essentially a book review of Ratey and Hagerman's (2009) book – *Spark* – on the subject of how exercise improves the brain.[166]

This is how we commented towards the end of our paper:

"If you value your brain, and want to keep it in good shape, then exercise is going to appeal more and more to you. Why? Because: 'The better your fitness level, the better your brain works', say Ratey and Hagerman (2010, page 247). They mention that research from epidemiologists to kinesiologists confirms this connection (between fitness and brain functioning) repeatedly. They also mention that: 'Population studies including tens of thousands of people of every age show that fitness levels relate directly to positive mood and lower levels of anxiety and stress'.

"Jeannine Stamatakis writes: 'To see how much exercise is required to relieve stress, researchers at the National Institutes of Mental Health observed how prior exercise changed the interaction between aggressive and reserved mice'. If the reserved mice had a chance to do some exercise before encountering the aggressive mice, then they were a lot less stressed by that conflict experience. 'Although this study was done in mice, the results likely have implications for humans as well. Exercising regularly, even taking a walk for 20 minutes several times a week, may help you cope with stress. So dig out those running shoes from the back of your closet and get moving'. (Scientific American Mind, Vol. 23. No.3, July/August 2012; page 72).

~~~

Professor Sapolsky on exercise for stress

Finally, in this section, the views of Robert Sapolsky on the benefits of exercise will be summarised. He has been researching and writing about the effects of stress on human beings for many years. He is a professor of biology, neuroscience and neurosurgery at Stanford University, and a research associate with the Institute of

Primal Research, National Museum of Kenya. He is the author of a book titled, *'Why Zebras Don't Get Ulcers', (2010)*[167], which is a guide to stress and stress-related diseases, and how we cope with them.

When Sapolsky describes the techniques he uses to control his own stress, he starts with exercise, and states that he uses this technique most frequently. And in his book he describes the many benefits of physical exercise. In relation to blood pressure and resting heart rate, for example, he states that regular exercise will lower them both, and increase lung capacity at the same time.

Exercise also reduces the risk of a range of cardiovascular and metabolic diseases, and so lessens the chance of stress making them worse.

Exercise makes us *feel* better, and uplifts our *mood*, and this is because of the release of beta-endorphins. These are neurotransmitters, which are chemicals that pass along signals from one neuron to the next. Neurotransmitters play a crucial role in the function of the central nervous system, and in mood change; and beta-endorphins are more powerful than morphine. (See Bryant, 2010)[168].

New imaging methods have allowed researchers to study the pattern of behaviour of neurotransmitters in the body, and the flow of endorphins as they interact with human brain cells, confirming that they play a part in the 'feel-good effect that we get from exercising'. So they are natural pain-killers and mood-lifters - (according to Charles Bryant, 2010).

In addition, Sapolsky (2010) states that you reduce physical tension in your body by doing challenging physical exercises. And there is also evidence that if you are well-exercised, then your reaction to psychological stressors is reduced considerably.

Significantly, because you are keeping to your self-chosen exercise regime, you get a sense of achievement and self-efficacy, which is very rewarding.

However, Sapolsky points out that there are several provisos, in his opinion:

(1) You will get a more cheerful mood and a reduced stress response if you exercise – but this will only last for a period of time that can vary from between two hours up to a day after the exercise session. So the benefits wear off if the exercise is not repeated regularly.

(2) He also makes the point that you will *only* reduce your stress levels through exercise if you *want* to do it. Sapolsky states:

"Let rats voluntarily run on a running wheel and their health improves in all sorts of ways. Force them, even when playing great dance music, and their health worsens". (Page 491)

The research studies, according to Sapolsky, show very clearly that moderate aerobic exercise, (which you can do whilst talking, without getting too much out of breath), is better than anaerobic exercise - (which is short-lasting, high-intensity activity, where your body's demand for oxygen exceeds the oxygen supply available, and you use energy that is stored in your muscles).

Sapolsky recommends that exercise be done in a consistent, regular pattern and for a prolonged period of time: *"It's pretty clear that you need to exercise a minimum of twenty or thirty minutes at a time, a few times a week, to really get the health benefits."* (Page 402).

And finally he recommends that you don't overdo it.

However, if you were to *never* exercise, then there would (obviously) be no benefit for you, because exercise is really good for your health.

On the one hand, Sapolsky is saying that a big amount of exercise improves your health a great deal. On the other hand, he cautions against doing *excessive* amounts of exercise as this could damage various physiological systems in the body.

~~~

7. The search for the ideal exercise routine

Choosing the right exercise for yourself is a very personal process. It can take time to find the right one for you and there are now a dazzling array of sports and exercises to choose from. Experimenting with them and finding the ones that suit you best, can be very rewarding, whether it's a team game like football, volleyball, or basketball; or more sedate group exercises like Tai Chi or Qigong. And many people have gained a great deal from yoga and Pilates, or simple walking.

(We [Renata and Jim] like to do Qigong (pronounced Chi Kung) every morning after meditation. Plus some calisthenics, like press ups and sit backs; the plank; and I [Renata] also like to do some Yoga stretching exercises. Jim runs on the spot, for one minute every fifteen minutes, during the work day, and does some leg circling exercise, to overcome the negative effects of engaging in sedentary work. [From time to time, we both 'lose' these habits, and have to start all over again to re-establish them!]).

One thing is clear – we need, and greatly benefit from, exercise. We benefit both mentally and physically. Physical exercise enriches our lives, helps us to resist diseases, enables our brains to develop, and reduces the impact of the many stresses and strains we are all subject to in the modern world. And as shown above, physical exercise contributes to emotional control – which means reducing our tendencies towards anger, anxiety and/or depression. For these reasons, we recommend that their clients do an average of thirty minutes of physical exercise per day, for at least five days per week. Happy exercising!

~~~

Copyright © Renata Taylor-Byrne and Jim Byrne – June 2016

~~~

Part 3: Dr Jim´s Stress and Anxiety Diet

Copyright © Jim Byrne 2016

1. Introduction and disclaimer

This information is intended for *educational* purposes only, and does not purport to be medical advice. Bear in mind that each individual body is probably pretty unique, because of its unique nutritional journey through life. So it seems unlikely that we could ever produce a 'universally valid' diet! But it is certainly true that some foods are simply bad for us, causing blood-glucose problems, inflammation problems, and stress-hormone problems, all of which can and will have negative effects upon our mood and emotions.

We are changed by the foods we eat, and some experts would say we 'are what we eat'. There are many expert nutritionists available today, at reasonable fees; and you would be well advised to see a nutritionist, or other medical practitioner if you are concerned there might be a link between your current emotional state and your diet.

2. Personal experience of diet and emotional distress

Whereas Renata Taylor-Byrne has formally studied diet and nutrition at diploma level, I (Jim Byrne) got involved in researching my own diet, and its effects upon my body-mind, because of an illness I had developed.

Between 1970 and 1976, I was married to a woman who had studied biochemistry, and also took some training as a cordon beau cook. Therefore, unthinkingly, I was well fed, and kept away from foods that might be bad for my health (by and large!)

In 1976, my first wife and I divorced, and I became a mindless bachelor. I bought only 'convenience foods', and ate out all the time, apart from Sunday lunch, which was a 'family event' with the people with whom I shared a house in Oxford.

Every morning I got up and went to the corner store and bought a pint of milk and a pork pie. (Milk is full of lactic acid, or milk sugar, which selectively feeds our unfriendly bacterial, including Candida Albicans. And pork pies are made from pig meat, and pigs are pumped full of antibiotics to prevent diseases in the herd; but those same antibiotics, in my gut, killed off my friendly bacteria).

My lunches varied (though I did have a lot of eggs; and non-organic eggs contain a lot of antibiotics, which kill off friendly gut bacteria, and allow for Candida overgrowth. They also contain a lot of arachidonic acid (a variety of omega-6 fatty acids, which causes inflammation; while organic eggs are high in omega-3 fatty acids, which quell inflammation. And inflammation is a cause of physical and emotional health problems).

Every evening I had the same thing for my dinner/tea: 'Bhuna Chicken'. (Bhuna chicken was sold in the Bengali restaurant down the road from where I lived. It was made from factory-farmed chicken, which is full of antibiotics, to prevent diseases killing off the flock; but the same antibiotics, in my guts, killed off what was left of my friendly bacteria, and allowed unfriendly bacteria – like Candida Albicans – to flourish. And the most prominent taste of the Bhuna chicken was sweetness: from the handfuls of sugar in which it was cooked. And sugar is a neurotoxin, which suppressed my immune system for hours after eating it).

After one year of living like this, I went to work in Bangladesh. Firstly, I had to submit to a range of vaccinations, each of which probably impaired my immune system (and I have since worked with a homeopath to reverse some of that damage!) Then, upon arriving in Bangladesh, I hired a cook, who fed me rice three times per day. Sweet Bengali Pudding, for breakfast; rice with curried vegetables, and polluted river prawns for lunch; rice with curried vegetables, and polluted river prawns for evening meal; followed by a sweet. Yes: Sweet Bengali Pudding!

After one year in Bangladesh, I had a massive allergic reaction. My body became covered with hot hives. Even my tongue and eyeballs were erupting with urticaria. Some friends and I were on a steam-boat, half way to Khulna, and the boat would not turn back. So we had to travel to Khulna, stay overnight, and then take the first steam-boat back to Dhaka the following day. By the time I arrived in Dhaka, I was delirious. My friends took me to a private doctor (British trained!) I believe the doctor panicked, and instead of placing me under observation for twenty-four hours, and doing some proper diagnostic tests, he simply got a big hypodermic syringe, sucked some antibiotic into it; followed by adrenaline; and then some cortisol. And he pumped this concoction into my right hip.

I was high as a kite for days. I felt like god. But when I came down my energy was half what it had been; and I had permanent dhobi itch; or what the Americans call jock itch; and indeed, on very hot and humid days, I got intense itchiness in all moist parts of my body. My mood was also lower than it had been.

It took three or four years for me to learn that this is a problem called 'systemic Candidiasis', which most western doctors did not understand at that time, and perhaps that has not change much (for all I now know). This condition is perhaps now included under the newer heading of 'dysbiosis', or imbalanced or unbalanced gut flora and fauna.

Fortunately, I got some advice from the late Kevin Benson, a specialist in herbal remedies, at *Food Therapy*, in Halifax, in 1981, or '82. I learned that the Candida spore has a negative effect upon our body and mind, and it's normally held in check by our friendly gut bacteria. We need to reduce sugar and yeast in our diets, and to take an anti-fungal substance (caprylic acid), and also to supplement with friendly bacteria, like Acidophilus Bifidus, and others. I also read a book by Leon Chaitow on the nature of Candida Albicans, and how to control it using dietary restrictions[169]. That was the beginning of my journey into researching the effects of gut bacteria on health, including mood and emotion. (See Jacobs, 1994; and Trowbridge and Walker, 1989)[170].

Because I was sensitized to the gut-brain-mind connection through my personal experience of diet and ill health, I was alert to new research coming out about similar unconventional insights; including the information that trans-fats are linked to problems of lack of control of anger[171]; and research showing that British prisoners who were switched to a diet high in omega-3 fatty acids experienced a reduction in aggressive incidents, fights, etc., with their fellow prisoners.

I then, also found that I occasionally got a depressed or anxious client who had no apparent psychological problem as the cause or stimulus for their condition, but who was on a high sugar and yeast diet, and who was, in fact, suffering the effects of Candida Albicans overgrowth. Once they changed their diets, their depression and anxiety problems cleared up.

So I learned about the gut-brain-mind connection the hard way; the personal way; and I also collected empirical evidence of the truth of those insights from my counselling practice!

3. No universal agreement regarding diet

As far as I can tell, after years of personal research, there is no universal agreement about the precise kind of diet which will promote or reduce stress, although we have some pretty good ideas of some of the major culprits, and some of the main forms of 'best practice'.

As suggested by many other sources of advice, it is advisable to eat lots of fresh fruit and vegetables (if you know you can *tolerate* the fruit!). And, actually, this guideline should be expressed the other way around: Eat *lots of vegetables* and *less* fruit. Fruits contain sugars, and even though they are 'natural sugars', they can still cause problems for our blood-sugar management system. So do not over-consume them. (High GI [glycaemic index] foods push our blood sugar levels too high. See section 4[b] above).

Sugars also occur naturally in vegetables, and some people are so sensitive to sugars that they have to reduce their consumption of those vegetables which are highest in such elements as fructans, oligosaccharides, disaccharides, monosaccharaides, and polyols. These elements are normally referred to by the acronym of FodMaps; and there are some online information sites regarding the nature of FodMaps, and which foods contain them.

4. Schools of thought on diet

There are many schools of thought on diet and health; perhaps several dozen; or even more. There are many different types of diet in circulation today. (See section 3 of Part 1, above, for more detail). Vegetarian diets; the Atkins, Ketogenic and Paleo diets (high in meat and fats, and low in carbs); Semi-vegetarian diets; raw-food diets; wholefood diets; macrobiotic (beans) diet; Weight control diets; Low-calorie diets; high calorie diets; Very low calorie diets; Low-carbohydrate diets; high carb diets; Low-fat diets; high fat diets; crash diets; detox diets. And, of course, the *Metabolic typing diet* ([Atkinson, 2008, pages 50-54]: which I tried but found both unhelpful to me, and difficult to implement).

Dr Atkinson's general (non-metabolic typing) advice is probably sound: He suggests that we:

#Avoid trans-fatty acids (found in junk foods);

minimize (meaning 'eat in moderation') saturated fats (found in meat, dairy, (organic) eggs and seafood products); avoid refined carbohydrates (like white bread, white rice, white pasta, cakes, biscuits, sweets, bottles of juice and pop drinks, and most breakfast cereals);

avoid sugar (including the sugars found in junk and processed foods);

avoid artificial sweeteners;

avoid refined soya products (because refined soya is [no joke!] seen as unfit for feeding to piglets, as it damages their guts!)

restrict salt consumption to six grams (or one-eighth of an ounce) per day;

avoid or limit mercury-laden fish. (The only really safe fish that is left on the planet is Wild Alaskan salmon!) Occasional sardines, or a piece of white fish may be tolerable, but levels of pollution are very high indeed! And some people suffer from adult-onset fish-allergy, which is visible on their skin, but most likely also affects their moods and emotions. So do not overdo the fish consumption. To fish meals per week is probably optimal.

Eat at least five portions of vegetables and fruit per day (seven or eight would be better!) But again, there are no 'totally safe' foods. Some vegetables contain high levels of various *sugars* (fructans, oligosaccharides, disaccharides, monosaccharides and polyols [collectively called FODMAPS]); and others contain excessive amounts of *lectins*; both of which can cause inflammation in the bowel

Drink filtered water – at least six to eight glasses per day, to stay hydrated.

Eat as much of your food from organic sources as possible.

And, take nutritional supplements, including a complete multivitamin complex, B-complex, omega-3 fatty acid supplement (like krill oil or cod liver oil); and friendly gut bacteria (like Acidophilus).

"Your health and mood is intimately linked to the food choices that you make". Dr Mark Atkinson (2008)

~~~

There is *no universal agreement* about what works for anybody, and some researchers now believe that a diet has to be personalized to the individual, because we each have an individual history of environmental effects which impact our genes.

Many experts recommend the ***Mediterranean diet*** - high in vegetables, fish and olive oil, and low in meat consumption[172]. See, for example: www.nhs.uk/Livewell/Goodfood/Pages/what-is-a-Mediterranean-diet.aspx.

Or (occasionally, but ***not*** long-term) the ***Paleo diet*** - high in meat, fish, vegetables, fruit; and excluding (most) grains and dairy. See: thepaleodiet.com/what-to-eat-on-the-Paleo-diet/)[173]. (But this diet probably involves eating too much meat, according to Dr Michael Greger, 2016). Meat contains the essential fatty acid (omega-6), but it seems from Dr Greger's argument that we should not have too much of this fatty acid – even though it's essential. It seems we need to watch the ratio of omega-3 to omega-6. (See Simopoulos, 2002)[174]. So the emerging Nordic diet may be worth considering; or the Mediterranean diet, because they both favour fish over meat, with the Nordic involving more fish.

Eating organic foods is one way of minimizing the chemical pollutants that get into our bodies and impair our ability to function healthily in the face of the pressures and strains of daily life, according to Bart Cunningham, PhD.[175] There is also recent research which suggests a link between trans-fats (including hydrogenated fats in processed foods) and aggression, irritability and impatience.[176]

5. Stress management advice

The Stress Management Society gives the following advice: "*If you want a strong nervous system, boost your intake of vitamins B, C and E, together with minerals magnesium and zinc. The best source of these nutrients is from food, rather than supplements. So eat a balanced diet of meat, nuts, seeds, fresh fruit and vegetables and oily fish. If you need to snack during the day, try pumpkin or sunflower seeds and fruit, particularly (greenish) bananas. Fresh organic food is the best source. If you can't get fresh, frozen vegetables are a reasonable alternative as much of their nutritional content is retained.*" [177]

We suggest you follow most of this advice, except for the supplementation of vitamins and minerals. Unless you are on a wholly organic diet, your food will be largely denatured and devoid of much nutritional value; you may not know what to eat in order to have 'a balanced diet'; and it you cook your food, you will lose some of the nutrients that are in it; therefore you need to use vitamin and mineral supplements of a good, natural-source quality.

The Stress Management Society also rightly emphasizes the importance of drinking lots of water over the course of the day: "*If you want to deal with stress, drink water. It hydrates every part of the body and brain and helps you to better cope with stressful situations. A good rule is to take a few sips every 15 minutes. The best source is room-temperature still water bought in glass bottles (some plastic bottles can leach chemicals into the water inside) or use a jug filter system that you fill from the tap."* (Stress Management Society, 2012/2016).

6. Proportions of food groups

How much protein, carbohydrate and other foods should we eat? There is a lot of emphasis today on having five (six, or seven) portions per day of fruit and vegetables. Before that particular campaign began, the Department of Health (in Britain) and many nutritionists were recommending that about fifty to seventy percent of our daily intake of food should come from complex carbohydrate, such as brown rice, pasta, wholemeal bread, millet, potatoes, and so on. (And this kind of ratio is maintained in the US to this day). About twenty-five percent (they said) should be unsaturated fats, from sources like oily fish, nuts, seeds, cold-pressed oils, like olive oil, flaxseed oil, and so on.

And ideally you need about fifteen percent of your food intake to be in the form of protein sources such as grass fed meat, (especially liver); fish (especially oily varieties [which contain more omega-3 fatty acid], though some white fish is very good for the brain); and eggs (preferably organic free range). Keep the meat proportion low and the fish proportion high, to reduce the omega-6/omega-3 ratio (Simopoulos, 2002).

Increasingly, we see recommendations that about 80% of your dinner plate should be vegetables, with a small amount of protein. Or, in the case of current UK guidelines: 35% grains and legumes; 35% vegetables and fruit; and the remaining 30% split into three groups: milk and dairy foods (10%); meat, fish and alternatives (10%); and foods containing fat, and foods containing sugar (10%).

The best and safest sources of protein are probably wild Pacific salmon, or wild Alaskan salmon; grass fed lamb; organic, free range chicken; and organic eggs.

7. Food combining, or not

Some theorists believe that combining complex carbohydrates with a protein can reduce stress and provide a solid fuel for daily energy requirements: (Atkinson, 2008: page 57). This, however, contradicts the **Hay Diet**, which recommends keeping carbohydrates and proteins separate, in meals separated by at least four hours! (However, there does not seem to be any scientific studies supporting the Hay approach to food combining – although Renata and I have found it very helpful in reducing indigestion, and promoting efficient elimination).

Others argue that too much carbohydrate, especially refined forms, could cause stress (e.g. Gangwisch, J. et al. (2015) in *ScienceDaily*, 2015)[178]. On the other hand, oily fish, like salmon, mackerel and sardines, with green vegetables and complex carbohydrate are believed to be particularly beneficial. There *are* scientific studies to support the claims about the impact of oily fish on the reduction of panic attacks. For example, Perretta, 2001, page 90).[179]

Cunningham (2001) maintains that fast foods, which are normally high in fats and sugars "*...are stressful to our systems*". (Page 201)[180]. So eliminating fast foods would seem like a sensible precaution as part of a stress management programme. And getting rid of sugar and salt in general from our diets is sometimes said to be a good idea, though some theorists think *a small amount of salt* is needed by the body to function normally. In general, however, western diets are overloaded with salt and sugar, and a vast reduction seems to be called for, as high blood sugar levels are bad for stress levels, and high salt levels are implicated in heart attacks and strokes (according to some experts, and some studies). And caffeine, sugar and alcohol are stressful to the body-brain-mind.

The **Ph Diet** is an interesting one, which emphasizes the general guideline that about 75% of the content of each main meal should comprise vegetables. Pasta, rice and potatoes should never be taken as more than a *small* side dish! Avoid pizzas, burgers and other processed foods. Additionally, as Nicki Woodward writes: "*Acidifying foods should be reduced in the diet as much as possible*". According to C Vasey, author of The Acid-Alkaline Diet... "*These foods are primarily rich in proteins, carbohydrates and/or fats. Cheese, vegetable oils, hard animal fats, bread, pasta, white sugar all fall into this category*".[181] Sugar and sugary foods are bad; avoid processed foods (especially pastries, pastas and white bread); salt; and minimize saturated dietary fat (as in meat, cheese and eggs).

~~~

8. Drinks and drinking

As a general rule, we can definitely say that you could benefit from minimizing your consumption of caffeine (coffee, tea, cocoa, and cola drinks). Also, avoid sugary drinks (like colas, sodas, pops and power drinks/energy drinks). All of these drinks tend to stoke the build-up of anxiety. And avoid alcohol, if you have Candida overgrowth problems. And minimize it otherwise, which means about one unit of alcohol three times per week. Preferably red wine with a meal.

Green tea is good for you. Camomile tea is very calming of the central nervous system.

Minimize milk, as it contains high levels of lactic acid, which is a sugar that feeds candida, and thus triggers depressed feelings. (Very little research has been done, apparently, on the effect of milk upon the emotional states of *adult* humans. However, a significant degree of research has been done on the effect of milk, via migraine reactions, on *children's moods and behaviours*, and the effects can be quite negative and disruptive of brain-mind functioning)[182].

It is important to drink at least six or eight glasses of water per day, preferably mineral water, or a combination of mineral water and filtered water. (Tap water is bad for your health, because of various forms of pollution, like heavy metals and agricultural chemical run-off).

Avoid sugary cola and pop drinks. And minimize alcohol consumption, as suggested above. (Alcohol can trigger anger, aggression, and suicidal ideation and self-harm acts; and it feeds the unfriendly bacterium, Candida Albicans). Perhaps one unit of alcohol three times per week might be tolerable (especially a red wine). More than that and you will damage your health. Alcohol is a depressant which also disturbs your sleep, which has a negative effect upon your mood the following day. Some nutritionists are concerned that 'green smoothies', or regular 'fruit smoothies' may be bad for us, because they give us a quick spike of sugar (fructose and other forms) which raises our stress level. (For example: Dr Thomas Campbell recommends that you, *"Use your mouth and your teeth the way nature intended and put the smoothies aside or have them just as treats."*[183]

9. Fats and oils

Fats are one of the three macronutrients, which are essential for physical and mental health. The other two are protein and carbohydrates. We also need two micronutrients: vitamins and minerals. And we need water.

We need fat for current energy needs; plus energy storage (for later use); and for the building and rebuilding of our cells, including our brain cells; and to produce myelin, which is essential for transmitting signals from brain cell to brain cell. And certain essential fatty acids (EFA's) are important for brain and emotional health.

But even though we need fat, we can also have *too much*.

Most of the important questions about fat remain unanswered (according to Campbell and Campbell, 2006). The 'diet wars' are as much about fat as any other macronutrient or food group.

Butter is probably quite bad for you (because it is 100% animal fat, and animal fat (and animal-based foods in general) are bad for our general health [according to the China Study, by Campbell and Campbell, 2006]). And margarine is even worse (even though it is vegetable fat – and even though vegetable fat tends to promote health while animal fat reduces it [Campbell and Campbell, 2006: pages 66, and 129-130]). And the reason for the problem with margarine is the chemicals that are used to harden it and colour and flavour it. Most margarines are made from, or contain, trans-fatty acids, which are bad for your body and brain. Some of the chemical processes used in the manufacture of margarine (like bleaching!) are clearly not good for human health! (Source: The Real Food Guide (2017))[184].

A McDonald's Double Cheeseburger is 67% animal fat, and whole cow's milk is 64% animal fat. Very small amounts of animal fat are probably going to be okay, but we have to keep it low. (Campbell and Campbell, 2006).

So small amounts of extra virgin olive oil dribbled on your (gluten free) bread might be better (as demonstrated by the Mediterranean diet), but keep the quantity to about one teaspoon per day, as processing fats uses up your body's water content, which results in dehydration. (You could also try Extra Virgin Coconut Oil, which is solid at room temperature, and can be spread like butter. [However, Patrick Holford recommends cold-pressed seed oils, like flaxseed oil or hemp oil]. But, again, watch out for dehydration by keeping oil consumption low [or you could significantly increase your water consumption?!]).

Avoid all trans-fats, which are found in junk foods, processed food, and most take-way foods. (See Part 1 of this book, section 4(a), above).

According to Campbell and Campbell (2006), we should probably keep our total fat consumption below 30% (although this has not been established as a 'vital threshold'). It is also difficult for us to figure out how much fat we are eating in any case! It's not easy, since all of the main food groups, in the UK National Food Guide, and the US Food Guide Pyramid (renamed My-Pyramid), contain some fat. So, as a general guideline, it is probably best to keep your animal product consumption low, since there is *a strong parallel between increasing animal products and increasing total fat consumption*. And there is also a strong link between increasing the consumption of animal products and increasing disease! (Campbell and Campbell, 2006: page 83, and page 129-130).

We recommend that you keep your dairy products and meat consumption low or very low. You should probably aim for less than 10% of your total calorie consumption from this food group. (You will still be getting plant based fats from the other food groups, and plant based fats are probably better [based on the results of the China Study]).

Make sure you get at least as much omega-3 fatty acid as omega-6. Again this is difficult to calculate and maintain, because most of our foods contain lots of omega-6 fatty acids, and very few contain much omega-3. The best way to do this is to eat oily fish (like salmon, mackerel, tuna and sardines) at least twice each week. And eat lots of nuts and seeds on a regular basis. Since it is very difficult to measure the fats we are eating, it is probably best to choose a good, healthy, balanced diet, like the Mediterranean or the Nordic diets, and stick to those general guidelines. Perhaps also get cookbooks for those diets, and try to be guided by the types of food recommend therein. (But mainly go for plant based foods, and keep meat and dairy products very low).

What about other uses of oils in the kitchen?

For salad dressings, it is probably best to use olive oil.

And what about frying? We tend not to fry anything. I (Jim) usually poach our salmon fillets, in herb-flavoured water, instead of frying them.

But what do the experts say? One BBC blog reported on some recent frying experiments (by Professor Martin Grootveld, at De Montford University) like this:

'Firstly, try to do less frying, particularly at high temperature. If you are frying, minimise the amount of oil you use, and also take steps to remove the oil from the outside of the fried food, perhaps with a paper towel.

'To reduce aldehyde (which are noxious chemical products of the frying process) go for an oil or fat high in monounsaturated or saturated lipids (preferably greater than 60% for one or the other, and more than 80% for the two combined), and low in polyunsaturates* (less than 20%).

'He thinks the ideal "compromise" oil for cooking purposes is olive oil,

> "because it is about 76% monounsaturates, 14% saturates and only 10% polyunsaturates - monounsaturates and saturates are much more resistant to oxidation (which produces trans-fats) than are polyunsaturates".' (Source: Mosley, M., 2015)[185].

If we (Renata and Jim) - very occasionally - fry anything, then we add some butter to the olive oil, which is even better at resisting the oxidation process (which is what produces the aldehydes). And rapeseed oil and goose fat were also found by Prof Grootveld's study to resist the oxidation process (and thus produced a healthier friend food result).

~~~

10. Never skip breakfast

Don't skip your breakfast, no matter how late or busy you might be, as you need a solid supply of *food-derived-glucose*, **burning slowly** throughout the morning, to keep your blood sugar level at a suitable and fairly constant level. Porridge or cooked fish make a good, slow-burning breakfast; or wholemeal brown toast and organic eggs. Make sure you eat at least three nutritious meals every day; and have a light snack mid-morning and mid-afternoon, to keep your blood sugar level up. Always eat in a relaxing environment. And avoid simple sugars, as they are seen to over-boost blood sugar levels, precipitating insulin release, and a quick fall back in blood sugar levels, thus reducing energy, concentration, and potentially boosting stress levels via the release of adrenaline.

Some people are so sensitive to sugar that they cannot even cope well with fruit sugar, and those individuals fare better on a diet of seven portions of vegetables per day, and no fruit at all.

The worst kind of breakfast is no breakfast at all!

The next worse kind of breakfasts is one of refined carbohydrate and simple sugars, such as white toast, or any kind of bread made from refined flour; sugary cereals; jams and marmalades; and so on.

The best kind of breakfast (according to some theorists) consists of complex carbohydrate, such as porridge or muesli, combined with a couple of pieces of fresh fruit (if you can tolerate the fructose), such as apples or bananas. (However, in relation to carbohydrate consumption, watch out for *gluten intolerance* in yourself - and it is advisable to only eat gluten-free breakfast cereals (complex, not refined or processed). Also watch out for food intolerances - allergic reactions - and eliminate those foods to which you are currently allergic). You can always consult a nutritional therapist regarding what to eat for your particular needs and problems.

A couple of times per week, a protein breakfast would be good, such as grilled mackerel, kippers, or traditional (organic) bacon and egg, etc. It is best to eat like a "king/queen" at breakfast, to fuel your morning's work. Then have a reasonable lunch, to carry you through the afternoon. And finally, have a light meal in the evening.

PS: Actually, for several months now, I have been having salad for breakfast, with nuts and seeds and some low-sugar berries. And I seem to be thriving on that!

11. Snacks, supplements and raw food

Mid-morning and mid-afternoon, it is important to have both (small) snacks and (10 minute) naps. The best forms of snacks are probably a handful of nuts or seeds, and a piece of fruit, with a bottle of mineral water or a herbal tea. Brazil nuts are particularly high in selenium and magnesium, which are both calming. Dr John Briffa believes that just three or four Brazil nuts per day can stabilize the moods of anxious individuals.[186]

If you prefer to take a magnesium supplement, then 400 milligrams per day is probably a good level to take. Some theorists believe milk is particularly helpful, because its calcium content is calming. However, it also contains lactose, which is a form of sugar, and it has been shown to cause emotional problems (Brown, 2017); so watch the consumption level. And the Paleo theorists think dairy products cause inflammation in the guts, which can then cause mood swings. (80 or 90% of the serotonin in our bodies is, apparently, produced in our guts!) There is no doubt that many people are lactose intolerant, and we have included a reference to research that shows milk can have a negative impact on mood, emotions and behaviours in children, and, by implication, in adults also.

Raw food is very important, as much cooked food is very low in nutritional content, and especially enzymes, which are essential for digestion: so at least one salad meal per day would seem to be sensible. Furthermore, eating lots of salad vegetables seems like a good idea. The Chinese would not agree with that, as they think the digestion process is aided by lightly stir-frying vegetables.

~~~

12. Find out for yourself

However there really is no alternative to experimenting with these ideas, and trying to map the effects of particular kinds of food on your energy level and your mood. We do know from scientific studies that caffeine and alcohol are particular causes of concern, in that they stimulate the sympathetic nervous system, pushing your stress level up, causing irritability and anger, anxiety, panic attacks, depression and insomnia. (Perretta, 2001, page 88)[187].

Smoking also tends to increase stress levels, and some recreational drugs are also stressors. Therefore, many alternative health practitioners and nutritionists advocate giving up smoking; reducing alcohol consumption; avoiding stimulants; and restricting your intake of caffeine to two cups of fresh ground coffee per day, or four cups of tea. (Cunningham, 2001). Dr John Briffa recommends *complete elimination* of caffeine for individuals who are "*on the anxious side*". We recommend that you reduce or eliminate smoking; alcohol consumption; and breathing polluted air.

Most practitioners recommend consuming less than two units of alcohol every other day, as a maximum, for men, and half of that for women; and also slowly getting off tobacco completely. Marijuana has also been implicated in the causation of panic attacks and paranoia.

13. Supplements and healthy foods

Because modern methods of agriculture have resulted in reduced levels of nutrition in our foods, and many of these foods are further denatured by the food-processing industry, you are strongly advised to take a good quality multivitamin and mineral supplement, plus a full spectrum B-complex, including B5 and B2; iron, magnesium and calcium.

You will also benefit from extra vitamin C (at least one gram per day). Perretta (2001) recommends the following foods in particular: avocado; mushrooms; spring greens and spinach; liver; millet; guava and papaya. And a friendly bacteria supplement will support your gut health.

~~~

14. Finale

Green vegetables are recommended by many nutritionists, and the British Department of Health. And don't forget the oily fish! It aids all brain functions, including managing stress. Best oily fish: Wild Alaskan salmon, (or Wild Pacific salmon) which is available fresh (chilled) or in tins at Marks and Spencer, UK; tinned sardines, which can be with tomato sauce for taste purposes; grilled fresh mackerel; or trout.

And finally, lettuce is a natural tranquillizer[188], so it seems sensible to eat lots of it; and drinking Chamomile tea may also calm the nervous system, and reduce insomnia[189]. But be careful. Everything we put in our digestive system has the potential to produce side-effects; and some investigators have reported anecdotal evidence that Chamomile tea can interfere with antidepressant medication! (See 'Health Unblocked' blog[190]). (Not that we can recommend antidepressant medication, which seems to be no better than a placebo, and has some very nasty side effects which will, predictably, affect a high proportion of the users of these drugs. 'Food is the best medicine'!)

~~~

See also my web page titled, 'More on Diet and Brain Functioning' page, at: http://web.archive.org/web/20160322040504/http://www.abc-counselling.com/id270.html.

~~~

If you want to check out the areas of agreement and disagreement among medical practitioners on the subject of diet and emotional wellbeing, then take a look at this debate: 'Sugar, Gluten, Paleo, Vegan: 3 Doctors Debate The Best Way To Eat', here: http://www.mindbodygreen.com/revitalize/video/sugar-gluten-paleo-vegan-3-doctors- debate-the-best-way-to-eat

And remember: This is not *medical* advice. It is *educational* information. For medical advice, please see your medical practitioner, GP, or holistic, complementary or alternative health physician; or your health coach. For professional advice and help with your diet, please see a registered nutritional therapist or nutritionist.

~~~

Part 4: Nutritional deficiencies and emotional disorders – The link

By Jim Byrne

Copyright (c) Jim Byrne, 3rd April 2017

Section A: The science of nutritional deficiency

1. Introduction

There is now a growing consensus that there is a significant link between diet/nutrition - on the one hand - and 'mental health' or emotional wellbeing - on the other. (For examples, see Korn 2016, and Enders 2015, and Holford 2010).

I first began to take these emerging insights into account in dealing with my clients, perhaps fifteen or more years ago. Out of my curiosity about this link, I created what I called my Stress and Anxiety Diet. (See Part 3, above).

I recently reviewed Part 1 of a three part webinar on 'Nutrition and Mental Health', by Dr Bonnie Kaplan, a professor in the Cumming School of Medicine, University of Calgary, Alberta, Canada[191].

In her webinar, Dr Kaplan reviews 2,600 years of folklore and modern science to explore the link between nutrition and mental health.

2. The science of nutritional deficiency

In the realm of science, she presents evidence that, just as deficiencies in single nutrients can cause physical diseases (e.g. scurvy), they can also cause psychological/psychiatric symptoms.

She begins her science section with a look at the dire consequences of citrus deficiency: the development of a disease called scurvy, which killed 40% of the crews of ships that sailed without lemon juice. In 1774, citrus was shown, in a randomized control trial of six potential treatments, to be superior. But it took *264 years* before citrus was made routinely available to all sailors.

Subsequent studies showed that single nutrient deficiencies could, and would, cause psychiatric symptoms, of which Kaplan mentions four:

> \# Thiamine/ B1 deficiency causes the conditions called Wernicke's encephalopathy[192] and Korsakoff's psychosis[193].

> \# Cyanocobalamin/ B12 deficiency causes Psychosis of pernicious anaemia[194].

> \# Iodine deficiency causes 'Myxoedema madness'[195]. And:

> \# Niacin/B3 deficiency causes Pellagra[196].

The widespread recognition that these psychiatric conditions can be caused by *single nutrient deficiencies* is beyond dispute. As Dr Kaplan points out, the DSM acknowledges that niacin deficiency can cause neurocognitive disorders.

How do we know that **most** so called psychiatric symptoms are *not* a result of single or multiple vitamin or mineral deficiencies? Or a result of nutritional deficiencies **plus** dehydration? Or nutritional deficiencies, *sugar overload*, and *inflammation* due to gluten allergies? The answer is: *We Don't!*

But there is a growing field of nutritional medicine emerging which seems to cohere around one central theme: *Food is the best medicine!* (Brogan, 2016[197]; Perlmutter, 2015[198]; Ross, 2002[199]; Enders, 2015[200]).

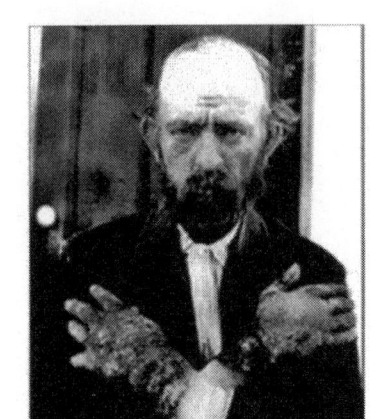

~~~

3. Vitamin B3 deficiency and the disease of Pellagra

If you suffer from an insufficiency of vitamin B3, you will almost certainly contract a disease called Pellagra. The most obvious symptom of Pellagra is rough skin, or dermatitis of an extreme form. According to Dr Kaplan, this disease was first described in 1735 in Spain. But it was not until 1914 that Dr Joseph Goldberger realized that it was not an infectious disease, but that it was linked to diet. By 1937, it was precisely linked to niacin (or Vitamin B3) deficiency. As a result, some governments began to fortify food with vitamin B3, to prevent this disease.

However, as mentioned earlier, Pellagra symptoms were not restricted to the skin, but also affected the brain-mind of the victim, causing mental disturbances sufficiently sever for sufferers to be admitted to psychiatric hospitals. And Dr Kaplan cites one American hospital which estimated that 1 in 5 admissions from 1930-32 were solely due to Pellagra psychosis.

Much of this psychosis was caused by over-reliance on maize as the staple of the 'poor man's diet'.

What does this tell us about the stigma of 'mental illness'? Are we misrepresenting nutritional deficiencies as 'madness'?

My (Jim's) own mother was hospitalized for depression when I was about twelve years old. The one thing I know for sure about those years is this: *We were all seriously malnourished!* (Of course, we must not get into the trap of swapping one 'single cause' of emotional distress for another. We subscribe to a holistic model, in which diet, exercise, self-talk, relaxation, meditation, sleep pattern, family of origin, current relationships, environmental stressors, economic circumstances, housing circumstances, and so on, all play a role in determining the individual's capacity to regulate their emotions; and certainly there were a lot of stressors [financial and relational] in my mother's life at that time!)

~~~

4. Nutritional treatment of emotional problems

Dr Kaplan, in 2007, co-authored a paper on Vitamins, Minerals and Mood[201]. This is what the abstract said:

"In this article, the authors explore the breadth and depth of published research linking dietary vitamins and minerals (micro-nutrients) to mood. Since the 1920's, there have been many studies on individual vitamins (especially B vitamins and Vitamins C, D, and E), minerals (calcium, chromium, iron, magnesium, zinc, and selenium), and vitamin-like compounds (choline). Recent investigations with multi-ingredient formulas are especially promising. However, without a reasonable conceptual framework for understanding mechanisms by which micronutrients might influence mood, the published literature is too readily dismissed. Consequently, 4 explanatory models are presented... These models provide possible explanations for why micronutrient supplementation could ameliorate some mental symptoms[202]."

Dr Kaplan next moves on to present the result of the **Minnesota Starvation Experiments**, from 1950, which demonstrated that, when a group of normal, healthy students were deprived of a nutritious diet, and placed on 50% of normal nutritional levels, they developed symptoms of depression, hysteria, irritability, self-mutilation, apathy and lethargy, social withdrawal, and inability to concentrate. (Keys, et al, 1950)[203].

The link between nutrition and mental health is therefore, quite clearly, beyond dispute[204].

~~~

Section B: The Minnesota Starvation Experiment

1. Introduction

Above, I reviewed the scientific evidence, presented by Professor Bonnie Kaplan, that nutritional deficiencies can and do result in mental health or emotional wellbeing problems.

In particular, we saw that *single nutrient deficiencies* – like vitamins B1, B3, B12, and iodine, resulted in psychiatric disorders, or mental health difficulties.

At the end of her presentation of the scientific evidence of the importance of nutrition for mental health, Dr Kaplan raises this question: **What happened next?**

And her answer? *Nothing! Or: 5+ years of virtual silence on the role of nutrition in mental health in the realm of psychiatry or clinical medicine.*

She then wonders: **'Why?'**

Her first inference is that this was the era of *the development of pharmaceuticals!* (Which we now know to be little better than a placebo, but with hugely damaging side effects! [More on that later in this series!])

And she also mentions that psychologists and mental health workers were taught that *nutrition was not important!*

But that claim is spurious, and contradicts the scientific evidence presented by Dr Kaplan.

~~~

2. Evidence from the Minnesota Starvation Experiments

In an effort to keep a tight focus upon the research on single nutrient deficiencies, in the previous section, I skipped Dr Kaplan's presentation on the Minnesota Starvation Experiment. I now want to return to that subject:

The results of the Minnesota Starvation Experiment have been summarized as follows, by two authors at the American Psychological Association[205]:

"Amid the privations of World War II, 36 men voluntarily starved themselves so that researchers and relief workers could learn about how to help people recover from starvation.

*"They reported fatigue, **irritability, depression and apathy**. Interestingly, the men also reported **decreases in mental ability**, although mental testing of the men did not support this belief." And their sex urge disappeared completely."* (Professor Bonnie Kaplan, who has studied the reports carefully, expands this list as follows: *"Depression, hysteria, irritability, self-mutilation, apathy/lethargy, social withdrawal and inability to concentrate".*)[206]

Given the insights of this research, why should anybody feel any sense of stigma about 'mental health issues'? What if all of their problems could be cleared up by working on their diet, their gut health, and their general level of stress? (And perhaps re-writing or re-thinking their personal and family history?)

"The Minnesota Starvation Experiment ... reminds us that in psychology studies of mind and body, science and practice can converge to deal with real problems in the real world."[207]

Despite the fact that the American Psychological Association knows of this research, in which semi-starvation, or extreme nutrient deficiency, resulted in fatigue, irritability, depression and apathy, *no significant evidence exists that counsellors and psychotherapists normally take the diet of their clients into account.* (A junk food diet is a form of semi-starvation from the point of view of nutrient-deficiency! And there is now evidence that trans-fats and high sugar content results in emotional disturbances, such as angry outbursts and depression).

~~~

3. Summing up

Bonnie Kaplan has presented a range of evidences that nutritional deficiencies affect mental health. I am very careful to eat a balanced diet – but, also in line with her thinking – to use a range of good quality micronutrients (vitamins and minerals) to compensate for the poor quality of much agricultural soil today; to compensate for the fact that I do not know for sure how to compile a day's menu which will give me adequate amounts of all the essential nutrients I need for my physical and mental functioning.

I would recommend that you follow this pattern. Follow a good guide to nutritious eating – probably something like the Nordic or Mediterranean diet; with perhaps some elements of the Paleo Diet, for short periods of time (with reduced meat and fat).

Or have seven or eight portions of vegetables and fruit per day; with plenty of water (about two litres per day); plus some wholegrain cereals; plus some nuts and seeds; plus some cheese or organic eggs.

And, no matter what diet you evolve for yourself, you will need a good strong multivitamin and mineral supplement; a strong (and preferably yeast free) vitamin B complex; a good quality digestive enzyme supplement (especially if you are over the age of forty years, when you digestive enzymes show a marked decline); and perhaps talk to a good nutritional therapist who can advise you on other supplements you might benefit from.

We also try to eat at least 50% organic; and we currently keep our wholegrains and dairy products well below our vegetable and fruit consumption (and when we eat grains, they are mostly wholegrains, and gluten-free. [PS: Update - And I have recently had to eliminate almost all grains from my diet; though Renata can still tolerate a small amount]).

The simplest way for you to proceed might be to use the guidelines outlined in section 3(a) above, which are produced by the Food Standards Agency. Or experiment with our variation of those guidelines.

But most important of all, do you own research. Find out for yourself. Become your own physician!

Section C: The role of inflammation in emotional disturbance

1. Introduction

In Section 1 of this Part (4), I reviewed the scientific evidence, presented by Professor Bonnie Kaplan, that nutritional deficiencies can and do result in mental health or emotional wellbeing problems.

Then, in Part 2, I reviewed the Minnesota Starvation Experiment[208]. The results of the Minnesota Starvation Experiment have been summarized as follows, by two authors at the American Psychological Association:

"Amid the privations of World War II, 36 men voluntarily starved themselves so that researchers and relief workers could learn about how to help people recover from starvation.

*"They reported **fatigue, irritability, depression and apathy**. Interestingly, the men also reported **decreases in mental ability**, although mental testing of the men did not support this belief.*[209]*"* And their sex urge disappeared completely. (Professor Bonnie Kaplan, who has studied the reports carefully, expands this list as follows: "Depression, hysteria, irritability, self-mutilation, apathy/lethargy, social withdrawal and inability to concentrate"[210].)

And now, in Part 3, I want to move on to review the end of Dr Bonnie Kaplan's webinar[211], which concludes her argument that nutrition is centrally important to good mental health, especially via the link between inflammation and depression.

Blood, brain and nutrition

People like to blame genes for mental illness. But genes cannot do anything in the absence of a facilitating or retarding environment. Genes are switched on or off depending upon the environmental signals they receive. In 1974, in an article in Science, Linus Pauling stated that the genes for mental illness are likely *"...the genes that regulate brain metabolism of essential nutrients"*. That is to say, when mental illness manifests, we should be looking at the environmental factors that are swathing on those symptoms, and we should look at the impact of essential nutrients upon brain metabolism.

Which aspect of the brain's environment should we consider?

The most important one is the blood that flows through our brains at a rate of sixty (recycled) pints per hour. This blood is constantly bathing our brains, and it contains the chemical elements that we have been able to extract from our food.

So, thinking about the chemicals that bathe your brain, are they good chemicals from a healthy diet and nutritional supplements, or are they bad chemicals from a junk food diet. (And how much oxygen is being carried in your blood – which is a function of your level of exercise?)

When our blood is deficient in good quality nutrients, we suffer three major impacts:

1. Impaired functioning of our cells (including the mitochondria), resulting in fatigue and other somatic complaints and mental illness;

2. Excessive inflammatory responses, which causes all kinds of diseases, and there is a direct link to depression from inflammation;

3. Impaired neurotransmitter synthesis and uptake, and we need those neurotransmitters to communicate between the brain and the rest of the body; and to control our moods.

Impaired mitochondrial function is also a problem, because they are "our natural defence against inflammation", and so there is an additional impact upon the initiation of depression symptoms.

2. Depression is associated with inflammation

Professor Kaplan draws attention to a particular academic paper, by Berk, Williams and others, and here is the abstract from that paper:

> "Abstract
>
> "Background
>
> "We now know that depression is associated with a chronic, low-grade inflammatory response and activation of cell-mediated immunity, as well as activation of the compensatory anti-inflammatory reflex system. It is similarly accompanied by increased oxidative and nitrosative stress (O&NS), which contribute to neuroprogression in the disorder. The obvious question this poses is 'what is the source of this chronic low-grade inflammation?'
>
> "Discussion
>
> "This review explores the role of inflammation and oxidative and nitrosative stress as possible mediators of known environmental risk factors in depression, and discusses potential implications of these findings. A range of factors appear to increase the risk for the development of depression, and seem to be associated with systemic inflammation; these include psychosocial stressors, poor diet, physical inactivity, obesity, smoking, altered gut permeability, atopy, dental cares, sleep and vitamin D deficiency.
>
> "Summary
>
> "The identification of known sources of inflammation provides support for inflammation as a mediating pathway to both risk and neuroprogression in depression. Critically, most of these factors are plastic, and potentially amenable to therapeutic and preventative interventions. Most, but not all, of the above mentioned sources of inflammation may play a role in other psychiatric disorders, such as bipolar disorder, schizophrenia, autism and post-traumatic stress disorder." (Berk, Williams, et al, 2013)[212].

3. The sources of inflammation

So where does the inflammation come from, which causes depression and other forms of emotional distress and mental illness? The main answers seem to be:

1. Stress and trauma

2. Suboptimal diet (derived from nutritional epidemiology studies)

3. Sedentary behaviour (so exercise!)

4. Obesity (which is 'an inflammatory state')

5. Gut health! (Which can benefit from both nutrients and friendly bacteria, like lactobacillus supplements)

6. And perhaps other sources...

Item 1 above is greatly helped by talking therapies and other forms of stress management, like relaxation and meditation. Items 2 and 3 depend upon a healthy diet and adequate physical exercise. Items 4 and 5 also benefit from a healthy diet and an active lifestyle, and an effective approach to stress management.

The mitochondrial function of our cells seems to need every single micronutrient know to us; that is to say, all the common vitamins and minerals; plus co-enzyme Q10; and omega-3 fatty acids.

And now that mitochondrial function has been linked to inflammation, the Big Pharma drug companies are promoting the idea that drugs can help; and many academics are obliging them by advocating the development of anti-inflammatory drugs. But our mitochondria are our *natural defence* against inflammation, and they depend upon the whole range of vitamins, minerals and other supplements, all of which can come from a healthy, nutrient dense diet, plus nutritional supplements. Therefore, it makes more sense to treat emotional disorders with nutritional therapies, plus some talking therapies, plus regular physical exercise, and a good stress management strategy.

~~~

For more, see the paper on Nutritional Mental Health, by Bonnie Kaplan, Julia Rucklidge and colleagues[213]. Here is the abstract:

"We live in a transformational moment for understanding the etiology of mental disorders. The previous leap in understanding occurred 60 years ago, which led us to incorporate psycho-pharmacology into our curricula to address the chemical basis of neurotransmitter function, especially as explained through the then-popular catecholamine hypothesis. The current revolution is broader, consisting of the rapidly accumulating knowledge of how inflammation, microbiome imbalance (gut dysbiosis), oxidative stress, and impaired mitochondrial output affect brain function. Suitable interventions for fighting inflammation, restoring normal gut function, reducing oxidative stress, and improving mitochondrial metabolism incorporate lifestyle variables, including nutrients and probiotics. This article invites readers to stay abreast of this emerging model of the biological basis of mental illness, given that it has particular relevance for those readers interested in alleviating the suffering of individuals with mental disorders. This overview describes the basis for a new field in mental health: nutritional psychiatry/ psychology".

~~~

PS: It seems likely that inflammation is as important as external sources of stress in producing emotional distress, including depression and anxiety. Perhaps the mechanism through which external sources of stress impact us is also through the inflammation process. And therefore, we could all benefit from managing our physical activity levels to reduce stress hormones, and managing our diets so that we eliminate common sources of inflammation. That makes it difficult, because the Paleo theorists say grains and dairy and legumes are the main sources of inflammation in our bodies. While Dr Michael Greger says that grain-fed meat is probably the main cause of inflammation, and that we should eat lots of whole grains, vegetables, and legumes instead. And Dr Joseph Mercola warns that many vegetables contain lectins, which cause intestinal inflammation!

So we have to find out for ourselves, through personal experimentation: *Which kinds of meals work best for me? How do I feel twenty-four hours after eating a meal of a particular type? How has it affected my guts, my skin, my level of energy and my moods?*

And if we get stuck, we can benefit from consulting a nutritional expert, to get some guidance. But we should reserve to ourselves the *final decision* as to what we will eat and drink, and why. Because every nutritional expert will subscribe to one or other school of thought, and there is *no universal agreement!*

~~~

Part 5: Summing Up

By Renata Taylor-Byrne

Part 1 of this book looked at a number of questions about the ways in which nutrition affects our body-brain-mind and emotions. In this section, I want to pull together some of the key points that emerged from those considerations:

Firstly, we can't function properly without food, and inadequate nutrition impacts our ability to live, work, communicate, heal, and fight off all the viruses and germs which are present in the atmosphere. We need to have a diet which has all the essential amino acids, vitamins and minerals, complex carbohydrate, fats, and fibre. These should come from healthy sources of unprocessed food, plus some nutritional supplements. The Mediterranean diet is highlighted, plus the Nordic diet, as potential models to follow; or rather to build upon. Some others were also commended, for short-term use; such as (aspects of) the Paleo, Atkins, and Ketogenic diets – which might, unfortunately, be too high in meat content, which causes inflammation, which is linked to mood disorders.

Some of the evidence in favour of the high-fat, low carb diets may be misinterpreting the findings (e.g. Elliott, 2014). Although Elliott goes along with the idea that it is the high-protein, high-fat content of the Atkins/Paleo-type diets that reduces depression; Mozes (2015), looking at the effect of carbohydrates on the incidence of depression, shows a better understanding. Alan Mozes reports that *"The study (under consideration) involved 70,000 women aged 50 to 79. The findings, the investigators said, only show an association between 'refined' carbs and elevated depression, risk, rather than a direct cause-and-effect relationship"*.

But could it not be the case that the Atkins/Paleo diets work, not because of the high fat, high protein end of the equation, but because of the 'low carb' end of the equation; which must (most often) also be 'low refined carbs', as opposed to 'low wholegrains and vegetables'?

Certainly the research cited by Mozes (2015) seems to suggest that as a valid interpretation, where he writes that *"...the women who consumed diets higher in vegetables, fruits and whole grains had a lower incidence of depression"*. (However, this does not prove that *everybody* can tolerate grains!)

Complex carbs, in the form of vegetables, and whole (gluten free and gliadin free) grains, seem to be okay (for many people, much of the time), and not at all in need of being replaced by proteins and fats! By eliminating *refined carbs*, in the form of junk foods and highly processed foods, the Atkins/ Paleo diets make it impossible to evaluate the impact of protein and fats *per se!* Some new research is clearly needed to separate out these competing interpretations. (And some people may need to avoid all grains, at least some of the time; and some will have to permanently exclude them. But they should do this by experimentation, under the guidance of a qualified nutritional therapist!)

~~~

So, at the moment, there is no universal agreement about the ideal, balanced diet. However, we know (some of) what is bad for us, and we have some clues as to what may often be good for people, but we have to allow for individualized diet and nutrition plans.

~~~

Secondly, there are foods whose toxicity is very high, and it is only in the last twenty years or so that people have been able to gain access to research studies and investigations which have looked at those 'foods' which, though always on sale in the supermarket and shops, are really bad for our bodies and brains.

The first culprit is transfats (also called hydrogenated fat, and nicknamed "Frankenfats"). They begin life as harmless vegetable oils, which are then industrially processed by superheating processes which add hydrogen atoms to the oils. Why are these vegetable oils put through this damaging process? Because it makes the fat much easier to use in manufacturing bread, cakes, biscuits, snack bars; and it is preferred by fast food shops and restaurants. And it is much cheaper than real butter or natural vegetable oils. These trans-fats last longer than healthier fats, which means processed foods can last longer on supermarket shelves – but the effects on the body are grim!

Because the trans-fat is created by being boiled at very high temperatures, this affects its chemical structure. The fat is thus unnatural and (wo)man-made and causes chaos in our body and brain on a cellular level. It affects the enzymes that we have which fight cancer, and these have been implicated in a major study which showed a connection between rage and the consumption of trans-fats. They also interfere with the insulin receptors on the body's cell membranes, which causes obesity. And they cause major blocking of the arteries!

The second enemy of our body-brain-mind is sugar. It's described as the enemy of the immune system, which takes four hours to recover from the effects of sugar. It reduces the ability of the immune system to protect us properly; increases inflammation in the body; interferes with the proper functioning of our brain cells; and makes our blood sugar levels fluctuate wildly. It creates fat around our internal organs; causes obesity and diabetes; attacks the collagen in our skin; stiffens our skin and causes wrinkles; and increases blood pressure! It is also implicated in heightening the stress response, when we face any difficulty in life.

The third enemy? It's alcohol, described by Patrick Holford as 'the brain's worst enemy'. Its effects include: unhelpfully dissolving essential fatty acids[214] in the brain; negatively impacting the way our memory works; draining certain B vitamins, vitamin D and calcium from our body; and damaging our ability to get a good night's sleep. It leaches water from the cells of our body, creating dehydration and creating large amount of 'free radicals', which increase the risk of hormonal cancers, particularly breast cancer. It is also implicated in depression and suicide ideation, suicide completion, and self-harm.

Caffeine is next in line in terms of its harmful effects: it overstimulates the heart, stomach, pancreas and intestines. And it reduces calcium, potassium, zinc, vitamin C and the B vitamins. It also alters the acid/alkaline balance in the body, plays a part in premature ageing and affects our sleep. Its main negative effect on our emotions is to simulate anxiety, and trigger panic attacks.

Processed food is the next problem (and much processed food is also 'junk food'). When people are short of time, they are very tempted to get processed food for meals, because of the convenience. Processed foods are normally faster to prepare, but if they have been altered in any way, apart from being washed and packaged, then they normally become suspect of being 'junk foods'. Junk food (which is most processed food) is food which has been altered from its raw, natural state by chemical or physical means. It is sold in jars, tin cans, bottles, and boxes. And it has very dodgy add-ons, like sugar and transfats, and artificial flavours and colours. They also often have constituents that are low in nutrition. Because there can be so much fat, sugar and salt in processed food, this increases the risk of high blood pressure; and the increase in sodium increases the risk of stroke. Furthermore, processed foods create constipation due to lack of fibre. And they can increase the risk of depression, according to a research study by Akbaraly et al (2009), which compared the level of depressive symptoms of middle-aged people on diets which were *either:* high in processed food; or high in wholefoods. Those on a diet high in processed foods had a 58% increased risk for depression over a five year period, according to the research findings. (Wholefoods are normally bought in the state in which they came out of the ground or off the trees and bushes [fruits and vegetables]; or they have remained minimally harvested and left in their natural state [like wholegrains, legumes, etc.]).

What about gluten? This is an enemy for our bodies because of the way gluten behaves when it's in our intestines. Gluten is actually the name of the mixture which is formed (or expanded) when cereal flours (like wheat, rye or barley [or contaminate oats]) are mixed with water. When these two substances are mixed together they expand the chains of proteins called gliadins and glutenins. These substances tend to create inflammation, and to pull the cells in the gut walls apart, producing a condition called 'leaky gut'. This allows whole molecules of food to escape into the blood stream, and travel to the brain. And, according to Dr Giulia Ender's (2015) book on the guts, this also tend to break down the blood-brain barrier, and allow food particles to affect the brain, causing inflammation. (Inflammation is now recognized as the main cause of all the major diseases, including the emotional problem of depression, and possibly other emotional problems, like anxiety). Many people are gluten intolerant. This is called Celiac disease, and people with this condition have to avoid all forms of gluten, otherwise they will further damage their guts. Some other people (perhaps 26% of us) have non-Celiac gluten sensitivity

(NCGS), which damages our brains, but not our guts. And people with neurological damage of unknown origin should therefore always be tested for NCGS. There may be other people who have a form of non-Celiac gluten sensitivity which causes abdominal discomfort, pain, and gas. And there may be people who think they have gluten sensitivity, but actually have gut problems resulting from the Fructans in fruits and vegetables, or other food stuffs.

Because of this situation, many people are not opting to avoid gluten. The official advice to those people is to get themselves tested, for both Celiac disease and NCGS, to make sure they are treating the right condition!

Technically, the gliadin within gluten draws apart the 'tight junctions' between the cells in our intestines. This leads to an increase in the space between the cells, allowing toxins and larger molecules of food, (which would normally pass through the intestines, and be eliminated), to be released into the blood system of our bodies, causing havoc in the form of bowel problems, celiac disease, headaches, anxiety and depression. Apparently there are many thousands of people suffering from the effects of gluten, according to Julia Ross (2002); and researchers have found that symptoms of depression tend to disappear when wheat and other grains have been taken out of the diet. (But we can always use gluten-free whole grains, if we find, by experimentation, that we can tolerate them in our diet)[33].

~~~

We then went on to look at nutritional supplements, like vitamins, minerals, Co-Q-10, gut bacteria, and so on. The question as to whether nutritional supplements actually help us improve our physical and emotional well-being, was addressed. The findings show a range of opinions on their effectiveness. The NHS Direct UK, considers that they are *unnecessary* unless there are specific *reasons* why someone may need extra nutrients, such as pregnant women, and women who may be breastfeeding, and also young children who may have a lack of variety in their diets. Also doctors may prescribe specific nutrients e.g. iron supplements being recommended when a patient has iron deficiency anaemia.

We reject this view as ill-informed, because most people do *not* eat a balanced diet; would not know what a balanced diet *looked* like; and would find it hard to get all the nutrients they need from modern, processed, *denatured* foods!

There are contrasting views held by the following experts: a professor at the Yale School of Public Health's Division of Chronic Disease Epidemiology; Patrick Holford; and Dr David Perlmutter. Susan Taylor-Maine considers them to be inappropriate because: 'They deliver vitamins out of context' (Ballantyne, 2007); and Patrick Holford considers them to be *essential* as we need good nutrition for the creation of optimum mental health.

~~~

For us, the most powerful arguments are these:

(1) Much of our food is now denatured, and low in nutritional value.

(2) Most people would not know how to put together a balanced diet for a day, not to say a week, so they tend to miss out on many nutrients.

(3) Nutritional deficiencies are definitely implicated in the causation of not just physical diseases, but also emotional problems. Therefore it makes sense to take multivitamins and minerals, plus vitamin C and vitamin B complex, and a strong, natural source vitamin E (400 iu), even if it could be shown that some proportion of those supplements are then urinated out of the body. This is a safer option than relying on an inadequate diet for our full range of nutritional needs.

Furthermore, Dr David Perlmutter considers that we need to use probiotics (or live, friendly bacteria, like Acidophilus Bifidus), as supplements, if we want to have a healthy gut and brain. He was inspired by the views of Nobel Laureate Elie Mechnikov, who considered that a proper balance of good and bad bacteria in the gut was an essential factor in making sure human beings live a long and healthy life.

Since Mechnikov has put this theory forward his views have been confirmed by many scientific studies. Perlmutter states the view that the research results confirm that *'Up to 90% of all known human illness can be traced back to an unhealthy gut.'*

~~~

Our experience of anxiety, anger and depression is affected by the nutrients in our bodies. This is the core subject of this book.

Firstly, this book examined how nutrients can affect the experience of anxiety, which is defined by the Oxford dictionary as a *'Feeling of unease or concern'*. It can be an invaluable warning signal, part of our physiological/psychological make-up that can alert us to danger in our immediate environment, but which can also send false alarms! We can experience anxiety because of false fears; a build-up of stress hormones in our bodies; and also due to the condition of our guts, and the nature of the foods and drinks that we consume.

Dr Perlmutter (a board-certified neurologist and fellow of the American College of Nutrition, and President of the Perlmutter Health Centre), has done extensive research on this subject and presents compelling evidence. The condition of the gut, its ability to process food, and the bacteria which is present in the gut, all have a role to play in the creation of anxiety disorders. Our guts apparently contain 70 – 80% of our immune system and they can maintain control over the production of cortisol and adrenaline (which are the main stress hormones). Perlmutter cites evidence from two research studies, one conducted in 2011 - (published in the Proceedings of the National Academy of Sciences, and conducted by J.A. Bravo et al., 2011), and one conducted at Oxford University in 2014 (by K. Schmidt et al., 2014). Both experiments confirm that the use of 'prebiotics' and 'probiotics' lower the levels of corticosterone and cortisol in the gut of animals and humans, thus reducing the stress response. (Prebiotics are foods that promote the growth of good [or 'friendly'] bacteria in the gut; and probiotics are microorganism which, when eaten (normally in capsule form), maintain or reinstate beneficial bacteria in the digestive tract.

In his book titled 'Brainmaker' (2015), Dr Perlmutter describes a client called Martina who started a regime of gluten free food, an oral probiotic programme with probiotic foods, vitamin supplementation, and changes in her lifestyle, such as aerobic exercise and more sleep. After six weeks, when she came back to see him, "She was transformed....she looked radiant". She had no more chronic anxiety, and was off all her medication (anti-depressant and non-steroid anti-inflammatory drugs). Dr Perlmutter and his colleagues always take pictures of their clients at the start of their treatment and at the end. If you would like to see the "Before" and "After" pictures of Martina then they are on his website at www.DrPerlmutter.com.

Jenny Sansouci, a nutritional researcher, found that the top offenders for the creation of anxiety in the human body are caffeine, sugar, artificial sweeteners and alcohol.

~~~

We have considered anxiety. But what about anger? This emotional state is also affected by nutrition to a surprising extent, which the findings of Dr Julia Ross (2003) confirm.

Ross is a psychotherapist and director of Recovery Systems, a clinic in California that treats mood, eating and addiction problems with nutritional therapy and biochemical rebalancing. And her findings are mirrored by the research findings of Patrick Holford (Chief Executive of the Food for the Brain Foundation, in the UK, and a leading nutrition expert).

Both of these experts quote research results which show that angry, aggressive behaviour can originate from chemical imbalances in the body, and they give examples of aggressive behaviour being transformed when nutrients were given to people suffering from low levels of serotonin or who were suffering from hypoglycaemia. For example, there were some astonishing results from the work done by Professor Stephen Schoenthaler, with 3,000 prison inmates in California in 1983. There was a massive reduction in aggressive behaviour when the research study participants, the inmates, were given a diet which was stripped of refined food and sugar.

Schoenthaler's research findings were later replicated in a double-blind study of 1,482 juveniles and several follow-up studies confirmed his findings, which revealed strong, unequivocal evidence of the link between anger and aggression, on the one hand, and the consumption of sugar, processed food and transfats, on the other.

~~~

What about depression? Can the foods that we eat cause depression, or is it our life circumstances? There are many factors to take into account in understanding depression, which are all considered in this book. People can easily confuse depression with grief, and if someone has a bereavement, and they are still suffering from deep feelings of loss and sadness after eighteen months have elapsed, then this is a sign that their grief may be stuck. They may be resisting feeling their grief, and this becomes stuck depression

Dr Kelly Brogan, a practising psychiatrist in America, considers depression to be a grossly misunderstood state. She explains that having one in four American women in their 40's and 50's using psychiatric drugs shows that medication is being given without a proper understanding of the role of lifestyle factors, including dietary habits, and the physiological state of the client's body, especially their guts.

"If you think a chemical pill can save, cure or 'correct' you, you're dead wrong. This is about as misguided as taking aspirin for a nail stuck in your foot", she states. She considers it to be essential to get a full picture of her client's biological make-up and their lifestyle, dietary habits, level of sugar consumption, the state of their guts, hormone levels, genetic variations in their DNA, and their beliefs about their own health.

Both Dr Kelly Brogan and Dr David Perlmutter consider that the state of our guts is a very important determinant of our well-being, and that our guts play a role in the experience of depression. For example Perlmutter cites a research study in which scientists gave people, who had no signs of depression whatsoever, an infusion to precipitate inflammation, which would begin in the guts. And apparently classic depression symptoms developed immediately, in response to that physical inflammation.

As 70-80% of our immune system is in our guts, we need to keep our guts in a good state of health. Our guts play a crucial role in keeping our levels of cortisol and adrenaline in check. Those stress hormones can cause mayhem in the body when they are continually stimulated. So taking care of your intestines is very important, and being aware of the effects on our guts of the food and drink that we consume is part of that process.

Finally, Robert Redfern (2016), who is a nutritionist, author and broadcaster, has publicised the findings from research done at the University of Eastern Finland, in the publication 'Naturally Healthy News'. A study examined the diets of 2,000 men and when the participants ate a diet free of processed food, and instead eat a healthy selection of food, there were fewer symptoms of depression. They also discovered that eating processed food (or 'junk' food), and sugar, increased the symptoms of depression.

~~~

The take away message from this examination of the links between anxiety, anger and depression, on the one hand, and diet and nutrition, on the other, is this: the state of our bodies, our lifestyle, and the food and drink that we consume, all contribute a great deal to the creation of emotional distress. And these insights about nutrition need to be taken into account in the understanding and treatment of emotional and mental problems in counselling, psychotherapy, psychiatry, health coaching, and alternative health advice support services.

~~~

Part 2 of this book was about the relationship between physical exercise and emotional well-being; and the power of exercise to reduce the incidence of anxiety, anger and depression.

The effectiveness of exercise in reducing stress in all its forms was explored. The opinions of the NHS in the UK and the Mayo Clinic in America were cited; and two forms of exercise which are highly rated (Chinese and Indian), were examined.

Normally, when we experience stressful events in our daily lives, if we also have an *active* lifestyle, this physical activity can burn off the stress hormones which would otherwise accumulate in our bodies.

In an emergency (or an apparent emergency), our internal protective mechanism, the *'fight or flight response'*, will normally mobilise our body-brain-mind, by pouring very powerful stress hormones into our system to empower us to get moving and to resolve the problem we are faced with, in a physical way. This is called *activation of the **sympathetic** system*. We automatically either fight our way out, or flee; or sometimes freeze.

When we get to a safe place, or have resolved the emergency, and can breathe more easily, the *'rest and digest'* system kicks in and our bodies slowly return to a relaxed state and our digestion returns to normal. This is called *activation of the **parasympathetic** system*.

But if we don't give our bodies a chance to work off the stress hormones, with physical activity, then anxiety can accumulate and this can become a habitual anxiety problem (which some would call 'an anxiety disorder'. But it should not be given such an apparently 'medical' label!) This habitual state of anxiety means that we can feel stressed even when there is no danger in our immediate environment.

How is this problem of excess anxiety solved?

Partly the answer is to adjust the client's diet. Partly it involves helping them to rethink their *perceptions* of danger. And partly it has to do with *keeping **physically** fit*. Sometimes one of these approaches will do the trick; sometimes it takes two; and sometimes we need to address all three aspects (the dietary, the exercise program, and the self-talk, or inner dialogue).

How effective is the exercise component on its own? This question was answered by the research findings from Joshua Broman-Fulks who recruited two groups of students, 54 in total, and got them exercising. Both sets of students had generalised anxiety disorder and high levels of anxiety, and they exercised less than once a week. One group ran on treadmills (at 60-90% of their maximum heart rates) and the second group walked on treadmills at a rate that was equal to 50% of their maximum heart rates. Each of these two groups had six sessions of the exercise (twenty minutes in length) spread over two weeks.

As a result of the exercise sessions, both groups of students became less sensitive to anxiety, and the more physically demanding exercise produced beneficial results in a shorter period of time.

But why did the exercising work? In a nutshell, the exercise reduces the tension levels in your muscles (stopping the *anxiety feedback loop* going to your brain). So you stop feeling anxious about feeling anxious! Or, you stop having psychological feeling about your physical sensations.

~~~

Can anger be reduced by exercise? How about taking easily-angered people and seeing if exercising has any effect on their levels of annoyance and irritation?

This is exactly what was done by Reynolds (2010), at the University of Georgia, and presented at the Annual Conference of the American College of Sports Medicine. It was described in the *New York Times* Sunday Magazine, as follows:

Sixteen University of Georgia students were selected on the basis of their responses to a questionnaire on their moods. The questionnaire results revealed that the students were easily enraged or hypersensitive.

These easily-angered students were shown a sequence of slides which were deliberately designed to really annoy them. But they were in fact shown them at two different time intervals. One group of students had exercised before viewing the second set of slides, and the other group hadn't. The group of students who hadn't exercised became angry when viewing the slides for a second time.

In contrast, the students who *had* exercised, before seeing the slides for a second time, kept the same level of emotional arousal and annoyance, and there was no increase in their level of anger when seeing the slides for a second time. The lead researcher, Nathaniel Thom, stated that: *"Exercise, even a single bout of it, can have a robust, prophylactic (therapeutic) effect against the build-up of anger."*

Thom reported that, when the students (the study participants) didn't exercise, they were weak in the face of emotional provocation, and were unable to manage their anger. But after the exercise, the students were able to show calm self-assurance when confronted with the provocative, anger-arousing slides used in the experiment.

~~~

Finally, in relation to depression (the effects of which can be devastating), its apparent from the research findings reviewed in this book that exercise has an invaluable part to play.

A key research study was undertaken by Blumenthal et al. (1999 and 2012). The goal of the research project was to compare the effectiveness of exercise against an anti-depressant called Sertraline (which is called Lustral in the UK and Zoloft in the US). It is one of a group of drugs known as selective serotonin reuptake inhibitors (SSRI's). Three groups of participants (156 people in total) were randomly assigned to three different research conditions. Group 1 received Zoloft for their depression. The second group were given exercise activities to do. And Group 3 was given a combination of Zoloft and exercise.

The results showed that all of the three groups showed a distinct lowering of their depression, and approximately half of each group had recovered from their depression by the time the research project had finished. Thirteen percent had reduced symptoms but didn't completely recover.

Then six months later Blumenthal et al. examined the health of the research participants and found that over the long haul, 30% of the exercise group remained depressed as opposed to the 52% on medication, and 55% in the combined treatment group.

A year later there was a second study, identical to the first one, and when the participants were reassessed a year later (by Hoffman and his colleagues), they found that, regardless of the treatment group the participants had been in, the participants who described doing regular exercise, after the research project had finished, were the least likely to be depressed a year later. And this study was about major depression – not mild depression!

The NHS in the UK, on their website, support the view that exercise is good for mild or moderate depression, but they don't clarify that it can also be invaluable for major depression, which was demonstrated by Blumenthal's 1999 and 2012 research findings.

In their book, *'Spark'*, (2009) - on the science of exercise and the brain - Ratey and Hagerman comment upon the findings of Blumenthal's and Hoffman's research, like this:

"The results (of this research, showing the effectiveness of exercise in reducing depression) should be taught in medical schools and driven home with health insurance companies and posted on the bulletin boards of every nursing home in the country, where nearly half of the residents have depression" (page 122).

~~~

Dr Robert Sapolsky, who is a professor of biology, neuroscience and neurosurgery at Stanford University in America, has been studying stress management for many years and uses exercise as his favourite way to manage stress.

He points out that the value of keeping to an exercise regime, whatever the type of exercise might be, is very good for providing individuals with a sense of achievement and self-efficacy. In addition, he makes two key points:

(1) The stress reducing benefits of exercise will wear off if they are not repeated; and:

(2) If you do not want to exercise, but are forced to do it, then it won't help your health.

Sapolsky (2010) writes: *"Let rats run voluntarily on a running wheel and their health improves in all sorts of ways. Force them, even when playing great dance music, and their health worsens."* (Page 491)

Finally he recommends that you have a consistent, regular pattern for a prolonged period of time (a minimum of twenty to thirty minutes per session, several times a week) and that you don't overdo it (because it is possible to harm yourself while exercising. For example, by pulling a muscle).

~~~

We wanted to look at specific approaches to physical exercise in this book. Although brisk walking has been shown to reduce depression and anxiety symptoms, we wanted to look at some of the more formal systems which claim to help with emotional problems.

Therefore, we examined evidence about the value of Qigong (Chi Kung) and yoga, and found that they both have lots of evidence supporting their ability to help people manage anxiety, anger and depression.

~~~

In this summary, I have reviewed the reasons why food is vitally important for our physical and mental health. The evidence is clear: without a balanced range of nutritious foods of decent quality, our bodies and brains can't function properly in the long term. Some foods are toxic to the body-brain-mind, and some are enhancing of physical and mental health.

There are particular body and mind toxins being sold to us, as if there is nothing wrong with them: transfats, sugar, alcohol, caffeine, processed (junk) foods, and gluten, to take a few examples. Becoming aware of the effects of these toxins is crucially important if we are to protect our physical health and emotional wellbeing. For example, anxiety, anger and depression are affected by the types of food we eat, and the liquids we consume.

The take away message from this examination of the causes of anxiety, anger and depression, is that the state of our bodies, our lifestyle, and the food and drink that we consume, contributes a great deal to our emotional state – positive or negative. All those contributing factors need to be taken into account in the understanding and treatment of emotional and mental problems.

Part 2 of this book was about the relationship between physical exercise and emotional well-being and the power of exercise to reduce the incidence of anxiety, anger and depression. The effectiveness of exercise is demonstrated; the opinions of the NHS in the UK and the Mayo Clinic in America are referred to; and two forms of exercise which are highly rated (Chinese and Indian), are examined.

Finally the recommendations of Robert Sapolsky (2010) are mentioned: the personal benefits to be gained from creating an exercise plan and sticking to it, (which includes a feeling of achievement and self-efficacy); the importance of a lack of outside coercion in relation to doing exercise (otherwise our health will deteriorate); and not to do too much of it.

The crucial well-being message for you, the reader, for Parts 1 and 2 is this:

Do not eat, drink and be merry; for tomorrow we may all be very much alive, but very, very ill!

Eat for health and happiness! Nutritious food can be very pleasurable.

To overcome anger, anxiety and depression: eat well; exercise often; and develop a good, calm, mindful philosophy of life. And, take extremely good care of yourself!

~~~

In Part 3, of this book, Dr Jim Byrne introduced his stress and anxiety diet. This came out of his years of struggling with the side-effects of Candida Albicans overgrowth, which include low energy and low mood, plus anxiety. He described how he used supplements and a particular diet to overcome those side effects, and to boost his mood and stabilize his emotions. The anti-Candida diet eliminates most sugar, yeast and fermented foods: (see Chaitow, 2003; Jacobs, 1994; and Trowbridge and Walker, 1989). But you still have to find a way to balance your consumption of protein, carbohydrates and fats.

From this experience of managing his own gut-brain-mind interactions, he was sensitized to any new research he came across, on any aspect of the body-brain-mind and emotions, and he passed this learning on to any of his counselling clients who showed an interest, or a need to know about it.

He then describes certain pieces of advice, from the Stress Management Society, and other authors; and from the Paleo, Nordic and Mediterranean diets; which can normally be expected to have a positive effect upon mood and emotions; but watch out for the down side of the Paleo diet.

Some of his key recommendations included: Don't skip breakfast; eat a balanced diet (which has to be established by trial and error); avoid sugar, caffeine, alcohol, gluten, and dairy products. Close to 70% percent of your diet should be in the form of low-sugar vegetables (and grains and legumes, if you can tolerate them), with fibre intact; plus 10% in fats; 10% nuts and seeds; plus the remainder in the form of meat, fish and alternative forms of protein (like tofu). Try to eliminate all *processed* grains (e.g. white bread, white pasta, etc.), but keep whole grains (if you can healthily tolerate them!) at about 20% to 25% of your diet (and make sure they are gluten free)[33]. He also talks about the importance of adequate water consumption, meaning six to eight glasses per day of filtered tap water, or glass-bottled mineral water.

Eating snacks (like nuts and seeds) mid-morning and mid-afternoon is also an important form of blood-sugar management.

Raw food is very important, because cooking kills so many nutrients. And organic vegetable are best, and should be emphasized ahead of fruit, because fruit sugars, taken in excess, can cause physical and emotional health problems. For some people, who are particularly sensitive to sugar, even vegetables have to be selected for low-sugar content (the Low FodMaps diet). (Some people are fructose ***intolerant***, and have to avoid it. While some are fructose ***sensitive***, and have to reduce its consumption).

Jim recommends various supplements, especially vitamin B, C and E, for stress management; plus a good strong multivitamin supplement, with the full range of minerals. The body needs every single nutrient known to science (according to Leslie Korn, 2016). One of the best ways to proceed is probably to take a good, complex multivitamin and mineral supplement every morning; plus a yeast-free B-complex tablet; and a couple or more grams of vitamin C powder in water per day. Plus a natural source vitamin E capsule (400 iu's); plus omega-3 fatty acids (in the form of foods and supplements). Plus a friendly bacteria supplement, like Acidophilus, or preferably a multi-strain variety, in capsule form.

~~~

In Part 4, Jim writes about old and new research on nutritional deficiencies, and what those studies have taught us about the effect of even single nutrient deficits on our physical health and our emotional states. The most stunning finding is that depression is (or can be) linked to (meaning *caused by*) inflammation, which is also the main cause of most chronic physical diseases. And according to the Paleo diet theorists, all grains and dairy products, and legumes, cause inflammation. Of course, a person on the Paleo diet, who has little or no inflammation in their body could still experience depression for psychological reasons, such as the loss of a child, a marriage partner, or a significant material loss, like a job. Or even a symbolic loss, like a sense of loss of *assumed* social status.

But much of the modern explosion of depression and anxiety may well be caused by inflammation coming from junk food and other dietary mistakes! In addition, Dr Michael Greger has highlighted the problem with diets which contain too much omega-6 and too little omega-3 fatty acids. It seems omega-6 fatty acids cause inflammation, and a common source of this problem in America is too much grain-fed meat consumption. (This may also be on the increase in the UK). Much of the current explosion in depression may be a result of over-consumption of omega-6 through red and white meaty diets. So largely vegetarian diets, with small amounts of Wild Alaskan salmon, plus nuts, seeds and perhaps organic eggs, might be a good way to go. According to Dr Michael Greger, *"Higher consumption of vegetables may cut the odds of developing depression by as much as 62 percent"*[215]. And the China Study established that people who ate the most vegetables were the healthiest, while the people who ate the most meat were the least healthy.

However, you have to find out for yourself, through trial and error, which foods suit your body-brain; and perhaps you can get some help from a nutritional expert. (But always preserve your own judgement!)

~~~

Part 6: How to change for good

By Jim Byrne and Renata Taylor-Byrne

Copyright (c) Jim Byrne and Renata Taylor-Byrne, 2017

~~~

Section 1: Introduction to habit change

By Jim Byrne

In this section, and the next, we intend to give you all the tools you need to implement the behaviour changes which have been recommended in the main body of this book.

1. General theory

In our system of coaching, counselling and therapy (known as the E-CENT[216] perspective), humans are seen as creatures of habit, rather than rational thinkers. (Or, rather, we are *both*; but the emotional past most often proves to be *more powerful* than our present, surface thinking; which is how and why we have survived for so long. We don't have to sit around thinking about how to respond to potential threats. We just automatically do what has kept us safe in the past!) Whatever we did before, you can bet most humans will tend, normally, to repeat in the present – except sometimes. Sometimes we may step outside of our past performances, but *not normally*.

In this sense – the sense of being creatures of habit – humans are clearly **products** *of the past;* **shaped** by the past; **driven** by past experiences; and **acting out** scripts and stories which they **constructed in the past** in response to 'present time' stimuli which they experience *as if they were a* **repetition** *of the past*.

Because we humans are **dominated** *by the past* – all our knowledge and skill and habitual behaviour comes to us from our past, which is stored in our body-brain-mind in the present moment. We cannot 'dump the past'; cannot step away from the past; or behave as if we do not have a specific, personal, historical past.

We learned to eat from our mothers; and we often copy our parents' attitudes towards exercise and alcohol and smoking, and so on.

So change has to be *gradual*, because it involves the *breaking* of powerful habits. And it requires *self-discipline*, and some kind of *support system*.

~~~

2. The benefits of exercise and dietary self-management skills

Diet is not about weight loss, in the main, but about eating healthily; and not just for physical health, but also for emotional wellbeing. Our guts and our brains communicate constantly, and when we eat the wrong foods, we tend to disrupt our normal gut flora and friendly bacteria, which then produces negative effects upon our brain-mind, and thus upon our moods and emotions, and our ability to think straight. Excess sugar causes stress; gluten damages our guts and disrupts our brains. Caffeine speeds up our nervous systems, by secreting stress hormones. And sedentary lifestyle allows the build-up of stress hormones, and slows down the lymphatic drainage of toxic substances from our bodies.

Exercise is important because it affects the electro-chemical functioning of the whole body-brain-mind, reducing stress hormones, releasing happiness chemicals, and promoting oxygenation of every cell, plus the movement of lymphatic fluid; and thus promoting physical *detoxification* and improving physical health and emotional wellbeing through *stress reduction*.

~~~

3. Our approach to behaviour change

We believe in *gradual* change!

We do not want to encourage you to *overload yourself* with self-change action lists! Or, to put it better: We do not want you to believe that you *have to change* **everything** on your self-change list *today, right now,* **immediately** and totally!

You cannot do it anyway. Because we are creatures of habit, if we try to change too much too quickly, the deeply emotional, habit-based part of us will panic, and rebel; and not allow it to happen. It's too scary.

So, therefore, change takes time.

Change take effort.

Change takes commitment.

And the best way to proceed is slowly, incrementally, and self-supportingly!

4. A personal example

To make this point well, I (Jim) would like to present an example from my own life:

About fifteen years ago, I found I had lost all my self-discipline in relation to daily physical exercise. I had gone from being a regular exerciser to a regular procrastinator! I could not bring myself to do any exercise whatsoever. So, for a long time I was stuck in this 'pre-contemplation' stage. I was not planning to change anything!

Then, as the weeks and months drifted past, I became more and more annoyed with myself, because I knew I was risking serious damage to my physical health and my emotional wellbeing. At this point I became a 'contemplator'. I was contemplating, or thinking about, change, but I could not quite bring myself to do anything about it. I kept 'planning' to change; or 'trying' to change; but I did not change!

Then one morning I felt so bad about my procrastination, that I became 'determined' to do something about it. This is, obviously, called the 'Determination Stage' of behaviour change. (Prochaska, Norcross and DiClemente, 1998)[217]. That was when I remembered the *Kaizen* method of 'gradual improvement'[218]. This system, introduced to Japan by some American teachers, including W. Edwards Deming, at the end of the Second World War, teaches a process of gradual refinement and progress, instead of huge jumps and big goals.

So I decided on the smallest goal I could come up with, which would be acceptable to me. I felt I could run on the spot, right by my armchair, for thirty seconds, and then sit down. I stood up – (this is the Action step) - feeling hopeless, and I did it. I ran on the spot to the count of thirty. That is to say, when my left foot hit the floor, I counted '1'. Then, when my right foot hit the floor, I counted 'And'. When my left foot fell again, I counted '2'. And so on, up to thirty foot falls; like gentle jogging, but on the same spot. Then I sat down. *I felt great!*

I felt such a sense of self-efficacy – of self-esteem – that I was amazed. Such a small step forward, and such a big reward in terms of how good I felt about myself.

So, the next day, I decided to run on the spot for the count of sixty (foot lifts and falls). When I sat down, I felt even better.

The third morning, I could not stop when I reached 60, or 120, or 240. I was hooked.

I had persuaded the resistant, emotional, non-conscious part of myself that I would not die, or fall apart, if I did my physical exercises; so I went back to doing my old Judo club calisthenics, my Chi Kung, and my press-ups and sit-backs.

And this is the key point: This is how we want you to tackle whatever personal-change goals you come up with, as a result of reading Part 1 and Part 2 of this book.

We do not want you to demoralize yourself, by *aiming too high*, too soon, only to fail; and then to abandon all attempt at personal change. We want you to be *realistic*, and we want you to give yourself the best chance of *succeeding* in making those changes you choose for yourself!

~~~

5. A second example: Using rewards and penalties

The second story I want to tell you follows on from the first.

So, I did my exercises four or five mornings each week, for quite some time, but then I began to skip them, if I was 'too busy'; or if I was 'running late'. So, I remembered another very important principle of behaviour change: rewards and penalties!

So I made this commitment to myself:

"Every morning that I do my exercises, I will give myself permission to read six pages of a novel that I like, as a reward. And if I fail to do my exercises, I will immediately take *two £1 coins* (which totals close to $3 US) from my bookcase shelf, and go out into the street, and drop them both down the nearest drain, so they become irretrievably lost!"

Needless to say, I did not skip any exercise sessions from that point onwards!

~~~

In Section 2 of this, the sixth part of this book, below, Renata presents an even more powerful system of behaviour change, which you can use to make those changes you want to make to your diet and exercise regimes.

~~~

6. The stages of change

So now, we hope, you have an understanding that change has to be *gradual*.

Change begins at the ***Precontemplation*** stage, when you are not planning any change at all. Then it proceeds through ***Contemplation***, when you are *thinking about* changing something. Then on to becoming ***Determined*** to change something. Then you take ***Action***. And even after that, you can slip back. So you have to work at ***Maintenance*** of the new habit. When you feel yourself slip back, you have to repeat whatever process you used to make the change. And you have to be vigilant, to make sure you don't slip back too easily.

The important point is this: You cannot make any changes until you reach the *'determination'* stage; and it's best to have a system of *rewards* and *penalties* in place.

One of the best rewards, of course, is the realization that – when you manage your diet and exercise programs well - you are adding years to your life; adding to your physical health and your mental health; and improving your moods and emotions. (And you will also look more attractive, and be more creative, and be more successful in your relationships, at home and in work!)

~~~

7. How to use this book to promote change

In Part 1 of this book, in Section 3, we introduced you to the idea of a balanced diet, and the problem of figuring out what a balanced diet would look like for you. This is a challenging task, but far from impossible. If you know that you have to change your diet, for the sake of your physical and mental health - and that those changes will improve your emotional wellbeing, on a day to day basis - then that can provide the motivation to do the hard work of making the necessary changes.

The best way to proceed has to be determined by you. But we would like to make a few supportive suggestions here, for our three categories of readers:

Firstly, for professionals

1. If you are a professional, wanting to improve your capacity to help your clients, by understanding the dietary and exercise elements that would help their emotional functioning, then you might consider these ideas:

- ❖ Think of a specific client that you want to help. Ask yourself, which bit of this book is most likely to contain the most helpful advice and support for that client.

- ❖ Turn to that section, and read it. From that section, try to identify *one or two small changes* that your client could make (if they had reached the 'determination stage' of behaviour change).

- ❖ Teach your client (at your next meeting) the lessons on behaviour change outlined above, or those that you normally teach; and then introduce them to one or two ideas that you have found which might be most helpful to them at this point in time. See if they are willing to contemplate such changes. If they are, help them to build up their own case for those changes. Do not try to 'sell' the change to them; and certainly do not try a 'hard sell' on it. Stay at the stage they are at. When they say they are determined to take action, then help them to set up the rewards and penalties that they will need to keep themselves on track.

- ❖ Repeat this process with a second client; and a third; and so on. Proceed slowly and methodologically, and do not expect earth-shattering changes in yourself or your client!

~~~

Secondly, for students

2. If you are a student of counselling, psychotherapy, psychology, or some related field that makes the study of this book important to you, then you might consider proceeding like this:

- ❖ Read Part 1, making notes in the margins, and on a note pad.

- ❖ Re-read Part 1 another two times, improving your notes each time.

- ❖ Then, try to summarize your notes on a few file cards, as if preparing to do a presentation to a group of fellow students. Try to identify the most important seven points.

- ❖ When you're happy you've mastered Part 1, move on to Part 2, and use the same approach. Reward yourself – with a little treat - for methodological study; and penalize yourself (say, by burning a £5 note [or $7 US]) for not keeping up your study practice.

~~~

And finally, for self-help enthusiasts

3. If you are a self-help enthusiast, who wants to improve your own physical/emotional wellbeing, by improving your diet and exercise regimes, then you might want to consider the following ideas:

- ❖ Begin with Section 4 of Part 1 – the foods to avoid.
- ❖ Read through the whole of that section, and make a list of the foods you still need to exclude from your daily diet (given that you may already have excluded some).
- ❖ Do not attempt to exclude all of them at once.
- ❖ Choose the *one item* of toxic food that you intend to exclude first, and then proceed as follows.
    - o Let us assume that you've decided to exclude sugar from your diet. Then:
        - Firstly, acquire a good supply of a safe, sugar substitute, such as *stevia*.
        - Secondly, start using the stevia as a sugar substitute for alternate uses – e.g. alternative cups of (preferably decaffeinated) tea.
        - Once you are used to the stevia, drop the sugar altogether, and always use stevia instead.
        - Reward yourself (with a little treat) for making this substitution; and penalize yourself (by burning a £5 note [or $7 US]) if you slip back to using sugar (for example, in cafes). Make sure you carry a supply of stevia with you when you are out and about, or visiting other people's homes.
- ❖ Once you are comfortably off the sugar, move on to the next toxic food item on your action list. Find an acceptable substitute. Introduce the substitute for alternate uses. Reward yourself for this halfway house position. Then make the full exclusion. Reward yourself for making the full transition. (This pattern is related to the system of habit change which Renata describes in Section 2, below).

~~~

- ❖ When you are ready to move on to working on your physical exercise regime, proceed according to the kaizen approach which I have described above, when I was writing about how I got back into doing my own daily exercise, very slowly and gradually (in Part 6, Section 1, sub-section 4).

Using nutrition and physical exercise

- o You could begin with 30 *seconds* of running of the spot; and build that up to five minutes over a period of days or weeks.

- o You could begin by walking out of your home, after breakfast each morning, and walking *briskly* for just five minutes, then turn around and briskly walk home again. Increase this to ten minutes when you are ready to do so. And slowly built that up to twenty minutes and then to thirty minutes, over a period of weeks.

❖ Once you are doing a reasonable amount of home-based exercise each day, or at least five days per week, you could then consider adding on something else:

- o You could go swimming with some friends or family members, a couple of times per week. Make it a social event, and make it a rule that if one person fails to turn up (unless they are actually unwell) then the whole group is penalized. (The penalty could be that the whole group has to make a monetary donation to the most obnoxious political group in your locality!) Loyalty to the group (rather than group coercion) will most likely help to keep you motivated. (Coercion does not work!)

- o You could join a yoga or Tai Chi, or Chi Kung class, which would probably be for a couple of hours each week, for about twelve weeks. You could join with a family group, or a group of friends, to support each other, and prevent drop-out. The advantage of such a class is this: After twelve weeks, you can begin to do the exercises at home, for free! And if you attend with a family member, you can reinforce each other's commitment to keep up the exercises, by taking turns, from day to day, to 'lead' the process. You can inspire each other, rather than coercing each other. (Coercion does not work!)

~~~
Next we will present Section 2 (of Part 6): How to change your negative habits, below.
~~~

Section 2 (of Part 6): How to change your negative habits

By Renata Taylor Byrne - Copyright © Renata Taylor-Byrne 2016-17

~~~

1. The nature of habits

What are habits? Here are two definitions from the Merriam-Webster dictionary:

> (1) Habit is "... (a) *behaviour pattern acquired by frequent repetition or physiologic exposure that shows itself in regularity or increased facility of performance"* and/or:
>
> (2) It's *"...An acquired mode of behaviour that has become nearly or completely involuntary."*

~~~

And here is the viewpoint of one of the fathers of American psychology:

> *"All our life, so far as it has definite form, is a mass of habits".*
>
> *William James, 1892*

~~~

We are habit-based human beings, and the more we know about how we form habits, the *easier* it will be for us to change old ones that aren't working for us, and to create new ones.

A researcher at Duke University in 2006 discovered that more than 40% of the activities people engaged in every day were habits, and not decisions they had made. And some theorists would say that our habit-based functioning is as high as 95% (Bargh and Chartrand, 1999)[219].

Throughout the animal world, habit based behaviour is the norm. This has served survival well, which is why it is ubiquitous.

Humans have the greatest capacity of all animals to change our habits, but we will never become habit-less.

Our brains have developed the ability to create habits because they allow our brains to save effort, and to function more efficiently without having our minds cluttered with the mechanics of the many basic behaviours we have to follow each day.

2. The structure of a habit

In his book, *The Power of Habit,* Charles Duhigg[220] looked very closely at the specific features of what makes up a habit. In his view, a habit is like a loop that has three parts: the cue; the routine; and the reward. Here is a picture of that loop:

```
     Routine
Cue           Reward
```

Firstly, there is a *cue* (a trigger that starts off a *routine*: e.g. the sound of the alarm clock in the morning is a cue, which triggers the routine of getting up).

Here's *an example of a cue* that I recently found in the *Sunday Times Magazine*, in an article by Viv Groscop (who performed her one-woman show at Edinburgh in August this year [2017]). Viv stated that, to make her exercise routine strong, she started keeping her workout clothes and trainers next to her bed, so they were *the first things she saw- the cue! - in the early morning*, as soon as she woke up. (She lost 3 stone [or 42 pounds in weight] in one year through changes in her exercise and nutrition habits).

2. Secondly, this cue is followed by *a routine*.

A routine is here defined as *any* pattern of behaviour. Examples include: eating, going to the pub, watching a TV programme, going to the gym, doing homework, buying clothes, smoking, placing a bet, etc.

3. Finally, there is a *reward* – the most important part of the loop.

All habits have a *reward* at the end of them. Here are some examples of rewards:

(1) The feeling of comradeship when drinking at the pub;

(2) the rush of pleasure after you have just done a bout of exercise;

(3) giving yourself a cup of (decaffeinated!) coffee when you've done your daily exercise. And:

(4) seeing the *good, pleasurable results* of any difficult task.

~~~

3. The importance of craving!

*For habit change to work you have to **crave** the reward.*

This is an important alert: You have to *really crave* the reward, or you *won't* have the incentive to change your behaviour. Charles Duhigg describes a research project undertaken by the National Weight Control Agency. The agency examined the *routines* for eating food that had been created by people who were successful dieters. They investigated more than 6,000 people's routines.

What was discovered was that *all* the successful dieters eat a breakfast (which was cued by the *time* of day). But they also had very real, *very desirable **rewards*** in place for themselves if they stuck to their diet plans – and it was the reward that they craved. (For example, being able to fit into new clothes in a smaller size; or having a flatter belly, etc.)

And if they felt themselves *weakening* in their commitment, they **changed** *their focus onto the rewards* that they would get if they *kept* to their plans. This visualisation, of the very real rewards they would get, kept them strong in the face of temptation.

Apparently people who started new exercise routines showed that they were more likely to follow an exercise routine if they chose a *specific cue* (first thing in the morning, or as soon as they get in from work, or before bedtime).

*So having a cue in place is **crucial** to initiating the new behaviour (or routine).*

The new behaviour (or **routine**) follows from the cue.

Let me give you a personal example: Jim and I get up in the morning, and the first thing we do is to have breakfast, because we *crave* the pleasure of raw salad with seeds and nuts, and minor embellishments.

The *end of breakfast **cues*** us to meditate, and we crave the rewards of meditation, (a lot of which have to do with stress management, health and happiness, plus creativity).

Then, *the end of meditation **cues*** us to begin our physical exercise (Chi Kung [or Qigong], the Plank, some press-ups and sit-backs, and so on]) which we **crave** because of the physical and mental health benefits that we gain.

So, the **reward** is what people crave at the end of their routines. Some of the *rewards* mentioned in Duhigg's research were having a (small amount of) beer, or an evening of watching the TV without guilt.

As my own experiment, I (Renata) wanted to establish a daily habit of exercising my arm muscles, to firm them up. Therefore, I set up a **cue** which is the start of the BBC TV programme **'Pointless'**, at 5.15pm every day.

When I hear the theme music for *Pointless*, I get out our "Powerspin" device – which simulates weight training - and do a pre-planned (recommended) set of exercises.

This exercise **routine** is designed to strengthen my arms and back muscles, and core (stomach); and it is very simple, but involves some physical exertion.

And the **reward** for me (which I *crave* strongly – otherwise it won't work) is the knowledge that my arms and back and core muscles are getting stronger and fitter, and that this will keep me fit and able to carry heavy objects into old age! And so far, so good – I've only missed a few times!

~~~

4. Duhigg's own experiment

Charles Duhigg did a really interesting personal experiment to see if he could change one of his own habits. He was eating too many cookies (or biscuits) and he was starting to put on weight. He did an explanation and a description of his experiment which you can see on YouTube. He broke the habit, by working out what the reward was (and it had nothing to do with cookies/biscuits). Once he knew what the reward was, he found it very easy to substitute a new routine which did not involve eating junk foods! Here is the address of his video clip at YouTube: https://youtu.be/W1eYrhGeffc

~~~

5. The importance of substitution

What if we have a habit that we want to change? Can we get rid of it?

How do we go about it? Charles Duhigg states that we **can't** get rid of old habits – but what we can do is *substitute* new routines for the old ones, and get the same rewards.

He explains that a golden rule of habit change, which has been validated by repeated studies for a long time, is as follows:

"To change a habit, we must keep the old <u>cue</u>, which delivers the old <u>reward</u>, but **change the routine.**

"That's the rule: if you use the same cue, and provide the same reward, you can shift the routine and change the habit. Almost any behaviour can be transformed if the cue and reward stay the same". (Page 62)

He gives the example of someone who wants to give up cigarettes. If the person wanting to quit smoking fails to find something else to do (a new routine), when they start to crave nicotine, then they will be unable to stop! It will be *too hard* for them. That's why, in Section 1 of Part 6 above, Jim emphasizes substituting stevia for sugar, before giving up the sugar. The reward is the sweetness. The cue may be thirst. But the routine does not have to involve sugar, so long as it involves some sweetness; and stevia is a safer form of sweetness.

6. Stopping addictions

Charles Duhigg states that the organisation called *'Alcoholics Anonymous'* (**AA**) is effective in helping people reduce their drinking habits because it examines and shines a very clear light on the **cues** which trigger drinking in people; and the **AA** program deliberately encourages people to **identify** the **cues** and **rewards** that encourages their alcoholic habits, and then *assists them* as they try to find new behaviours (or routines).

So the implied question that **AA** asks an alcoholic is: *"What rewards do you get from alcohol?"*

"In order for alcoholics to get the same rewards that they get in a bar, AA has built a system of meetings and **companionship** *– (the individual 'Sponsor' that each person works with) – that strives to offer as much escape, distraction and catharsis as a Friday night bender." (Page 71)*

If someone wants to get support from another person, they can receive this by talking to their *sponsor* or by going to a ***group meeting***, rather than "toasting a drinking buddy".

A researcher called J. Scott Tonigan has been looking at the work of **AA** for more than ten years, and he states that if you look at Step 4 of the 12 step program, (which is to make a *'searching and fearless inventory of ourselves and to admit to God, to ourselves* and *another human being the exact nature of our wrongs'*), you will see that something crucial is taking place, which he sums up like this:

*"It's not obvious from the way they are written, but to complete those steps, someone has to create a list of **triggers** for all their alcoholic urges. When you make a self-inventory, you're figuring out all the **things** that make you drink…"* The ***cues!***

7. The rewards of drinking

The **AA** organisation then asks alcoholics (or alcohol dependent individuals) to look really hard for the **rewards** they get from alcohol, and the **cravings** that are behind the behaviour. And what is discovered?

*"Alcoholics crave a drink because it offers escape, relaxation, companionship, the blunting of anxieties and an opportunity for emotional release….the **physical effects** of alcohol are one of the least rewarding parts of drinking for addicts."* (Page 71)

So what **AA** does is gets you to create *new routines* for your spare time *instead of going out drinking*. You can relax and talk through any worries or concerns you might have at the meetings.

*"The triggers (cues) are the same, and the payoffs (rewards) are the same, it's just the **behaviour** that changes,"* states Tonigan.

8. The result of one experiment

To summarise the value of one particular experiment, Duhigg showed that the former alcoholics in the study only succeeded in eliminating their drinking behaviour because they developed new routines which followed the old *triggers* (or ***cues***), and gave them their comforting ***rewards***.

Apparently the techniques that were developed by the **AA** for changing habits have also been successfully applied to children's temper tantrums, sex addictions and other types of behaviour.

The **AA** is described in Duhigg's book as an organisation which creates techniques to change the habits associated with the use of alcohol:

"AA is in essence a giant machine for changing habit loops and though the habits associated with alcohol consumption are extreme, the lessons AA provides demonstrates how almost any habit – even the most obstinate – can be changed." Charles Duhigg

He makes it clear in his book that overeating, alcoholism, or smoking, are ingrained habits that take real commitment to change. But if you know how your habits are working, this makes it easier to experiment with new behaviours.

~~~

9. Analysing your own habits

If you look very carefully at the **cues** that cause you to avoid physical exercise, or to eat foods that you now know to be bad for your physical and emotional health, and you work out the rewards that you currently get from the *avoidance routine*, or the *consumption routine*, then you can easily identify a new **healthy routine** to substitute for the old unhealthy routine.

It might be best to begin with exercise, because this may help you to find the commitment to change other habits, including some eating habits.

Why is this?

~~~

10. Creating 'keystone habits'

Exercise seems to be a 'keystone habit' that has a beneficial, 'knock-on' effect. When people begin exercising, and it can be as little as once a week, they begin to change other, unconnected habits in their lives. It has been discovered that they reduce their smoking, spend money less, and have more understanding for their family and the people they work with.

"Exercise spills over", stated James Prochaska (a University of Rhode Island researcher). *"There's something about it that makes good habits easier."*

Other studies have revealed that families who are in the habit of having their meals together regularly – which is another 'keystone habit' - raise children with higher school grades, more emotional control, better homework skills and increased confidence.

Apparently making your bed every morning is also a keystone habit, which has a spill over effect. It is correlated with a higher level of happiness, stronger skills at sticking to a budget and a higher level of productivity.

So, by beginning to use the kaizen approach (described in Jim's section above), to get in the habit of doing a few minutes exercise each day, you will be starting a cascade of potential change. Over time, you can learn how to exclude all of the toxic foods; to get on to an exciting, healthy and enlivening diet; and to be happier, healthier and more creative. (But do it slowly, gradually, incrementally. And reward yourself at every step)

~~~

11. Habit reversal

Here is a quote by Nathan Azrin, who was one of the people who developed habit reversal training:

*"It seems ridiculously simple, but once you are aware of how your habit works, once you recognise the **cues** and the **rewards**, you're half-way to changing it."*

Today, habit reversal is used to treat gambling, depression, smoking, anxiety, procrastination, and sex and alcohol addiction etc. And you can now use it to change your exercise and dietary habits too.

Charles Duhigg makes the point that although the habit process can be simply described, it doesn't mean that it's *easily* changed. As Mark Twain argued, a habit cannot be flung out of the window by any person, but has to be coaxed downstairs a step at a time! You cannot eliminate habits that no longer serve, you can only *replace them* with new habits that support your goals. You have to be aware of what you want (the implicit reward – the thing that you crave), and work to create new habits (or routines) that will get you what you want.

Charles Duhigg states:

"It's facile to imply that smoking, alcoholism, over-eating or other ingrained patterns can be upended without real effort. Genuine change requires real work and self-understanding of the cravings driving the behaviours. No one will quit smoking because they can sketch a habit loop.

"However, by understanding habits' mechanisms, we gain insights that make new behaviours easier to grasp. Anyone struggling with addiction or destructive behaviours can benefit from help from many quarters, including trained therapists, physicians, social workers and clergy.

*"Much of those changes are accomplished because people examine the cues, cravings and rewards that drive their behaviours and then find ways to **replace** their self-destructive **routines** with healthier alternatives, even if they aren't aware of what they are doing at the time. Understanding the cues and cravings driving your habits won't make them suddenly disappear – but it will give you a way to change the pattern."* (Page 77)

It may also help to get you from the 'contemplation stage' of behaviour change to the 'determination stage'.

Once you are determined, you are halfway there. And if you know what the reward will be – and you put secondary rewards and penalties in place – then you are on the home run!

~~~

12. Conclusion

In Part 6 of this book, we have given you all you need to change any of your habits related to diet and/or exercise. All you need now is the *determination* to use this information to bring about the changes that you want to see.

Do you crave release from anger, anxiety or depression? If so, which of your unhelpful dietary routines, or lack of activity routines, do you want to change first? What can you substitute for that routine which you would find rewarding? Once you know the cue, the routine and the reward, all you have to do is make the substitution.

If you want 'belt and braces' support, then set up an additional reward and penalty (as described by Jim in Section 1 of Part 6, above) to make sure you stick to the new routine! And try to get social support for your changes. Good luck!

Renata Taylor-Byrne

~~~

References

ABC

Agarwal, U., Suruchi Mishra, Jia Xu, et al (2015) 'A Multicentre Randomized Controlled Trial of a Nutrition Intervention Program in a Multi-ethnic Adult Population in the Corporate Setting Reduces Depression and Anxiety and Improves Quality of Life: The GEICO Study. *American Journal of Health Promotion, Vol 29, Issue 4*, pp. 245 - 254.

Akbaraly, T.N., Brunner EJ, Ferrie JE, Marmot MG, et al. (2009) 'Dietary pattern and depressive symptoms in middle age'. *British Journal of Psychiatry. 2009 Nov; 195(5):408-13*. doi: 10.1192/bjp.bp.108.058925. Available online at: https://www.ncbi.nlm.nih.gov/pubmed/19880930. Accessed: 22nd September 2017.

Alt Health (2017) 'Hay Diet'. A blog about food combining. Available online: https://www.althealth.co.uk/help-and-advice/diets/hay-diet/. Accessed: 11th October 2017.

Amen, D.G. (2013) *Use Your Brain to Change your Age: Secrets to look, feel, and think younger every day*. London: Piatkus.

Andrew (2017) 'Grains and Inflammation: What is the relationship between grains and inflammation?' The Paleo Munch! Blog. Available online at: http://paleomunch.com/the-paleo-diet/grains-and-inflammation/. Accessed: 4th October 2017.

APFHF (2008) 'The Links between Diet and Behaviour. The influence of nutrition on mental health'. Report of an inquiry held by the Associate Parliamentary Food and Health Forum (APFHF). London: All Party Parliamentary Food and Health Forum.

Atkinson, M. (2007) *The Mind Body Bible: Your personalised prescription for total health*. London: Piatkus Books.

Baker, D. and Keramidas, N. (2013) 'The psychology of hunger'. American Psychological Association: *Monitor on Psychology: October 2013, Vol 44, No. 9*.
Online: http://www.apa.org/monitor/2013/10/hunger.aspx

Ballantyne, C. (2007) 'Fact or Fiction? Vitamin Supplements Improve Your Health'. *Scientific American* (Online): http://www.scientificamerican.com/article/fact-or-fiction-vitamin-supplements-improve-health/May 17, 2007. Accessed 26th April 2016.

Bangalore, N.G., Varambally, S. (2012) 'Yoga therapy for schizophrenia'. *International Journal of Yoga 5(2):85-91*. [PUBMED: 22869990]

Barasi, M.E. (2003) *Human Nutrition: A health perspective*. Second edition. London: CRC Press/Taylor & Francis Group.

Bargh, J.A. and Chartrand, T.L. (1999) 'The unbearable automaticity of being'. *American Psychologist, 54(7): 462-479*.

Barrett J.S., Irving P.M., Gearry R, Shepherd SJ, and Gibson P.R. (2009) 'Comparison of the prevalence of fructose and lactose malabsorption across chronic intestinal disorders'. *Alimentary Pharmacology and Therapeutics, 2009;30(2): 165-74*

Beezhold, B. L., Johnston, C. S., & Daigle, D. R. (2010). 'Vegetarian diets are associated with healthy mood states: a cross-sectional study in Seventh Day Adventist adults'. *Nutrition Journal*, 9, 26. http://doi.org/10.1186/1475-2891-9-26

Behere, R.V., Arasappa, R., Jagannathan, A., et al (2011). 'Effect of yoga therapy on facial emotion recognition deficits, symptoms and functioning in patients with schizophrenia'. *Acta Psychiatrica Scandinavia, Vol 123 (2);* pp: 147 -53.

Benros, M.E.; and B.L. Waltoft; et al (2013) 'Autoimmune Diseases and Severe Infections as Risk Factors for Mood Disorders'. A nationwide Study. JAMA Psychiatry. 2013; 70(8):812-820. doi:10.1001/ jamapsychiatry. 2013. 1111. Accessed: 11th November 2017.

Benton, D. and G. Roberts (1988) 'Effects of vitamin and mineral supplementation on intelligence in schoolchildren'. *The Lancet, Vol 1 (8578),* Pages 140-143.

Berk et al. (2013) 'So depression is an inflammatory disease, but where does the inflammation come from?' *BMC Medicine 2013, 11:200* Available online: http://www.biomedcentral.com/1741-7015/11/200. Downloaded: 8th September 2017.

Blanchflower, D.G., Andrew J. Oswald and Sarah Stewart-Brown. (2016) 'Is Psychological Well-being Linked to the Consumption of Fruit and Vegetables?' Available online:
https://www.scribd.com/document/110654941/Psychological-Well-being-and-Consumption-of-Fruit-and-Vegetables# Accessed: 15th September 2017.

Blumenthal, J.A., Smith, P.J., and Hoffman, B.M. (2012) 'Is exercise a viable treatment for depression?' *American College of Sports Medicine Health & Fitness Journal. July/August; Vol. 16(4):* Pages 14–21. doi: 10.1249/01.FIT.0000416000.09526.eb.

Booth, M. (2013) 'The Okinawa diet – Could it help you live to 100?' The *Guardian* online: https://www.theguardian.com/lifeandstyle/2013/jun/19/japanese-diet-live-to-100

Boyd, D.B. (2003) 'Insulin and Cancer'. *Integrative Cancer Therapies. Dec 2003. Vol. 2(4):* Pages 315-329.

Bravo, J.A., P. Forsythe, M.V. Chew, E. Escaravage, H.M. et al (2011) 'Ingestion of Lactobacillus strain regulates emotional behaviour and central GABA receptor expression in a mouse via the vagus nerve'. PNAS 2011 108 (38) 16050-16055; doi:10.1073/pnas.1102999108; February, 2011: Available online: http://www.pnas.org/content/108/38/16050.long

Brewer, S. (2013) *Nutrition: A beginners guide*. London: Oneworld Publications.

Briffa, J. 'High Anxiety', *Observer Magazine,* 19th June 2005, page 61.

Broderick, J., Knowles, A., Chadwick, J.,... (2015) 'Yoga versus standard care for schizophrenia'. Cochrane Database of Systematic Reviews 2015, Issue 10. Art. No.: CD010554.DOI:10.1002/ 14651858. CD010554.pub2.

Brogan, K. (2016) *A Mind of Your Own: The truth about depression and how women can heal their bodies to reclaim their lives.* London: Thorsons.

Bryant, C.W. (2010) 'Does running fight depression?' HowStuffWorks.com. Available online: http://adventure.howstuffworks.com/outdoor-activities/running/health/running-fight-depression.htm. Accessed 16th June 2016.

Byrne, J.W. (2016) *Holistic Counselling in Practice: An introduction to the theory and practice of Emotive-Cognitive Embodied-Narrative Therapy.* Hebden Bridge: The Institute for E-CENT Publications.

Byrne, J.W. (2017) *Unfit for Therapeutic Purposes: The case against Rational Emotive and Cognitive Behavioural Therapy (RE & CBT).* Hebden Bridge: The Institute for E-CENT Publications.

Campbell, T.C. and Campbell, T.M. (2006) *The China Study: The most comprehensive study of nutrition ever conducted and the startling implications for diet, weight loss and long-term health.* Dallas, TX: Benbella Books.

Catassi, C., Bai, J., Bonaz, B., Bouma, G., et al. (2013) 'Non-Celiac Gluten Sensitivity: The New Frontier of Gluten Related Disorders'. *Nutrients, 2013 Sep 26;5(10):* 3839–3853. PMID 24077239 Available online: https://www.ncbi.nlm.nih.gov/pubmed/24077239. Accessed: 7th November 2017.

Chaitow, L. (2003) *Candida Albicans: The non-drug approach to the treatment of Candida infection.* London: Thorsons.

Christensen, L. (1991) 'The roles of caffeine and sugar in depression'. *The Nutrition Report 1991*: 9(5 Pt.1): Pages 691-698.

Coffman, M.A. (2016) 'The Disadvantages of Junk Food'. Available online at: http://healthyeating.sfgate.com/ disadvantages-junk-food-1501.html. Accessed: 30th April 2016.

Coleman, E. (2017) 'What is Arachidonic Acid?' The Fit Day blog. Available online: http://www.fitday.com/fitness-articles/nutrition/healthy-eating/what-is-arachidonic-acid.html. Accessed: 19th October 2017.

Collings, J. (1993) *The ordinary Person's Guide to Extraordinary Health.* London: Aurum Press Ltd.

Colman, A. (2002) *Dictionary of Psychology.* Oxford: Oxford University Press.

Columbia University Medical Centre (2015). 'Consuming highly refined carbohydrates increases risk of depression'. *ScienceDaily. ScienceDaily, 5 August 2015.* Available online:www.sciencedaily.com/releases/2015/08/150805110335.htm. Accessed: 3rd October 2017.

Cordain, L. (2011) *The Paleo Diet Cookbook.* Hoboken, NJ: John Wiley and Sons.

Corey, G. (2001) *Theory and Practice of Counselling and Psychotherapy.* Sixth Edition. Belmont, CA: Brooks/Cole.

Cummins, C. (2007) 'How to Start a Restorative Yoga Practice'. *Yoga Journal, Aug 28, 2007.* Available online: http://www.yogajournal.com/article/beginners/restorative-yoga/. Accessed: 17th June 2016.

Cunningham, J. B. (2001) *The Stress Management Sourcebook. Second edition.* Los Angeles: Lowell House.

DEF

Deleniv, S. (2015) 'Is serotonin the happy brain chemical, and do depressed people just have too little of it? *The Neuropshere.* Online: https://theneurosphere.com/ 2015/11/14/is-serotonin-the-happy-brain-chemical-and-do-depressed-people-just-have-too-little-of-it/

Duhigg, C. (2013) *The Power of Habit: Why we do what we do and how to change.* London: Random House.

Duraiswamy, G., Thirthalli J., Nagendra H.R. ... (2007). 'Yoga therapy as an add-on treatment in the management of patients with schizophrenia – a randomized controlled trial'. *Acta Psychiatrica Scandinavia, 116 (3);* pp: 226-32.

Edwards, M. (2014) 'The candida depression connection - How yeast leads to depression, anxiety, ADHD, and other mental disorders'. Available online at: https://www.naturalnews.com/047184 _candida_depression_gut_microbes.html#

Eggers, A.E. (2012) 'Extending David Horrobin's membrane phospholipid theory of schizophrenia: Overactivity of cytosolic phospholipase A(2) in the brain is caused by overdrive of coupled serotonergic 5HT(2A/2C) receptors in response to stress'. *Medical Hypotheses. 79.* 10.1016/j.mehy.2012.08.016.

Elliott, A.F. (2014) 'Can an Atkins-style diet really fight depression? Research suggests low-carb, high fat foods can drastically improve mental health'. Available online: http://www.dailymail.co.uk/ femail/ article-2590880/Can-Atkins-style-diet-really-fight-depression-Research-suggests-low-carb-high-fat-foods-drastically-improve-mental-health.html Downloaded: 2nd October 2017.

Enders, G. (2015) *Gut: The inside story of our body's most under-rated organ.* London: Scribe Publications.

Esposito K., and Giugliano, D. (2006) 'Whole-grain intake cools down inflammation'. *American Journal of Clinical Nutrition 2006 Jun; 83(6):* 1440-1441.

Esposito, K., Nappo, F., Giugliano, F., Di Palo, C., et al. (2003) 'Meal modulation of circulating interleukin 18 and adiponectin concentrations in healthy subjects and in patients with type 2 diabetes mellitus'. *American Journal of Clinical Nutrition 2003*; 78: 1135–40.

Evans, J. (2016) 'Natural vs medical'. *What Doctors Don't Tell You.* (Alternative health magazine). London: WDDTY Publishing. April 2016 (Page 70).

Evers, E. A. T., Tillie, D. E., van der Veen, F. M., et al (2005) 'Effects of a novel method of acute tryptophan depletion on plasma tryptophan and cognitive performance in healthy volunteers'. *Journal of Psychopharmacology, Vol 178, No. 1.* Pages 1432-2072.

Fife, B. (2005) *Coconut Cures: Preventing and treating common health problems with coconut.* Colorado Springs, CO: Piccadilly Books Ltd.

Fisher, R. (2016) 'What is the Paleo diet?' BBC Good Food blog. Online: https://www.bbcgoodfood.com/howto/guide/what-paleo-diet. Downloaded on 10th October 2017.

Food Standards Agency (2001) *Balance of Good Health: Information for educators and communicators.* London: Food Standards Agency.

Food Standards Agency (2004) 'National Diet & Nutrition Survey: Adults aged 19 to 64'. Volume 5. Available online: http://www.thehealthwell.info/ node/ 20299? &content= resource& member= 6744& catalogue=none&collection=none&tokens_complete=true

Ford, R.P.K. (2009) 'The gluten syndrome: A neurological disease'. *Medical Hypotheses, Volume 73, Issue 3*: Pages 438 - 440.

GHI

Gangwisch, J. et al. (2015) 'High Glycaemic Index Diet as a Risk Factor for Depression: Analyses from the Women's Health Initiative'. *American Journal of Clinical Nutrition, August 2015.*

Gesch, C.B. et al (2002) 'Influence of supplementary vitamins, minerals and essential fatty acids on the antisocial behaviour of young adults'. *British Journal of Psychiatry 81*: Pages 22–28.

Gilliland, K. and Andress, D. (1981) 'Ad Lib caffeine consumption, symptoms of caffeinism and academic performance'. *American Journal of Psychiatry, Vol 138 (4),* Pages. 512-514.

Goldacre, B. (2007) 'Patrick Holford's untruthful and unsubstantiated claims about pills': http://www.badscience.net/2007/09/patrick-holdford-unsubstantiated-untruthful/ Accessed 14th April 2016.

Goldacre, B. (2012) *Bad Pharma: How drug companies mislead doctors and harm patients*. London: Fourth Estate.

Goletzke, J, & Buyken, Anette & Joslowski, Gesa, et al. (2014). 'Increased Intake of Carbohydrates from Sources with a Higher Glycemic Index and Lower Consumption of Whole Grain during Puberty Are Prospectively Associated with Higher IL-6 Concentrations in Younger Adulthood among Healthy Individuals'. *The Journal of Nutrition*. 144.10.3945/jn.114.193391.

Golomb, B.A., Evans, M.A., White, H.L., and Dimsdale, J.E. (2012) 'Trans fat consumption and aggression'. Online: PLoS One. 2012; 7(3): e32175. doi: 10.1371/journal.pone. 0032175. Epub 2012 Mar 5.

Gomez-Pinilla, F. (2008) 'The influences of diet and exercise on mental health through hormesis'. *Ageing Research Reviews. Volume 7, Issue 1,* January 2008, Pages 49-62.

Grant, D. and Joice, J. (1984) *Food Combining for Health*. Wellingborough: Thorsons.

Greger, M. (2016) *How not to Die: Discover the foods scientifically proven to prevent and reverse disease*. London: Macmillan.

Hadjivassiliou, M., & A. Gibson, & G.A.B. Davies-Jones, et al (1996) 'Does cryptic gluten sensitivity play a part in neurological illness?' *The Lancet, Volume 347, Issue 8998, 10 February 1996*, Pages 369-371

Hadjivassiliou, M., Mäki, M., Sanders, D.S. et al. (2006) 'Autoantibody targeting of brain and intestinal trans-glutaminase in gluten ataxia'. *Neurology. 2006; 66*: 373–377

Hadjivassiliou, M., & Sanders, D.S., Grünewald, R.A. et al (2010) 'Gluten sensitivity: from gut to brain'. *The Lancet Neurology, Volume 9, Issue 3*, Pages 318 - 330.

Hadjivassiliou, M., & Sanders, D.S., Grünewald, R.A., et al. (2010) 'The neurology of gluten sensitivity'. *Lancet Neurol. 2010; 9*: 330–342.

Hahnemann, T. (2010) *The Nordic Diet*. London: Quadrille Publishing Ltd.

Halmos, E.P., Power, V.A., Shepherd S.J., et al. (2014) 'A Diet Low in FODMAPs Reduces Symptoms of Irritable Bowel Syndrome'. *Gastroenterology, 2014; 146(1):* 67-75

Hardy, R. (2013) 'Can food make you angry?' *The Guardian online*: https://www.theguardian.com/lifeandstyle/wordofmouth/2013/apr/24/can-food-make-you-angry

Hayes, N. (2003) *Applied Psychology (Teach Yourself Books)*. London: Hodder and Stoughton.

Healthcare Improvement Scotland (2017) 'Harmful drinking 3 – Alcohol and self-harm'. Downloadable PDF. Available online at: http://bit.ly/TbBYAX. Accessed 15th September 2017.

Healthline (2017) 'Why Refined Carbs Are Bad For You'. Available online: https://authoritynutrition. com/ why-refined-carbs-are-bad/. Accessed: 15th September 2017.

Hellmich, N. (2013) 'The best preventative medicine? Exercise'. Online: dailycomet.com. Accessed: 18th June 2016.

Hoffer, A. (1970) 'Pellagra and Schizophrenia'. *Psychosomatics, Volume 11, Issue 5*, Pages 522-525. Available online: http://www.psychosomaticsjournal.com/article/S0033-3182(70)71623-X/pdf

Hoffman, B.M., Babyak, M.A., Craighead, W.E., et al (2011) 'Exercise and pharmacotherapy in patients with major depression: One-year follow-up of the SMILE study'. *2011 Feb-Mar; Vol. 73(2):* Pages 127-133. doi: 10.1097/ PSY.0b013e31820433a5.

Holford, P. (2010) *Optimum Nutrition for the Mind*. London: Piatkus.

Isold, K. (2010) 'Anger and exercise: Anger is a normal, adaptive human emotion'. *Psychology Today blog*. Available online: https://www.psychologytoday.com/blog/hidden-motives/201008/anger-and-exercise. Accessed: 16th June 2016.

JKL

Jacobs, D.R., Andersen, L.F., and Blomhoff R. (2007) 'Whole-grain consumption is associated with a reduced risk of noncardiovascular, noncancer death attributed to inflammatory diseases in the Iowa Women's Health Study'. *American Journal of Clinical Nutrition 2007; 85:* 1606–1614. pmid:17556700.

Jacobs, G. (1994) *Candida Albicans: A user's guide to treatment and recovery*. London: Optima.

Jahnke R. (2002) *The Healing Promise of Qi: Creating Extraordinary Wellness through Qigong and Tai Chi*. Chicago, Il: Contemporary Books.

Jahnke, R. Larkey, L. Rogers, C. Etnier, J. and Lin, F. (2012) 'A Comprehensive Review of Health Benefits of Qigong and Tai Chi'. *American Journal of Health Promotion, Jul-Aug; Vol. 24(6),* Pages e1-e25.

James, O. (2007) *Affluenza: How to be successful and stay sane*. London: Vermillion.

Kaplan, B.J., and S.G. Crawford, C.J. Field and J.S.A. Simpson (2007) 'Vitamins, minerals, and mood'. *Psychological Bulletin, Sept; 133(5):* Pages 747-760.

Kaplan, B.J., Julia J. Rucklidge, Amy Romijn, and Kevin Flood (2015) 'The emerging field of nutritional mental health: Inflammation, the microbiome, oxidative stress, and mitochondrial function'. *Clinical Psychological Science, Vol. 3(6):* 964-980.

Keys, A., Brozek, J., Henshel, A., Mickelson, O., & Taylor, H.L. (1950). *The biology of human starvation*, (Vols. 1–2). Minneapolis, MN: University of Minnesota Press.

Khalsa, D.S. (1998) *The Mind Miracle: The revolutionary way to renew your mental powers*. London: Arrow Books.

Kiecolt-Glaser, J.K., Belury, M.A., Andridge, R., et al (2011) 'Omega 3 supplementation lowers inflammation and anxiety in medical students: A randomised, controlled trial'. *Brain, Behaviour, Immunity, Vol. 25(8).* Pages 1725-1734.

King, D.S. (1981) 'Can allergic exposure provoke psychological symptoms? A double-blind test'. *Biological Psychiatry, Vol. 16(1):* pages 3-19.

Korn, L. (2016). *Nutrition Essentials for Mental Health: A complete guide to the food-mood connection*. New York: W. W. Norton & Company.

Larkey, L., Jahnke, R., Etnier, J. and Gonzalez J. (2009) Meditative movement as a category of exercise: Implications for research. *Journal of Physical Activity & Health. 2009*; Vol. 6: Pages 230–238.

Lawrence, F. (2004*) Not on the Label: What really goes into the food on your plate*. London: Penguin Books.

Lazarides, L. (2002) *Treat Yourself: With nutritional therapy*. London: Waterfall 2000.

LeDoux, J.E., and Gorman, J.M. (2001) 'A call to action: Overcoming anxiety through active coping'. *Vol. 158, Issue 12*, December 2001, Pages 1953-1955. Available online at: psychiatry*online.org/* doi/10.1176/appi.ajp.158.12.1953

Lefevre, M.; Jonnalagadda, S. (2012) 'Effect of whole grains on markers of subclinical inflammation'. *Nutrition Review. 2012, 70,* 387–396, doi:10.1111/j.1753-4887.2012.00487.x.

Lindeberg, S., Jönsson, T., Granfeldt, Y. et al. (2007) 'A Palaeolithic diet improves glucose tolerance more than a Mediterranean-like diet in individuals with ischaemic heart disease'. *Diabetologia, September 2007, Volume 50, Issue 9*, pp 1795–1807. Available online: https://doi.org/10.1007/s00125-007-0716-y

Linder, K. and Svardsudd, K. (2006) 'Qigong has a relieving effect on stress'. *Lakartidningen.* (A Swedish Medical Journal) *2006; Vol. 103 (24-25):* Pages 1942-1945.

Logan, A. C. (2004) 'Omega-3 fatty acids and major depression: A primer for the mental health professional'. *Lipids in Health and Disease*, *3*, 25. Available online: http://doi.org/10.1186/1476-511X-3-25.

MNO

Masters, R. C., Liese, A. D., Haffner, S. M., et al. (2010). 'Whole and Refined Grain Intakes Are Related to Inflammatory Protein Concentrations in Human Plasma'. *The Journal of Nutrition, 140(3), 587–594.* http://doi.org/10.3945/jn.109.116640

Mayo Clinic (2016) 'Exercise and stress: Get moving to manage stress'. Available online: http://www.mayoclinic.org/healthy-lifestyle/stress-management/in-depth/exercise-and-stress/art-20044469) Accessed: 23rd February 2016.

Mayo Clinic Staff (2014) 'Depression and anxiety: Exercise eases symptoms'. Available online here: http://www.mayoclinic.org/diseases-conditions/depression/in-depth/depression-and-exercise/art-20046495. Accessed: 19th June 2016 and 15th September 2017.

Mayo Clinic Staff (2014) 'Anger management: 10 tips to tame your temper': Available online: http://www.mayoclinic.org/healthy-lifestyle/adult-health/in-depth/anger-management/art-20045434. Accessed 16th June 2016.

McGovern, C. (2017) 'B-Calmed'. (An article on stress, anxiety and vitamins). *What Doctors Don't Tell You, July 2017*, pages 28-34.

McLeod, J. (2003) *An Introduction to Counselling*. Third Edition. Buckingham: Open University Press.

Medina, J. (2015) 'How Yoga is Similar to Existing Mental Health Therapies'. Source: Psych Central website: http://psychcentral.com/lib/how-yoga-is-similar-to-existing-therapies/. Accessed: May 2016.

Mercola, J. (2010) 'Scientists Unlock How Trans Fats Harm Your Arteries'. (Health Blog). Available online: http://articles.mercola.com/sites/articles/archive/2010/11/16/scientists-unlock-how-trans-fats-harm-your-arteries.aspx. Accessed: 20th May 2016.

Mercola, J. (2013) 'Vitamin D — One of the Simplest Solutions to Wide-Ranging Health Problems'. Available online: http://articles.mercola.com/sites/articles/archive/2013/12/22/dr-holick-vitamin-d-benefits.aspx. Accessed 15 June 2016.

Michalak, J., Zhang, X.C., and Jacobi, F. (2012) 'Vegetarian diet and mental disorders: Results from a representative community survey'. *International Journal of Behavioural Nutrition and Physical Activity 2012: 9:67*. Available online: https://ijbnpa.biomedcentral.com/articles/10.1186/1479-5868-9-67

Montonen, J., Boeing, H., Fritsche, A., Schleicher, E., et al (2013) 'Consumption of red meat and whole-grain bread in relation to biomarkers of obesity, inflammation, glucose metabolism and oxidative stress'. *European Journal of Nutrition. 2013, 52,* 337–345, doi:10.1007/s00394-012-0340-6.

Morris, N. (2017) 'One in eight skips meals to pay bills'. ***The i*** *(newspaper, UK)*, Thursday 7th September 2017. Page 8.

Mosley, M. (2015) 'Which oils are best to cook with?' 28th July 2015. BBC: News: Magazine, Online: http://www.bbc.co.uk/news/magazine-33675975

Myers, A. (2016) 'Nine Signs you have a leaky gut', by Dr Amy Myers, Mind-body-green Blog: http://www.mindbodygreen.com/0-10908/9-signs-you-have-a-leaky-gut.html. Accessed: 13th June 2016).

Myhill, S. (2015) 'Healthy eating - Why grains are such a problem'. Dr Sarah Myhill's blog. Available online: http://drmyhill.co.uk/wiki/Healthy_eating_-_why_grains_are_such_a_problem. Accessed on: 21st November 2017.

National Health Service (NHS) (2016) 'Exercise for depression'. Available online: http://www.nhs.uk/conditions/stress-anxiety-depression/pages/exercise-for-depression.aspx. Accessed: 23rd February 2016.

Natural Health 365 (2017) 'The link between gum disease and Alzheimer's'. Available online at: http://www.naturalhealth365.com/alzheimers-disease-oral-health-1552.html. Accessed 15th September 2017.

Nelson, J.K. and Zeratsky, K. (2015) 'Are there whole grains that are gluten-free?' The Nutrition-wise blog. Healthy Lifestyle: Nutrition and healthy eating. The Mayo Clinic. Online at: http://www.mayoclinic.org/healthy-lifestyle/nutrition-and-healthy-eating/expert-blog/gluten-free-whole-grains/bgp-20056134/. Accessed: 17th October 2017.

Nelson-Jones, R. (2001) *Theory and Practice of Counselling and Therapy.* Third edition. London: Continuum.

NHS Choices (2016) 'Stress, anxiety and depression: How to control your anger'. Available online: www.nhs.uk/conditions/anger-management. Accessed 16th June 2016.

O'Connor, P.J., Herring, M.P. and Carvalho, A. (2010). 'Mental health benefits of strength training in adults'. *American Journal of Lifestyle Medicine, 4(5),* Pages 377-396.

Office for National Statistics (ONS) (1995) 'Surveys of Psychiatric Morbidity in Great Britain. Report 1 – The prevalence of psychiatric morbidity among adults living in private households'. London: The Stationery Office. Cited on: https://www.anxietyuk.org.uk/. Accessed 13th June 2016.

Ong D.K., Mitchell S.B., Barrett J.S., et al. (2010) 'Manipulation of dietary short chain carbohydrates alters the pattern of hydrogen and methane gas production and genesis of symptoms in patients with irritable bowel syndrome. *Journal of Gastroenterology and Hepatology. 2010 Aug; 25(8):* 1366-73

PQR

Perlmutter, D. (2014) *Grain Brain: The surprising truth about wheat, carbs, and sugar – your brain's silent killers.* London: Yellow Kite/Hodder and Stoughton.

Perlmutter, D. (2015) *Brain Maker: The power of gut microbes to heal and protect your brain – for life.* London: Hodder and Stoughton.

Perretta, L. (2001) *Brain Food: The essential guide to boosting brain power.* London: Hamlyn.

Perricone, N. (2002) *Dr Nicolas Perricone's Programme: Grow young, get slim, in days.* London: Thorsons.

Pickett, K. and Wilkinson, R. (2010) *The Spirit Level: Why equality is better for everyone.* London: Penguin.

Pinnock, D. (2015) *Anxiety and Depression: Eat your way to better health.* London: Quadrille Publishing.

Poulter, S. (2016) 'Don't eat our pasta sauce more than once a week'. *Daily Mail* online. April 14th 2016. Available online: http://www.dailymail.co.uk/health/article-3540217/When-sa-Dolmio-day-Just-week-Labels-advise-foods-high-sugar-salt-eaten-occasionally.html

Prochaska, J.O., Norcross, J.C. & DiClemente, C.C. (1998). *Changing for Good*. Reprint edition. New York: Morrow.

Punder, K. de, and Pruimboom, L. (2013) 'The Dietary Intake of Wheat and other Cereal Grains and Their Role in Inflammation'. *Nutrients 2013, 5, 771-787;* doi:10.3390/nu5030771. Available online: http://www.oalib.com/paper/2629517#.WgGOjFt-rcs. Accessed: 7th November 2017.

Qi, L., van Dam, R.M., Liu, S., et al (2006) 'Whole-grain, bran, and cereal fibre intakes and markers of systemic inflammation in diabetic women'. *Diabetes Care. 29.* 207-11. 10.2337/diacare.29.02.06.dc05-1903.

Radhakrishna, S. (2010). 'Application of integrated yoga therapy to increase imitation skills in children with autism spectrum disorder'. *International Journal of Yoga, 3 (1);* pp:26-30.

Radhakrishna, S., Nagarathna R., and Nagendra H.R. (2010). 'Integrated approach to yoga therapy and autism spectrum disorders'. *Journal of Ayurveda and Integrative Medicine, 1 (2);* pp: 120-4.

Ratey, J., and Hargerman, E. (2009) *Spark: The revolutionary new science of exercise and the brain.* London: Quercus.

Reder, A. (2007) 'Unmasking Anger'. *Yoga Journal.* August 28th 2007. Available online: http://www.yogajournal.com/article/yoga-101/unmasking-anger/. Accessed: 17th June 2016.

Redfern, R. (2016) 'The importance of nutrition for mental health'. *Naturally Healthy News, issue 30, 2016.*

Reynolds, G. (2010) 'Phys Ed: Can Exercise Moderate Anger?' August 11, 2010. Available online, here: http://well.blogs.nytimes.com/2010/08/11/phys-ed-can-exercise-moderate-anger/?_r=0. Accessed: 16th June 2016.

Romm, A. (2016) 'Five Steps to Heal a Leaky Gut Caused By Ibuprofen'. *Huffpost Healthy Living*: Available online: http://www.huffingtonpost.com/aviva-romm/5-steps-to-heal-a-leaky-g_b_5617109.html. Accessed: 13th June 2016)

Ross, J. (2003) *The Mood Cure: Take charge of your emotions in 24 hours using food and supplements.* London: Thorsons.

STU

Sadock, B.J. and Sadock, V.A. (2000) *Kaplan and Sadock's Synopsis of Psychiatry: Behavioural Sciences/ Clinical Psychiatry, 7th Edition.* Philadelphia, PA: Lippincott Williams & Wilkins.

Sanchez-Villegas, A., Almudena, M.A., *et al*. (2013) 'Mediterranean dietary pattern and depression: the PREDIMED randomized trial'. *BMC Medicine 2013, Vol.11: Article 208.*

Sánchez-Villegas, A., Verberne, L., De Irala, J., Ruíz-Canela, M., et al. (2011) 'Dietary Fat Intake and the Risk of Depression: The SUN Project'. PLoS ONE 6(1): e16268. doi:10.1371/journal.pone.0016268

Sandwell, H. and Wheatley, M. (2008) 'Healthy eating advice as part of drug treatment in prisons'. *Prison Service Journal, Issue 182.*

Sapolsky, R. (2010) *Why Zebras don't get Ulcers. Third Edition.* New York: St Martin's Griffin.

Sansouci, J. (2011) 'Nutrition and anxiety'. Healthy Crush Blog. Available at: http://healthycrush.com/nutrition-and-anxiety/. Accessed 20th May 2016.

Santer, M.J. (2011) 'Why Qigong Is So Effective Against Emotional Illnesses'. Available online at: http://qigong15.com/blog/qigong-exercises/why-qigong-is-so-effective-against-emotional-illnesses/. Accessed May 2015.

Schmidt, K., Cowen, P.J., Harmer, C.J., et al. (2015) 'Prebiotic intake reduces the waking cortisol response and alters emotional bias in healthy volunteers'. *Psychopharmacology* (2015) 232: Pages 1793-1801. Available online: https://link.springer.com/content/pdf/10.1007%2Fs00213-014-3810-0.pdf. Accessed: 15th September 2017.

Schoenthaler, S.J. (1983) 'The Northern California diet-behaviour program: An empirical evaluation of 3,000 incarcerated juveniles in Stanislaus County Juvenile Hall'. *International Journal of Biosocial Research, Vol 5(2),* Pages 99-106.

Schoenthaler, S.J. (1983) 'The Los Angeles probation department diet behaviour program: An empirical analysis of six institutional settings'. *International Journal of Biosocial Research, Vol 5(2),* Pages 107-117.

Schoenthaler S., et al (1997) 'The effect of randomized vitamin-mineral supplementation on violent and non-violent antisocial behaviour among incarcerated juveniles'. *Journal of Nutritional & Environmental Medicine 7:* Pages 343–352.

Schoenthaler, S., and Bier I. D. (2002) 'Food addiction and criminal behaviour – The California randomized trial'. *Food Allergy and Intolerance. 731–746.* Saunders. Cited in Sandwell and Wheatley (2008).

Scicurious (2010) 'If low serotonin levels aren't responsible for depression, what is?' *The Guardian*: Blog post: Online: https://www.theguardian.com/science/blog/2010/sep/28/depression-serotonin-neurogenesis. Accessed: 13th June 2016 and 15th September 2017.

Shapiro D., Cook I.A., Davydov, D.M., et al (2007) 'Yoga as a Complementary Treatment of Depression: Effects of Traits and Moods on Treatment Outcome'. *Evidence Based Complementary and Alternative Medicine, 4(4),* pp: 493-502.

Sharma, V.K., Das S, Mondal S, Goswami U and Gandhi A, (2006) 'Effect of Sahaj Yoga on neuro-cognitive functions in patients suffering from major depression'. *Indian Journal of Physiological Pharmacology*, Oct-Dec, 50(4); pp:375-83.

Sharma, V.K., Das, S., Mondal, S., et al (2005) 'Effect of Sahaj Yoga on depressive disorders'. *Indian Journal of Physiological Pharmacology*, Oct-Dec, 49(4); pp:462-8.

Shepherd, S.J., Parker, F.J., Muir, J.G. and Gibson, P.R. (2008) 'Dietary triggers of abdominal symptoms in patients with irritable bowel syndrome - Randomised placebo-controlled evidence'. *Clinical Gastroenterology and Hepatology. 2008; 6(7):* 765-771: http://www.sciencedirect.com/science/ article /pii/S1542356508001511

Simopoulos, A.P. (2002) 'The importance of the ratio of omega-6/omega-3 essential fatty acids'. *Biomedical Pharmacotherapy, Oct, Vol.56(8):* Pages 365-379. Online: https://www.ncbi.nlm.nih.gov/pubmed/12442909/

Simopoulos, A.P. (ed) (2004) 'Nutrition and Fitness: Mental health, aging, and the implementation of a healthy diet and physical activity lifestyle'. *World Review of Nutrition and Dietetics, Vol. 95.*

Skodje, G.I. et al. (2017, In press) 'Fructan, Rather Than Gluten, Induces Symptoms in Patients With Self-reported Non-celiac Gluten Sensitivity'. Gastroenterology, published online 1st November 2017. DOI: http://dx.doi.org/10.1053/j.gastro.2017.10.040) Accessed: 25th November 2017.

Small, G. (2010) 'Can Exercise Cure Depression? Exercise releases endorphins, the body's very own natural antidepressant'. Posted Sep 25, 2010. *Psychology Today blog*: Available online: https://www.psychologytoday.com/blog/brain-bootcamp/ 201009/ can-exercise-cure-depression. Accessed: 19th June 2016.

Sofi, F. & Ghiselli, L., & Cesari, F., et al. (2010) 'Effects of Short-Term Consumption of Bread Obtained by an Old Italian Grain Variety on Lipid, Inflammatory, and Hemorheological Variables: An Intervention Study'. *Journal of Medicinal Food. 13*. 615-20. 10.1089/jmf.2009.0092.

Stanfield, M. (2008) *Trans Fat: The Time Bomb in Your Food: The killer in the kitchen.* Souvenir Press: London.

St. Pierre, B. (2017) 'Settling the great grain debate. Can wheat and other grains fit into a healthy - and sane - diet?' Precision Nutrition Blog. Online: http://www.precisionnutrition.com/grain-wheat-debate. Accessed: 4th October 2017.

Stress Management Society (2012/2016) 'Nutritional stress and health: The "Think 'nervous'" box'. Available online: http://www.stress.org.uk/Diet-and-nutrition.aspx

Tahir, T. (2012 'Junk food and margarine among trans fats-laden food that "makes us angry".' *Metro* newspaper online: http://metro.co.uk/2012/03/14/junk-food-and-margarine-among-trans-fats-laden-food-that-makes-us-angry-351857/

Tighe, P., Duthie, G., Vaughan, N., Brittenden, J., et al. (2010) 'Effect of increased consumption of whole-grain foods on blood pressure and other cardiovascular risk markers in healthy middle-aged persons: A randomized controlled trial.' *The American Journal of Clinical Nutrition, Oct; 92(4)*:733-40. doi: 10.3945/ajcn.2010.29417. Epub.

Trowbridge, J.P. and Walker, M. (1989) *The Yeast Syndrome*. London: Bantam Books.

Tse, M. (1995) *Qigong for Health and Vitality*. London: Piatkus.

Uebelacker, L.A., Tremont G, Epstein-Lubow G, et al (2010) 'Open trial of Vinyasa yoga for persistently depressed individuals: Evidence of feasibility and acceptability'. *Behaviour Modification, May, 34(3)*; pp: 247-64.

VWXYZ

Vancampfort, D., De Hert, M., Knapen J, et al. (2011) 'State anxiety, psychological stress and positive well-being responses to yoga and aerobic exercise in people with schizophrenia: A pilot study'. *Disability Rehabilitation, 33(8)*; pp: 684-9.

Van der Veen, F. M., Evers, E.A.T., Deutz, N.E.P., and Schmitt, J.A.J. (2007) 'Effects of Acute Tryptophan Depletion on Mood and Facial Emotion Perception Related Brain Activation and Performance in Healthy Women with and without a Family History of Depression'. *Neuropsychopharmacology, Vol.32, Issue 1*, Pages 216-224.

Virkkunen, M. (1986) 'Reactive hypoglycaemic tendency among habitually violent offenders'. *Nutrition Reviews, Vol. 44 (Suppl).* Pages 94-103.

Visceglia, E. and Lewis, S. (2011) 'Yoga therapy as an adjunctive treatment for schizophrenia: A randomized, controlled pilot study'. *Journal of Alternative and complementary Medicine, 17 (7)*, pages: 601-7.

Vitaglione, P., Mennella, I., Ferracane, R., et al. (2015) 'Whole-grain wheat consumption reduces inflammation in a randomized controlled trial on overweight and obese subjects with unhealthy dietary and lifestyle behaviours: Role of polyphenols bound to cereal dietary fibre'. *American Journal of Clinical Nutrition 2015; 101*: 251–61.

Volta, U. and De Giorgio, R. (2010) 'Gluten sensitivity: an emerging issue behind neurological impairment?' *The Lancet Neurology, Volume 9, Issue 3*, pages 233-235.

Waite, M. (2012) *Paperback Oxford English Dictionary. Seventh edition*. Oxford: Oxford University Press.

Warwick University (2016) 'Seven a day for happiness and mental health'. Press release: http://www.2.warwick.ac.uk/newsandevents/presssreleases/7-a-day_for_happiness/ Accessed 2nd May 2016

WebMD (2017) 'Mediterranean Diet - Topic Overview'. The WebMD Blog. Online: https://www.webmd.com/heart-disease/tc/mediterranean-diet-topic-overview#1. Accessed: 11th October 2017.

Willcox, B.J., Willcox, D.C., and Suzuki, M. (2001) *The Okinawa Way: How to improve your health and longevity dramatically*. London: Michael Joseph/Penguin Group.

Wolcott, W.L. and Fahey, T. (2002) *The Metabolic Typing Diet*. New York: Broadway Books.

Woodward, N. (2006) 'Stress, Diet and Body Acidification'. *Cellular Chemistry, Issue 130, December 2006*. Available online at: http://www.positivehealth.com/article/alkaline/stress-diet-and-body-acidification

Woolfe, R., Dryden, W., and Strawbridge, S. (eds) (2003) *Handbook of Counselling Psychology*. Second Edition. London: Sage Publications.

Yu, W. (2012) 'High trans-fat diet predicts aggression: People who eat more hydrogenated oils are more aggressive'. *Scientific American Mind*, July 2012. Online at: https://www.scientificamerican.com/article/high-trans-fat-diet-predicts-aggresion/

~~~

Index

A

Adrenaline, 47, 48, 50, 63, 64, 72, 75, 104
Alcohol, 22, 25, 44, 47, 49, 58, 60, 62, 66, 77, 106, 131, 153
   and emotions, 22, 48, 49
   effects on body-brain-mind, 47–49
Amino acids, 57, 63, 82, 119
Anger, 13, 17, 22, 23, 46, 56, 60, 92, 94, 97, 127, 130
   and dietary considerations, 67–70, 76, 97, 106, 123, 124, 125, 129
   and exercise benefits, 87–91, 94, 126, 127, 154, 157
   multiple causes of, 21, 60
Antibiotics
   can facilitate the emergence of Candida Albicans overgrowth, 25
   damage friendly gut bacteria, 25
   in foods
      and Candida Albicans, 30
   in pork, chicken and eggs
      kills friendly bacteria, 95
Anxiety, 17–19, 21, 22, 25–26, 46, 47, 50, 54, 55
   and dietary considerations, 60–67
   and exercise benefits, 78–84
   multiple causes of, 21
Atkins diet, 30
Atkinson, Dr Mark, 9, 15, 19, 79, 98, 100, 149, 171

B

Balanced diet, 17, 129
   and supplements, 54, 56, 58, 63, 99, 111, 113, 123
   definition, 25
   difficulty of defining, 27–44, 120
BDNF
   and intestinal probiotics, 59
   and mental functioning, 13
   defined in footnote, 13
Blumenthal, James, 84, 85, 86, 128, 150
Body-brain-mind
   and alcohol, 120
   and bad foods, 25
   and caffeine, 121
   and diet, exercise and nutritional supplementation, 23
   and gluten, 121
   and good and bad foods, 129
   and nutrition, 26, 119
   and nutritional supplements, 122
   and physical exercise, 22, 79–80
   and processed foods, 121
   and social interactions, 11
   and sugar, 47, 120
   and the effects of trans-fats, 45
   and the stress response, 126
   interactionism, 19
Brain-derived neurotrophic factor. *See* BDNF
Bread. *See* Grains
   and problems with gluten, 54
Breakfast
   and depression, 71
   and high glycemic index foods, 96
   and self-management, 77
   cereals, 98
   guidelines, 104–5
   never skip it!, 104
Brogan
   Dr Kelly, 4, 110, 125
Butter. *See* Dairy

C

Caffeine, 22, 49, 50, 66, 77, 106, 129, 131, 151, 152
   and anxiety and panic, 61, 66, 124
   and irritability, anger, anxiety, panic attacks, depression and insomnia, 106
   and the body-brain-mind, 44
   effects on body-brain-mind, 25
   reduce coffee, tea, cocoa, cola drinks, 101
   the research findings, 49–50
Candida Albicans, 60
   and depression, 25, 61, 71, 97
   and diet, 30, 44, 95–97
   special anti-Candida diet, 130
Carbohydrate, 41
   and the Paleo diet theory, 42
   complex, or unprocessed, 41, 64, 100, 104
   refined carbs
      and depression, 119
   refined, or processed, 41, 64, 98, 100
Chi Kung. *See* Qigong
China Study, The, 151
   found veg better than meat for physical and mental health, 30, 38, 102, 103
Co-enzyme-Q-10
   and brain health, 39
   and mitochondrial function of our cells, 116
Coffee, 49, *See* Caffeine
   and anxiety, 66, 106

and depression, 49
link to anxiety and depression, 50
link to tiredness and headaches, 50
Cortisol
and the stress response, 65, 72, 96, 123, 124, 125, 158

D

Dairy, 42, 73, 98, 99, 105, 113, 117, 131
butter, 45, 103, 120
cheese, 60
milk, 42, 60, 95, 101, 105
Depression, 13
and alcohol, 48–49, 106, 121
and Candida Albicans, 97
and carbohydrates, 128–29
and coffee, 49–50, 106
and gluten, 121
and gut bacteria disruption, 22
and healthy gut bacteria, 125
and inflammation, 114–17, 125
and malnutrition, 110, 111–13
and medication, 125
and nutrient deficiencies, 17, 131
and nutritional mental health approaches, 19
and physical exercise, 84–86, 128–29
and processed food, 121, 125
and yoga, 88
causes and contributing factors, 11–12, 21, 25–26
Chi Kung and Tai Chi, 91
diet, nutrition, and lifestyle factors, 125, 129
drugs and placebos, 17
multiple causes, 125
Diet and nutrition
alcohol. *See* Alcohol
and balanced diet. *See* Balanced diet
and gut health, 17, 19, 23, 25, 61, 72, 105, 123, 125
and mental health, 3, 12–13, 17–19, 17, 21, 41, 57, 75, 76–77, 109, 111–14, 116, 122, 129
and nutritional treatments, 19
and other causes of emotional problems, 21
and social and economic deprivation, 20
and stress, 13, 17, 21, 22, 41–42, 46, 48, 50, 51, 56, 67, 95, 99–101, 106, 110, 115–17, 123, 130–31
and the harm done by food technologists, 22
and the need for government campaigns, 22

as one cause of emotional problems, 25
caffeine. *See* Caffeine
combined with counselling and therapy, 21
foods to avoid. *See* Food, foods to avoid
importance for body-brain-mind health, 25
link to emotional distress
personal experience, 95–97
more effective than drugs for mental health, 17
no universally agreed approach, 27, 43, 97, 99, 117, 120
nutritional deficiency or insufficiency
and mental health, 17, 54, 109–10, 112, 115
and nutritional treatments, 55–60, 76–78
and political factors, 20, 22
personalized to the individual, 95, 99, 120
promoting public awareness, 22–23
some dietary guidelines, 27–44, 40, 97–107
supplements and healthy foods, 17, 21, 41, 45, 54–60, 69, 76–77, 98–99, 106, 113, 114, 116, 119, 122–23, 130–31
what is nutrition?, 26
Diet types, 28–39, 97–99
Anti-Candida diet, 30
Atkins diet, 30, 60, 97
Candida diet. See Anti-Candida diet
FodMaps diet, 30
General dietary guidelines, 40–44
Hay diet, 31
Mediterranean diet, 32
Metabolic typing diet, 33
Nordic/Scandinavian diet, 34
Okinawa diet, 36
Paleo diet, 36
Perlmutter's dietary advice, 73
Personalized diet, 39
UK National Food Guide, 28–29
Vegetarian diet, 38
Drinks and drinking, 29, 47–50, 62, 75, 78, 98, 99, 101–2, 107
alcohol, 22, 25, 29, 44, 47–49, 60, 62, 66, 67, 77, 78, 102, 106, 120, 129
caffeine, 22, 25, 29, 49–50, 61, 66, 77, 101, 106, 121, 124, 129, 131
milk, 42, 60, 95, 101, 105
smoothies
fruit and/or veg, 102
sugary drinks, 29, 63, 75, 98, 101
water, 43, 44, 48, 58, 78, 98, 99, 101, 105, 113, 120, 131

Using nutrition and physical exercise

E

Eggs
  antibiotics and Candida Albicans, 95
  are high in saturated fats
    eat in moderation, 98, 101
  avoid non-organic varieties, 30
  non-organic eggs
    arachidonic acid and inflammation, 30, 41
  organic eggs (omega 3) quell inflammation, 95
  organic is better than 'omega-3 fortified', 30, 95
  should always be organic, 28, 100
Emotional distress or disturbance
  and Candida Albicans, 25, 30, 31, 60, 61, 71, 95–97, 101
  and gut problems, 23
  and inappropriate use of medication, 17
  and inflammation, 115, 117
  and junk food, 25, 30, 39, 41, 50, 61, 75, 112, 114, 132, 159
  and lifestyle factors, 126
  and poverty, 17
  and sedentary lifestyle, 10, 21, 23, 42, 71, 94
  multiple causes of, 21
  personal experience, 95
  promoting public awareness, 22
Enders, Dr Giulia, 4, 17, 22, 59, 109, 110, 152
Essential fatty acids (EFA's)
  cod liver oil as source, 33
  krill oil as a source, 33
Essential fatty acids (EFA's), 32, 35, 37, 38, 41, 45, 48, 62, 75, 82, 97, 116, 120, 132, 152
  effects on the brain-mind, 13, 27, 35, 38, 42, 48, 55, 57, 75, 99, 100, 106, 114
  omega 3
    and alcohol, 48
    and anger, 97
    and anxiety, 62–63
    and depression, 75
    and fish oil supplements, 32, 39, 45, 56, 98, 116
    and food sources, 32
    and Mediterranean diet, 32
    and oily fish, 42, 45, 55, 100
    and the Nordic diet, 35
    and the Paleo diet, 42
    and trans-fats, 45
    and vegetarian diets, 38
    omega 3/6 ratio, 35, 37, 99, 100, 132
  omega 6
    and animal products, 41, 99, 132
    and emotional wellbeing, 38
    and inflammation, 132
    in arachidonic acid form, 30, 38, 41, 151
    widely available, 32
Exercise systems
  aerobic exercise, 66, 79, 85, 86, 93, 124, 159
  Chinese exercise, 90–92
  flexibility and stretching, 79
  Indian yoga, 79, 88–90, 91, 94, 129
  running, 93, 129, 150
  swimming, 79, 87
  walking, 79, 85, 87, 88, 94, 129
  weight training, 79
Exercise, physical, 79–80
  and anger, 87–88
  and anxiety, 80–84
  and depression, 84–86
  and stress, 80
  and the brain-mind, 92–94
  western tradition, 79

F

Fast foods. *See* Food: foods to avoid
Fats and oils, 102–4
  as valuable macronutrients, 102
  butter, margarine and olive oil, 102
  cod liver oil. *See* Essential fatty acids
  essential fatty acids. *See* Essential fattty acids (EFA's)
  for frying, 103
  for salads, 103
  general guidelines, 103
  meat and dairy fats, 102
  oily fish, nuts and seeds, 103
  plant-based fats are best, 103
  saturated fats, relatively bad, 98, 101
  trans-fats. *See* Trans-fats
  unsaturated fats, relatively good, 32, 37, 42, 45, 100, 104
Fibre, 32, 46, 51, 73, 119, 121, 131
Fight or flight response, 83, 126
  parasympathetic nervous system, 81, 126
  sympathetic nervous system, 81, 106, 126
Fish
  and fish oil supplements, 69
    for reducing depression, 75
  and mental health, 76
  and the Atkins diet, 30
  and the Mediterranean diet, 32–33, 76
  and the Nordic diet, 34–36
  and the Okinawa diet, 36
  as low carb food, 73
  in a balanced diet, 99

163.

oily fish
- and fat intake, 42–43
- and omega-3, 39, 41–42, 45, 62, 100, 106
- and stress, 100, 106
- recommended varieties, 55
- polluted with mercury, 98
- reject 'fish and chips', 29

FodMaps diet. *See* Diet types: FodMaps diet

Food
- and anger, 124
- and anxiety, 123
- and brain chemicals, 114
- and depression, 125
- and gluten. *See* Gluten
- and nutrition, 123, *See* Diet types, *See* Diet and nutrition
- and organic wholefoods, 40
- and personalized dietary guidelines, 39
- and the The UK National Food Guide, 28
- as prebiotics and probiotics, 124
- as processed foods, 121
- foods to avoid, 44–54
    - animal-based food, 30
    - fast food, 101, 120
    - junk food, 22, 25, 30, 34, 39, 50–51, 54, 61, 75, 112
- foods to eat. *See* Diet types
- general dietary guidelines, 40–44
- is the best medicine, 110
- raw salads very nutritious, 131

Food Standards Agency
- and the UK National Food Guide, 28
- *Balance of Good Health*, 152
- National Diet and Nutrition Survey, 56

Fruit and vegetables
- *and balanced diet*, 99
- and mental or psychological well-being, 77, 150
- more veg, less fruit, 97
- most people don't eat enough of these, 56
- proportion of total food intake, 28
- recommended varieties, 40
- six or seven portions per day, 35, 77, 100
- too much fruit sugar is bad for us, 97

G

Gluten, 51–54, 121
- a description and definition, 51
- acts like an opiate in the brain, 53
- affects the gut and/or the brain, 52
- and avenin, in oats, 18
- and Dr Michael Greger's contested argument, 53
- and gluten free bread, 102
- and gluten-free grains, 18, 30, 34, 37, 77, 156
- and leaky gut syndrome, 17, 18, 52
- and leaky gut, and inflammation, 52, 65
- and neurological damage, 18, 52, 153, 160
- and Non-Celiac Gluten Sensitivity (NCGS), 18, 52, 151
- and the gluten syndrome, 52, 152
- and the Paleo view of grains, 37, 43–44
- and why it's a problem, 52, 73
- case study (Martina), 65, 124
- elimination, for mood and emotion improvement, 73
- intolerance and gluten sensitivity, 52, 121
- is a body-mind toxin, 129
- linked to anxiety and depression, 52, 74, 121, 122
- Three doctors debate gluten and sugar, 107

Glycaemic index, 38, 41, 152
- and blood sugar levels, 97
- low GI foods (beans and legumes), 38
- low GI fruit, 41

Grains, 28–29, 42, 43, 53, 54, 58, 60, 63, 73, 76, 77, 99, 113, 117, 119, 122, 131
- and inflammation, 17, 43
- in wholegrain form, 28–29, 40–44

Greger
- Dr Michael
    - and low meat diet good for emotional health, 38
    - and low meat, high veg diet, 41
    - and the omega-3-to-6 ratio, 99, 132
    - food and mood, 9
    - high veg diet cuts depression, 132
    - How Not to Die, 153
    - meat and arachidonic acid, 30, 41
    - omega-3 and brain health, 33
    - re vegetarian diet and exercise, 38

Gut bacteria
- and anti-Candida treatments, 96
- and anxiety
    - a healing solution, 64–66
- and anxiety reduction, 66
- and Candida Albicans, 96
- and curative diet changes, 39
- and human health and illness, 123
- and mental health, 65
- and mood control, 76
- and probiotic supplements, 59, 73, 116, 123
- and regulation of emotions, 150
- and supportive diet, 76

friendly and unfriendly varieties, 96
how to build up good bacteria, 60
linked to depression, 12
the five core probiotic species, 59

H

Hay diet, the, 31–32, 41, 64, 100, 149
Hippocrates
    knew diet and exercise important for health!, 12
Hoffer, Dr Abram
    influenced this book, 4
    on nutrient deficiencies and mental health, 17
    Pellagra and schizophrenia, 153
Hoffman, Benson, PhD
    exercise and depression, 85
    exercise and major depression, 86, 128
    journal article, 150
    second journal article, 153
Holford, Patrick
    and alcohol, 47, 48
    and dietary guidelines, 40
    and nutritional supplements, 57
    and recommended fish, 30
    and recommended seeds, 33
    and recommended vegetables, 40
    impact of caffein on brain chemistry, negative, 50
    influenced this book, 4
    nutritional supplements to balance neurotransmitters, 75
    on omega-3's and brain health, mood and emotion, 33
    on proportions and amounts of veg and wholegrains, 42
    violence and blood sugar problems, 68

I

Inflammation
    and arachidonic acid in meat and eggs, 30, 38
    and dairy products, 105
    and gluten, 18
    and gut bacteria, 72
    and 'leaky gut' syndrome, 52, 73
    and physical and mental health, 26
    and sluggish digestion, 64
    and sugar consumption, 46
    and trans-fats, 45
    linked to depression and anxiety, 19, 38, 72
    linked to omega-3/6 imbalance, 37
    may be linked to grain consumption, 43

mood and emotions, 95, 113–17
of the brain, linked to poor mental health, 41, 72
sugars and depression, 31

J

Junk foods. *See* Food: foods to avoid

K

Kaplan, Dr Bonnie, 109, 110, 111, 112, 113, 114, 115, 116, 154, 157
    and nutritional treatment of emotional problems, 111, 116
    and Pellegra psychosis, 110
    and the science of nutritional deficiency, 109
    nutritional deficiencies and mental health, 113
    on inflammation and depression, 115
    on inflammation and emotional disturbance, 113
    on nutritional mental health, 154
    on the Minnesota Starvation Experiment, 111, 112
    on vitamins, minerals and mood, 154
    vitamin B3 and schizophrenia, 110
Khalsa, Dr Dharma Singh, 4, 154
Korn, Dr Leslie
    and lifestyle approaches to treating mental health problems, 17
    and our level of nutritional need, 131
    Nutritional Essentials for Mental Health, 154
    on nutritional supplements and healthy foods, 17
    on the link between metabolism and mental health, 34
    the case for personalized diet, 39
    the link between diet/nutrition and emotional wellbeing, 109

L

Leaky gut syndrome
    and damage to blood/brain barrier, 74
    and inflammation, 52, 65, 73
    and NSAIDs, including painkillers, 65
    and the link to gluten, 52, 121
    damages mental health, 18
    five steps to heal this condition, 157
    nine signs of this condition, 156
LeDoux, Jospeh, 82

M

Mayo Clinic guidelines

for gluten-free grains, 18, 33, 34, 37, 44
on exercise for anger management, 87
on exercise for anger, anxiety, stress and depression, 155
on exercise relieving anxiety and depression, 86
on physical exercise for stress and anxiety, 86

McLeod, John, 155

meat
- minimize grain-fed meat consumption, 41

Meat
- and sluggish digestion problems, 31
- and undesirable antibiotic content, 30, 95
- arachidonic acid, inflammation and depression, 30
- as a proportion of food consumption, 28, 41, 43, 100, 103
- avoid processed meats, 44
- avoid salty delicatessen meats, 51
- eating less meat improves mental health, 38
- grain fed meats, omega-6 imbalance, and depression, 132
- low-meat, high-vegetable dietary guidelines, 41
- meat consumption and the omega-3/6 balance, 35, 100
- meat consumption linked to chronic physical and mental health problems, 30, 103
- *meat tolerance may be linked to genetic heritage*, 39
- minimize grain-fed meat consumption, 33, 64, 117
- Nordic diet minimizes meat consumption, 34–36
- processed meats linked to depression, 75
- proportion too high in Paleo diets, even if grass fed, 37
- small amount in Mediterranean diet, 32, 76

Meditation, 58, 71, 75, 77, 87, 88, 94, 111, 116

Mediterranean diet. See Diet types

Mental health
- *and arachidonic acid*, 41
- and government intervention, 22
- and gut health, 65
- and helpful diet, 76
- and neoliberal economic policy, 20
- and nutrition, 149
- and nutritional deficiency, 113
- and nutritional supplements, 57
- and yoga, 89

is damaged by nutritional deficiency, 109
is improved by physical exercise, 79
linked to diet and exercise
- a model, 12
- a second model, 19
linked to gut health, 23
linked to lifestyle factors, 17
linked to physical health, 25
multiple causes and cures, 20
the influence of diet and exercise, 153

Mercola, Dr Joseph, 45, 54, 55, 117, 155

Milk. *See* Dairy, milk

Minerals and vitamins. *See* Vitamin and mineral supplements

Minnesota Starvation Experiments. *See* Nutritional deficiency and insufficiency

Mutlivitamins and minerals. See Vitamin and mineral supplements

N

National Health Service (NHS - UK) guidelines
- *and nutritional supplements*, 54–55
- and the Mediterranean diet, 99
- regarding anger, 87
- regarding anxiety, 81
- regarding depression, 70, 86, 128

Nordic diet, 34–36, 153
- and fish, 33

Nutrition and nutritional. *See* Diet and nutrition

Nutritional deficiency and insufficiency
- and the Minnesota Starvation Experiments, 111–12

Nutritional deficiency or insufficiency, 109–11
- and emotional problems, 123, 131
- and inflammation, 114
- and mental health or illness, 109, 111, 113, 116
- and supplements, 113, 116
- nutritional treatment of, 110, 111, 124
- the scientific evidence, 109
- Vitamin B3 and Pellagra, 110

O

Okinawa diet, 36

Oligosaccharides
- and other food sugars, 60

Omega 3 fatty acid. *See* Essential fatty acids (EFA's)

Omega 6 fatty acid. *See* Essential fatty acids (EFA's)

P

Paleo diet

and the question of grains, 36–38
Perlmutter, Dr David
   and his dietary guidelines, 73
   and his two main books on the brain, 156
   and nutritional medicine, 110
   and probiotic and prebiotic supplements, 59, 66, 122, 123
   and sensitivity to gluten, 52
   on gluten and the gut wall, 66, 74
   on gut health and mental health, 72
   on probiotics, prebiotics and the stress response, 123
   on the gut-anxiety link, 64, 66
   on the link between inflammation and depression, 72, 125
   the gut as source of most illness, 59, 123, 125
Perricone, Dr Nicholas, 48, 156
Physical exercise. See Exercise, physical
Politics, social policy and mental health, 22
Poverty and mental illness, 20
Probiotics
   and Dr David Perlmutter's recommendations, 59
   and nutritional mental health, 116
   and stress reduction, 65, 123
   and the eating of prebiotic foods, 59
   for a healthy gut and brain, 123
   like Acidophilus bifidus, 73
Processed
   definition, description, advice to avoid, 50–51
Processed foods
   and aggression, irritability and impatience, 40, 124
   and our advice to avoid them, 29
   and the anti-Candida diet, 30
   and the Atkins diet, 30
   and the effects on the body-brain-mind, 25
   and the need for public education, 22
   as legally available toxins, 129
   avoidance of, reduces risk of depression, 75, 121, 125
   including trans-fats, 44–45
   or junk food, 50–51
   sugar rush, and anxiety, 63
   trans-fats, and aggression, 69
   what to eat and what to avoid, 43, 44–54, 77, 98, 99, 101, 103, 119, 121, 131
Protein
   a definition, 27
   and combining with carbohydrate, Hay diet, 31, 41, 64, 100
   and complex carbohydrates, 119
   and personalized diet, 39
   and the anti-Candida diet, 131
   and the Mediterranean diet, 32
   and the Metabolic typing diet, 33
   and the other macronutrients, 102
   and the Paleo diet, 36, 42, 119
   and the Ph diet (or acid/alkaline diet), 101
   and the stress and anxiety diet, 130
   for breakfast (occasionally), 105
   grains and gluten and inflammation, 51, 73
   grains and inflammation, the argument, 121
   grains, meat, gluten and inflammation, 18, 30, 41, 43, 95
   recommended proportion of diet, 100, 131
   very high in Atkins diet, 30

Q

Qigong (or Chi Kung)
   and anger, 92, 94
   and anxiety, 90
   and depression, 90
   flexibility and stretching exercises, 79
   for physical health and emotional wellbeing, 94
   our training, 10

R

Ratey, John and Hagerman, Eric
   on anxiety and exercise, 81–84
   on depression and exercise, 84–85
   on exercise and brain improvement, 92
Reactive hypoglycaemia
   and anger and depression, 69
   defined in footnote, 69
   Virkkunen on link to violence, 159
Ross, Dr Julia
   on caffeine as a serotonin killer, 49
   on gluten and mood problems, 52–53, 122
   on serotonin and anger, 67, 124
   on sugar and mood discorders, 46
   on supplements and nutritional therapy, 55

S

Salt
   reduce and restrict, 51, 77, 98, 101, 121, 157
Sapolsky, Robert
   on exercise for stress, 92–94, 129, 130, 157

Saturated fats. *See* Fats and oils: saturated fats
Schoenthaler, Prof Stephen
   on healthier diet and reduction in violence and anti-social behaviour, 69, 124, 158
Serotonin
   and negative effect of caffeine, 49
   and the link to anger and aggression, 67, 124
   and the link to GABA, 63
   and the link to wholegrains, 36
   and the negative effect of sugar, 66
   conflicting views of link to depression, 49, 75
   linked to exercise, 82
   manufactured in the guts, mainly, 23, 105
   negatively impacted by gluten, 53
Snacks
   as blood-sugar management, 131
   healthy types, 105
   mid morning and mid afternoon, 105
Starvation
   and the Minnesota experiments, 111–14
   in form of junk food dietl, 112
   nutritional deficiencies, and mental health, 111
Stress and anxiety diet
   by Jim Byrne, 95–107
Stress management
   advice, 41, 99, 101
   and inflammation, 116
   and lifestyle, 17
   and 'lifestyle medicine', 58–59
   and physical exercise, 86
   and Sopolsky on exercise, 129
   and vitamin and mineral supplements, 131
   mind and mood, 13
   water and body hydration, 44
Sugar
   and adequate blood sugar levels, 104
   and alcohol, 47
   and anger and aggression, 124
   and anxiety, 61, 63, 66, 124
   and blood-sugar management, 131
   and depression, 61, 75, 125
   and emotional disturbances, 112
   and mental illness, 72
   and physical and mental ill-health, 77
   and processed or junk food, 50
   and psychiatric symptoms, 110
   and stress, 101
   and the Anti-Candida diet, 30
   and the Atkins diet, 30
   and the FodMaps diet, 30
   and the Nordic diet, 35
   and the Okinawa diet, 36
   anger and anti-social behavioiur, 69
   anger and violence, 69
   as a body and mind toxin, 129
   as an enemy of the body-brain-mind, 120
   as cause of candida and depression, 97
   discussed by three doctors, 107
   in drinks linked to anxiety, 101
   in fruit smoothies are a problem, 102
   in green smoothies are a problem, 102
   in low-sugar vegetables, 131
   is a food to avoid, 46–47
   is a refined carbohydrate, 46
   miminize sugary foods, 28
Supplements
   a complete multivitamin complex, 98
   a range of perspectives, 54–60
   and nutritional deficiency, 69
   and omega-3 fatty acids, 33, 45
   and professional nutritional advice, 113
   and vegetarian diet, 38
   B-complex, 98
   evaluation, 122
   for anger, anxiety, depression, etc., 18
   for nutrition, Dr Leslie Korn, 17–19
   multivitamins and minerals, B-complex, omega-3, and Acidophilus, 98
   of friendly bacteria, for gut health, 21, 116
   the reasons for their usage, 26, 106
   vitamins B, C and E for stress, 39, 41, 99, 131

T

Trans-fats
   an overview, 44–46
   found in junk foods, 103
   how to avoid when cooking, 104
   linked to anger and aggression, 61, 69, 97, 99
   with sugar, linked to anger and depression, 112
Tse, Michael
   and training in Chi Kung, 10, 90, 91, 159

U

Unsaturated fats. *See* Fats and oils, unsaturated fats

V

Vegetables and fruit. *See* Fruit and vegetables
Vitamin and mineral supplements. *See* Supplements

definition of minerals, 27
definition of vitamins, 27
Vitamins B, C and E
   for stress, 39, 41, 99, 131

W

Water consumption. *See* Drinks and drinking
Weight training, 79
Wholegrains
   as proportion of diet, 31, 113
   in Parick Holford's optimum nutrition diet, 40, 42
   recommended gluten-free varieties, 18, 30, 37, 77, 113
   varieties to avoid
      wheat, rye, oats and barley, 18

Y

Yoga
   an overview, 22
   as a form of stress relief, 86
   as stretching and flexibility exercise, 79
   for anger management, 87, 88
   for anger, anxiety and depression treatment, 88
   for integrating emotional experiences, 89

Z

Zinc
   and the need for supplements, 99
   depleted by caffeine, 49, 121
   from food sources, 41
   plus a range of other minerals and vitamins needed, 111

Endnotes

[1] Campbell and Campbell (2006), *The China Study*.

[2] BDNF = "Brain-derived neurotrophic factor, also known as BDNF, is a protein that, in humans, is encoded by the BDNF gene. BDNF is a member of the neurotrophin family of growth factors, which are related to the canonical Nerve Growth Factor. Neurotrophic factors are found in the brain and the periphery."

"BDNF acts on certain neurons of the central nervous system and the peripheral nervous system, helping to support the survival of existing neurons, and encourage the growth and differentiation of new neurons and synapses. In the brain, it is active in the hippocampus, cortex, and basal forebrain—areas vital to learning, memory, and higher thinking." Source: https://en.wikipedia.org/wiki/Brain-derived_ neurotrophic _factor. Accessed: 4th October 2017.

~~~

[3] Gomez-Pinilla, F. (2008) 'The influences of diet and exercise on mental health through hormesis'. *Ageing Research Reviews. Volume 7, Issue 1, January 2008*, Pages 49-62. doi:10.1016/j.arr.2007.04.003. Early version (2007, in press) available online: http: //gettingstronger.org/wp-content/ uploads/ 2010/05 /Review-Hormesis-Diet-BDNF.pdf. (Hormesis is defined as: "the capacity of low doses of a potentially harmful stimulus to promote beneficial changes in adaptive plasticity" of body and brain cells).

[4] Atkinson, M. (2007) *The Mind Body Bible: Your personalised prescription for total health*. London: Piatkus Books.

[5] Korn, L. (2016). *Nutrition Essentials for Mental Health: A complete guide to the food-mood connection*. New York: W. W. Norton & Company. Summary: "This book is geared toward clinicians. It presents practical information on the complex interactions between the foods one eats and how they feel, think, and interface with the world around them. It seeks to provide the information clinicians need to provide nutritional counselling that will improve their clients' mental health and mood".

[6] McGovern, C. (2017) 'B-Calmed'. (An article on stress, anxiety and vitamins). *What Doctors Don't Tell You, July 2017*, pages 28-34. And:

Hoffer, A. (1970) 'Pellagra and Schizophrenia'. *Psychosomatics, Volume 11, Issue 5*, Pages 522-525. Available online: http://www.psychosomaticsjournal.com/article/S0033-3182(70)71623-X/pdf

~~~

[7] Microbiota: Collective term for microflora (i.e., any type of minute organism) that may be found within a given environment. For example, gut microbes; friendly and unfriendly organisms found in the human gut (and the guts of all animals).

[8] Source: Celiac.com: https://www.celiac.com/articles/23904/1/OatsDo-they-Contain-Gluten-Are-they-Safe-to-Eat/Page1.html

[9] Most Paleo diet theorists seem to be opposed to grains, and they have promoted the mantra that 'all grains cause inflammation'. But Michael Greger rejects this view.

For this reason, we went searching, online, for evidence that grains may or may not cause inflammation. We found a very interesting study - by Masters, Liese, Haffner, and colleagues (2010) - which looks at whole grain and refined grain intakes, and checks to see if they are related to inflammatory protein concentrations in human plasma (or blood samples). The bottom (rather technical) line was this:

"In summary, whole grain intake was inversely related to PAI-1 and CRP plasma concentrations, but these relationships were attenuated by the addition of metabolic variables to the model. Refined grain intake was positively independently related to plasma PAI-1 concentrations."

We believe this means: *When wholegrains were increased in the diet, two particular markers of inflammation were found to be reduced. This reduction, however, disappeared when some other relevant factors ('metabolic variables'), were factored in. On the other hand, when refined grains were increased in the diet, one of those markers of inflammation (PAI-1) was found to increase.*

This suggests that there may be a valid distinction to be made between **wholegrains** and **refined grains,** as causes of inflammation. So, eating wholegrain brown rice would be expected not to increase inflammation in the body, but eating **processed cereals** of any kind would. (However this might only apply to some people, and not to others. So find out for yourself if grains suit you, work for you, or cause you some physical or emotional problems.

Source: Masters, R. C., Liese, A. D., Haffner, S. M., Wagenknecht, L. E., & Hanley, A. J. (2010). 'Whole and Refined Grain Intakes Are Related to Inflammatory Protein Concentrations in Human Plasma'. *The Journal of Nutrition, 140(3), 587–594.* http://doi.org/10.3945/jn.109.116640

Next we went back to the books, and found some relevant research in Greger (2015). Dr Michael Greger begins by rejecting the online claims that all grains cause inflammation:

"Pick your indicator of inflammation", he writes. "Take C-reactive protein (CRP), for instance. CRP levels rise within the body in response to inflammatory insults, and are therefore used as a screening test for systemic inflammation. Each daily serving of whole grains is estimated to reduce CRP concentrations by approximately 7 percent". (Greger's footnote 8). "Furthermore, there's a whole alphabet soup of inflammation markers that appear to be improved by whole grains: ALT, GGT", (His footnote 9), "I:-6" (footnote 10), "IL-8" (FN 11), "IL-10" (FN 12), "IL-18" (FN13), "PAI-1" (FN14), "TNF-*a*", (FN15), "TNF-R2" (FN16), "whole blood viscosity, and erythrocyte filtration". (FN17). "Or, as presented in less technical terms in the American Journal of Clinical Nutrition, 'Whole-grain intake cools down inflammation'." (Footnote 18). "Even excluding heart disease and cancer, habitual wholegrain intake is linked to a significantly lower risk of dying from inflammatory disease". (Footnote 19). Source; Greger (2015; page 370).

Here are those ten footnotes, 8-19, from Greger (2015):

Greger's footnote 8: Lefevre, M.; Jonnalagadda, S. (2012) 'Effect of whole grains on markers of subclinical inflammation'. *Nutrition Review. 2012, 70,* 387–396, doi:10.1111/j.1753-4887.2012.00487.x.

(NB: We (Renata and Jim) took a look at the abstract of this paper by Lefevre and Jonnalagadda [2012] and found that the results were inconclusive, which weakens Dr Greger's overall argument to a dramatic degree. This is what we found: "... (the 13) Epidemiological studies provide reasonable support for an association between diets high in whole grains and lower C-reactive protein (CRP) concentrations. After adjusting for other dietary factors, each serving of whole grains is estimated to reduce CRP concentrations by approximately 7%. In contrast to epidemiological studies, (the 5) interventional studies do not demonstrate a clear effect of increased whole-grain consumption on CRP or other markers of inflammation". In other words, we have 13 studies that suggest a link between wholegrains and reduced inflammation, and 5 that do not. The case is far from proven! Indeed, we should reflect on this fact: The 13 studies which involve manipulating statistics, derived from self-report questionnaires, support Greger's argument; but the 5 that involve practical experiments to test the hypothesis all fail!)

Greger's FN 9: Montonen, J.; Boeing, H.; Fritsche, A.; Schleicher, E.; Joost, H.G.; Schulze, M.B.; Steffen, A.; Pischon, T. (2013) 'Consumption of red meat and whole-grain bread in relation to biomarkers of obesity, inflammation, glucose metabolism and oxidative stress'. *European Journal of Nutrition. 2013, 52*, 337–345, doi: 10.1007/s00394-012-0340-6.

(NB: According to the abstract of this paper: "...Vegan versus omnivorous diets tended to be associated with reduced risk (OR 0.89, 95% CI: 0.78–1.01, not statistically significant) while a lacto-ovo diet was associated with increased risk (OR 1.09, 95% CI: 1.01–1.18). In the incidence study, female gender, white ethnicity, higher education and BMI were predictors of hypothyroidism. Following a vegan diet tended to be protective (OR 0.78, 95% CI: 0.59–1.03, not statistically significant). In conclusion, a vegan diet tended to be associated with lower, not higher, risk of hypothyroid disease." This is not a straightforward proof that eating whole-grains will reduce inflammation *per se*. It may be that the research participants ate wholegrain bread as part of their diet; and they were less prone to hypothyroidism than those on a meat-milk omnivore diet. But again this is a relative gain, and not an absolute value. And again, this study was based on self-administered questionnaires, which lack verifiability, and are prone to subjectivity, and misreporting).

G FN 10: Goletzke, J, & Buyken, Anette & Joslowski, Gesa & Bolzenius, Katja & Remer, Thomas & Carstensen-Kirberg, Maren & Egert, et al. (2014). 'Increased Intake of Carbohydrates from Sources with a Higher Glycaemic Index and Lower Consumption of Whole Grain during Puberty Are Prospectively Associated with Higher IL-6 Concentrations in Younger Adulthood among Healthy Individuals'. *The Journal of Nutrition.* 144.10.3945/jn.114.193391.

G FN 11: Sofi, Francesco & Ghiselli, Lisetta & Cesari, Francesca & Gori, Anna Maria & Mannini, Lucia & Casini, Alessandro et al. (2010). 'Effects of Short-Term Consumption of Bread Obtained by an Old Italian Grain Variety on Lipid, Inflammatory, and Hemorheological Variables: An Intervention Study'. *Journal of Medicinal Food. 13.* 615-20. 10.1089/jmf.2009.0092.

(NB: This study seems to suggest that, if you switch from modern wheat to an older variety, inflammation goes down. This does not support Dr Greger's conclusion!)

G FN 12: Vitaglione, P., Ilario Mennella, Rosalia Ferracane, Angela A Rivellese, Rosalba Giacco, Danilo Ercolini, et al. (2015) 'Whole-grain wheat consumption reduces inflammation in a randomized controlled trial on overweight and obese subjects with unhealthy dietary and lifestyle behaviours: role of polyphenols bound to cereal dietary fibre'. *American Journal of Clinical Nutrition 2015; 101*: 251–61.

(NB: This is not saying much. If you switch somebody from a highly processed, junk-food diet to a wholegrain diet, they should show some signs of reduced inflammation. But that does not mean that if somebody went from their healthy, gluten-free diet to a wholegrain diet, they would reduce their inflammation!)

Greger's FN 13: Esposito, K., Francesco Nappo, Francesco Giugliano, Carmen Di Palo, Myriam Ciotola, Michelangela Barbieri, et al. (2003) 'Meal modulation of circulating interleukin 18 and adiponectin concentrations in healthy subjects and in patients with type 2 diabetes mellitus'. *American Journal of Clinical Nutrition 2003*; 78: 1135–40.

G FN 14: Masters, R. C., Liese, A. D., Haffner, S. M., Wagenknecht, L. E., & Hanley, A. J. (2010). 'Whole and Refined Grain Intakes Are Related to Inflammatory Protein Concentrations in Human Plasma'. *The Journal of Nutrition, 140(3),* 587–594. http://doi.org/10.3945/ jn.109.116640.

G FN 15: Same as 12 above: Vitaglione, P., Ilario Mennella, Rosalia Ferracane, Angela A Rivellese, Rosalba Giacco, Danilo Ercolini, et al. (2015) 'Whole-grain wheat consumption reduces inflammation in a randomized controlled trial on overweight and obese subjects with unhealthy dietary and lifestyle behaviours: role of polyphenols bound to cereal dietary fibre.' *American Journal of Clinical Nutrition 2015; 101:* 251–61.

(NB: This is not saying much. If you switch somebody from a highly processed, junk-food diet to a wholegrain diet, they should show some signs of reduced inflammation. But that does not mean that if somebody went from their healthy, gluten-free diet to a wholegrain [gluten-laden] diet, they would reduce their inflammation!)

Greger's FN 16. Qi, L., & van Dam, R.M., Liu, S., et al (2006) 'Whole-grain, bran, and cereal fibre intakes and markers of systemic inflammation in diabetic women.' *Diabetes Care. 29.* 207-11. 10.2337/diacare.29.02.06.dc05-1903.

(NB: This study was based on self-report questionnaires, which lack scientific validity and verifiability).

G FN 17. Same as 11 above: Sofi, Francesco & Ghiselli, Lisetta & Cesari, Francesca & Gori, Anna Maria & Mannini, Lucia & Casini, Alessandro et al. (2010). 'Effects of Short-Term Consumption of Bread Obtained by an Old Italian Grain Variety on Lipid, Inflammatory, and Hemorheological Variables: An Intervention Study'. *Journal of Medicinal Food. 13.* 615-20. 10.1089/jmf.2009.0092.

(NB: This study seems to suggest that, if you switch from modern wheat to an older variety, inflammation goes down. This does not support Dr Greger's conclusion!)

G FN 18: Esposito K, Giugliano D. (2006) 'Whole-grain intake cools down inflammation'. *American Journal of Clinical Nutrition 2006 Jun; 83(6):* 1440-1441.

(NB: Among Esposito and Giugliano's conclusions we found this: "...Increased consumption of high-density and low-quality foods, such as those rich in **refined grains** and poor in natural antioxidants and fibre, may cause an activation of the innate immune system, most likely by excessive production of proinflammatory cytokines associated with a reduced production of anti-inflammatory cytokines. This imbalance may favour the generation of an inflammatory milieu..." Which suggests that this field of study is concerned with showing how superior whole-grains are to refined grains (which is a **relative value**, and not an **absolute** value!); not at all considering how whole-grains compare with other foods/diets; and not at all looking at gluten! Again, this study does not particularly support Greger's strong position on grains).

Greger's FN 19: Jacobs DR, Andersen LF, Blomhoff R. (2007) 'Whole-grain consumption is associated with a reduced risk of noncardiovascular, noncancer death attributed to inflammatory diseases in the Iowa Women's Health Study'. *American Journal of Clinical Nutrition 2007; 85:* 1606–1614. Pmid: 17556700.

(NB: This study was based upon self-report questionnaires, and dealt with a whole range of foods in the diets of the participants, and evaluated those foods in terms of mortality rates after an average of 6.2 years. It was therefore impossible to separate out the effects of wholegrains from the other foods in the diets of these participants; and, as Jacobs et al admit: "...Given the observational study design, however, residual confounding cannot be completely ruled out." In other words, you cannot say the results are water-tight!)

But we have to watch out for the fact that some grains contain gluten and lectins which do cause inflammation, even in the wholegrain form! (Some of Greger's footnotes above seem to confirm this view).

And here is a source that we find particularly compelling evidence of the problem with gluten:

Punder, K. de, and Pruimboom, L. (2013) The Dietary Intake of Wheat and other Cereal Grains and Their Role in Inflammation. *Nutrients 2013, 5, 771-787;* doi: 10.3390/nu5030771. Available online: http://www.oalib.com/paper/2629517#.WgGOjFt-rcs. Accessed: 7th November 2017.

Here's the Abstract: "Wheat is one of the most consumed cereal grains worldwide and makes up a substantial part of the human diet. Although government-supported dietary guidelines in Europe and the U.S.A advise individuals to eat adequate amounts of (whole) grain products per day, cereal grains contain "anti-nutrients," such as wheat gluten and wheat lectin, that in humans can elicit dysfunction and disease. In this review we discuss evidence from in vitro, in vivo and human intervention studies that describe how the consumption of wheat, but also other cereal grains, can contribute to the manifestation of chronic inflammation and autoimmune diseases by increasing intestinal permeability and initiating a pro-inflammatory immune response."

So the takeaway message seems to be this:

Wholegrains and refined grains **which do contain gluten** – like wheat, rye, oats (which have been cross contaminated, and are not marked 'gluten free'), and barley, **will fairly reliably cause inflammation in the guts and bloodstream of the consumer**.

Wholegrains which are **gluten free**, most likely will **not** produce inflammation (or to a greatly reduced extent, since we also have to take account of lectins). This would include unprocessed whole-grain brown rice, unprocessed wholegrain teff, unprocessed whole-grain buckwheat (which is not a form of wheat!), unprocessed wholegrain amaranth, and some others.

But **refined grains** – which are what we get in processed cereal boxes, and in white bread, white pasta, and take-away meals – and much other processed foods - will most likely cause inflammation, **whether or not they are marked 'gluten free'**.

It's undeniably complex, but we can make some sense of it!

It may also be that gluten has become caught up in the 'diet wars', and everybody wants to claim that the science is complete: hence Greger's (2015) **ten sources** designed to prove that his position is verifiably true. However, the science is actually **in its infancy**, according to Catassi and colleagues (2013):

Catassi C, Bai J, Bonaz B, Bouma G, Calabrò A, Carroccio A, et al. (2013) 'Non-Celiac Gluten Sensitivity: The New Frontier of Gluten Related Disorders'. *Nutrients, 2013 Sep 26; 5(10):* 3839–3853. PMID 24077239 Available online: https://www.ncbi.nlm.nih.gov/pubmed/24077239. Accessed: 7th November 2017.

Here's the abstract from Catassi et al:

'Abstract

'Non Celiac Gluten Sensitivity (NCGS) was originally described in the 1980's and recently a "re-discovered" disorder characterized by intestinal and extra-intestinal symptoms related to the ingestion of gluten-containing food, in subjects that are not affected with either celiac disease (CD) or wheat allergy (WA). Although NCGS frequency is still unclear, epidemiological data have been generated that can help establishing the magnitude of the problem. Clinical studies further defined the identity of NCGS and its implications in human disease. An overlap between the irritable bowel syndrome (IBS) and NCGS has been detected, requiring even more stringent diagnostic criteria. Several studies suggested a relationship between NCGS and neuropsychiatric disorders, particularly autism and schizophrenia. The first case reports of NCGS in children have been described. Lack of biomarkers is still a major limitation of clinical studies, making it difficult to differentiate NCGS from other gluten related disorders. Recent studies raised the possibility that, beside gluten, wheat amylase-trypsin inhibitors and low-fermentable, poorly-absorbed, short-chain carbohydrates can contribute to symptoms (at least those related to IBS) experienced by NCGS patients. In this paper we report the major advances and current trends on NCGS'.

It may be quite some time before we (Renata and Jim) can say definitively what the overall linkages are between wheat, gluten, FodMaps, lectins, and other elements of this problematical, but clearly important, grain-gut-brain-mind conundrum. In the meantime, we will be staying away from gluten, and it looks like a growing percentage of the populations of the US, Australia and the UK are moving in the same direction, in the absence of clear scientific resolution. (The most conservative estimate that we've seen of the likely percentage of individuals who may be afflicted by neurological damage from gluten, which does not show any celiac symptoms in their guts, is about 26% [from Hadjivassiliou, 1996]). None of us can know if we are likely to be in that 26% (and it could be higher than 26%) so it would be foolhardy to ignore the risk!

~~~

[10] Foods that contain gluten – like wheat, rye, barley and contaminated oats – seem to cause inflammation: in the guts, in the case of celiac disease, and in the brain and central nervous system, in the case of Non-Celiac Gluten Sensitivity (NCGS). And we now know that inflammation is linked to the causation of depression, anxiety and other neurological problems. Therefore, it is not surprising to learn, from a major Danish longitudinal study, that people with a diagnosis of Celiac disease are almost twice as likely (1.91%, to be precise) to have problems with anxiety and/or depression, as a control group which has no autoimmune disease. Source: Benros and Waltoft et al (2013).

[11] Kaplan, B.J., Julia J. Rucklidge, Amy Romijn, and Kevin McLeod (2015) 'The Emerging Field of Nutritional Mental Health: Inflammation, the Microbiome, Oxidative Stress, and Mitochondrial Function'. *Clinical Psychological Science, Volume: 3 issue: 6,* Pages 964-980.

[12] Morris, N. (2017) 'One in eight skips meals to pay bills'. *The i newspaper,* Thursday 7th September 2017. Page 8.

[13] Definition of psychological trauma: "Trauma is an emotional response to a terrible event like an accident, rape or natural disaster. Immediately after the event, shock and denial are typical. Longer term reactions include unpredictable emotions, flashbacks, strained relationships and even physical symptoms like headaches or nausea. While these feelings are normal, some people have difficulty moving on with their lives. Psychologists can help these individuals find constructive ways of managing their emotions". Source: American Psychological Association (APA) website: http://www.apa.org/ topics/ trauma/. Accessed: 2nd October 2017.

[14] Enders, G. (2015) *Gut: The inside story of our body's most under-rated organ.* London: Scribe Publications. Pages 2-3.

[15] Dr Daniel Amen (2012) *Use your brain to change your life.* London: Piatkus.

[16] Edwards, M. (2014) 'The candida depression connection - How yeast leads to depression, anxiety, ADHD, and other mental disorders'. Available online at: https://www.naturalnews.com/047184_ candida_ depression_gut_microbes.html#

[17] Kris Carr; cited in: Pinnock, D. (2015) *Anxiety and Depression: Eat your way to better health.* London: Quadrille Publishing.

[18] Redfern, R. (2016) The importance of nutrition for mental health. *Naturally Healthy News, issue 30, 2016.*

[19] Dr Daniel Amen (2012) *Use your Brain to Change your Life.* London: Piatkus.

[20] Enders, G. (2015) *Gut: The inside story of our body's most under-rated organ.* Scribe Publications.

[21] Waite, M. (2012) *Paperback Oxford English Dictionary. Seventh edition*. Oxford: Oxford University Press.

[22] Brewer, S. (2013) *Nutrition: A beginners guide*. London: Oneworld Publications.

[23] "Protein is a macronutrient necessary for the proper growth and function of the human body. A deficiency in protein leads to muscle atrophy and impaired functioning of the human body in general.

"Athletes and those looking to build muscle might benefit from increased protein intake, but they should be aware of the risks. Excess protein is typically processed by the body, but may cause a strain on the liver and kidneys, and may also increase cancer risk (particularly from animal sources).

"The Daily Value (%DV) for protein is set at 50 grams per day, but individuals with more muscle mass may require more.

"Foods highest in protein per calorie include fish, cheese, turkey, chicken, lean beef, pork, tofu, yogurt, milk, beans, lentils, eggs, nuts, and seeds". Source: https://www.healthaliciousness.com/articles/foods-highest-in-protein.php

Protein is constructed in all plants, using nitrogen and carbon from the atmosphere and the soil. When those plants are eaten by animals, the proteins are concentrated in the animal muscle and animal products. But seeds, nuts and some vegetables are high in protein in their own right. Animal products are 'not essential', according to the China Study! But a 'low meat and other animals products' diet might be the most sensible compromise in terms of avoiding protein deficiency. But you have to find out for yourself, by experimentation, what works for your body!

~~~

[24] "Carbohydrates are found in almost all living things and play a critical role in the proper functioning of the immune system, fertilization, blood clotting, and human development. A deficiency of carbohydrates can lead to impaired functioning of all these systems, however, in the Western world, deficiency is rare. Excessive consumption of carbohydrates, especially refined carbohydrates like sugar or corn syrup, can lead to obesity, type II diabetes, and cancer. Unhealthy high carbohydrate foods include sugary cereals, crackers, cakes, flours, jams, preserves, bread products, refined potato products, and sugary drinks. Healthy high carbohydrate foods include vegetables, legumes (beans), whole grains, fruits, nuts, and yogurt. " Source: https://www.healthaliciousness.com/articles/foods-highest-in-carbohydrates.php

~~~

[25] "Fat is a type of nutrient, and just like protein and carbohydrates, your body needs some fat for energy, to absorb vitamins, and to protect your heart and brain health. Despite what you may have been told, fat isn't always the bad guy in the health and waistline wars. "Bad" fats, such as artificial trans-fats and saturated fats, are guilty of the unhealthy things all fats have been blamed for—weight gain, clogged arteries, and so forth. But "good" fats such as unsaturated fats and omega-3s have the opposite effect. In fact, healthy fats play a huge role in helping you manage your moods, stay on top of your mental game, fight fatigue, and even control your weight". Source: https://www.helpguide.org/articles/healthy-eating/choosing-healthy-fats.htm

~~~

[26] **Definition:** "Vitamins are nutrients your body needs to function and fight off disease. Your body cannot produce vitamins itself, so you must get them through food you eat or in some cases supplements. There are 13 vitamins that are essential to your body working well. Knowledge of the different types and understanding the purpose of these vitamins are important for good health.

"There are two types of vitamins: fat-soluble and water-soluble. Fat-soluble vitamins are stored in your fat cells, consequently requiring fat in order to be absorbed. Water-soluble vitamins are not stored in your body; therefore, they need to be replenished daily. Your body takes what it needs from the food you eat and then excretes what is not needed as waste. Here is a list of some vitamin types and common food sources:

"Fat-Soluble Vitamins

"Vitamin A - comes from orange coloured fruits and vegetables; dark leafy greens, like kale

Vitamin D - can be found in fortified milk and dairy products; cereals; (and of course, sunshine!)

Vitamin E - is found in fortified cereals; leafy green vegetables; seeds; nuts

Vitamin K - can be found in dark green leafy vegetables; turnip/beet greens

"Water-Soluble Vitamins:

Vitamin B1, or Thiamin - comes from whole grains; enriched grains; liver; nuts; seeds

Vitamin B2, or Riboflavin - comes from whole grains; enriched grains; dairy products

Vitamin B3, or Niacin - comes from meat; fish; poultry; whole grains

Vitamin B5, or Pantothenic Acid - comes from meat; poultry; whole grains

Vitamin B6, or Pyridoxine - comes from fortified cereals; soy products

Vitamin B7, or Biotin - is found in fruits; meats

Vitamin B9, or Folic Acid (Folate) - comes from leafy vegetables

Vitamin B12 - comes from fish; poultry; meat; dairy products

Vitamin C - comes from citrus fruits and juices, such as oranges and grapefruits; red, yellow, and green peppers".   Source: http://study.com/academy/lesson/what-are-vitamins-definition-types-purpose-examples.html. Accessed: 14th November 2017.

But because our food is largely denatured, and most people do not know what nutrients they are getting from their food, it makes sense to take a complete multivitamin, a B-complex, and extra vitamin C in supplement form, every day.

[27] "A list of minerals in foods may not necessarily include all of the minerals needed for health and wellness. There are 14 considered in the list below (which includes common minerals, like iron, copper, zinc, selenium, and so on – JWB). These 14 minerals are divided into two types: Macro minerals and trace minerals. A mineral is considered a macro mineral if your body requires over 100 mg of that particular element. Less than 100 mg and it's considered a trace element. Both types of minerals are important for health, but the body needs far greater amounts of macro minerals than trace minerals. The best source for both macro and trace minerals is whole foods containing plant digested minerals.

"The levels of all of minerals in foods vary depending on the nutrients of the soil where the food is grown. In the case of meats, the levels of minerals in the meat correspond directly to the amount of minerals contained in the plants that the animals have eaten." Source: http://www.wellness-with-natural-health-supplements.com/list-of-minerals-in-foods.html

[28] Source: The Good Animal blog, Available online at this address: https://good-animals.com/farm/chicken/should-you-be-eating-omega-3-fortified-eggs/7832/ Accessed: 6th November 2017

~~~

[29] See the following research papers, amongst others:

Shepherd SJ, Parker FJ, Muir JG and Gibson, PR (2008) 'Dietary triggers of abdominal symptoms in patients with irritable bowel syndrome - Randomised placebo-controlled evidence'. *Clinical Gastroenterology and Hepatology. 2008; 6(7):* 765-771:
http://www.sciencedirect.com/science/article/pii/S1542356508001511

Halmos, EP, Power, VA, Shepherd SJ, et al. (2014) 'A Diet Low in FODMAPs Reduces Symptoms of Irritable Bowel Syndrome'. *Gastroenterology, 2014; 146(1):* 67-75

Ong DK, Mitchell SB, Barrett JS, Shepherd SJ, Irving PI, Biesiekierski JR, Smith S, Gibson PR, Muir JG. (2010) 'Manipulation of dietary short chain carbohydrates alters the pattern of hydrogen and methane gas production and genesis of symptoms in patients with irritable bowel syndrome. *Journal of Gastroenterology and Hepatology. 2010 Aug; 25(8):* 1366-73

Barrett JS, Irving PM, Gearry R, Shepherd SJ, Gibson PR (2009) 'Comparison of the prevalence of fructose and lactose malabsorption across chronic intestinal disorders'. *Alimentary Pharmacology and Therapeutics, 2009; 30(2):* 165-74.

~~~

[30] See Grant and Joice (1984) *Food Combining for Health*.

[31] Alt Health (2017) 'Hay Diet'. A blog about food combining. Available online: https://www.althealth.co.uk/help-and-advice/diets/hay-diet/. Accessed: 11th October 2017.

[32] Julia Ross (2003) writes: "The rate of depression among individuals correlates precisely with the ratio of omega-3 fats to omega-6 in the brain". (Page 149).

[33] Here's the Mayo Clinic blog extract (2015):

"Here are five gluten-free whole grains, how to cook them and how to add them to your diet. Remember to aim for three servings of whole grains a day.

"**Amaranth:** About the size of a poppy seed, this pseudo-grain has a light peppery taste. Use 3 to 6 parts water to 1 part amaranth. Boil water, add grain and gently boil for 15 to 20 minutes. As it cooks, amaranth softens from the inside, releases a lot of starch and thickens the cooking liquid. Rinse cooked amaranth and let it drain before using. Use amaranth to thicken soups and stews. Add milk, fruit and a bit of honey for a healthy breakfast. You can even "pop" dried amaranth and make it into a granola-type bar.

"**Millet:** About the size of a small mustard seed, this grain has a mild flavour. Use 2 to 3 parts water to 1 part millet. Boil water, add grain and gently boil for 35 to 40 minutes. You may also "toast" millet in a hot pan before boiling to get a nuttier flavour. Top with cinnamon and peaches for breakfast. Or make a salad with halved grape tomatoes, radishes and chopped basil. Millet is also a great alternative to rice in casseroles, ground-meat dishes and stuffing.

"**Teff:** This smallest of grains is nutty and earthy in flavour. Use 3 parts water to 1 part teff. Boil water, add grain and simmer for 15 to 20 minutes. Its texture is like cream of wheat. Add cooked teff to soups or use teff as the main ingredient for polenta instead of cornmeal. Teff flour can be used to make pancakes.

"**Buckwheat:** Despite its name, buckwheat is not related to wheat. This-pseudo grain is pyramid shaped and known as kasha or buckwheat groats. To bring out its earthy flavour, cook 1 cup buckwheat with one egg in a large skillet over medium heat. Stir to keep from clumping until the mixture is dry and separated. Add 2 cups water or broth and cook uncovered over low heat for about 15 minutes. Mix cooked buckwheat with lentils, herbs and a bit of goat cheese. Or stuff peppers or acorn squash with cooked buckwheat. Buckwheat flour can be used to make pancakes.

"**Quinoa:** This pseudo-grain must be rinsed well before cooking to remove bitter-tasting saponins. You can also buy it pre-rinsed. The flavour is squash-like. Quinoa cooks in just 15 minutes. Use 2 parts water to 1 part quinoa. Mix with chopped fruit and drizzle with honey for breakfast. Or use quinoa instead of bulgur to make tabbouleh. Quinoa is also a good substitute for rice in rice pudding."

"Whether you are going gluten-free or not, these whole grains are good for you..."

Source: Nelson and Zeratsky (2015).

~~~

[34] Source: The Metabolic Typing Diet website: http://metabolictypingdiet.com/_Reat.htm

[35] Source: Christian Bates' blog about the Metabolic Typing diet: http://theperrymount.com/therapies/therapies/metabolictyping.html

[36] Source: http://www.goodtoknow.co.uk/wellbeing/440541/The-Nordic-Diet

[37] Source: The Woman and Home blog, available online at: http://www.womanandhome.com/galleries/diet-and-health/35358/3/0/the-nordic-diet

[38] Source: 'Preventing depression - can food rules help?' by Paula Goodyer. Online: http://www.smh.com.au/lifestyle/diet-and-fitness/preventing-depression--can-food-rules-help-20151022-gkfolu.html

[39] Korn (2016) and Eggers (2012).

[40] Source: Superfoods Scientific Research (2012) 'Phosphatidylserine Benefits and Side Effects'. Online: http://www.superfoods-scientific-research.com/natural-remedies/phosphatidylserine-benefits.html

[41] **Definition of legume**: "A legume is a plant or its fruit or seed in the family Fabaceae. Legumes are grown agriculturally, primarily for their grain seed called pulse, for livestock forage and silage, and as soil-enhancing green manure. Well-known legumes include alfalfa, clover, peas, beans, chickpeas, lentils, lupin bean, mesquite, carob, soybeans, peanuts and tamarind." (Source: Wikipedia).

[42] Tighe, Duthie, Vaughn and colleagues (2010).

[43] "What is the glycaemic index?" "The glycaemic index (GI) tells us whether a food raises blood glucose levels quickly, moderately or slowly. This means it can be useful to help you manage your diabetes. Different carbohydrates are digested and absorbed at different rates, and GI is a ranking of how quickly each carbohydrate-based food and drink makes blood glucose levels rise after eating them."

"The GI index runs from 0–100 and usually uses glucose, which has a GI of 100, as the reference. Slowly absorbed carbohydrates have a low GI rating (55 or below), and include most fruits and vegetables, milk, some wholegrain cereals and bread, pulses and basmati rice."

"Research has shown that choosing low-GI foods can particularly help manage glucose levels in people with Type 2 diabetes". And we have argued in this book that there is evidence that unmanaged blood-sugar level, resulting from eating too much high GI foods, damages mood control and emotion regulation.

~~~

[44] Michalak, Zhang and Jacobi, 2012, conducted a study of the link between vegetarian diet and mental disorders, because there is "...relatively little data... available on the associations between vegetarian diet and mental health". However, their study, in Germany, based on more than 4,000 participants, failed to find a positive correlation between vegetarianism and mental illness.

Here are their results and conclusions:

"Results: Vegetarians displayed elevated prevalence rates for depressive disorders, anxiety disorders and somatoform disorders. Due to the matching procedure, the findings cannot be explained by socio-demographic characteristics of vegetarians (e.g. higher rates of females, predominant residency in urban areas, and high proportion of singles). The analysis of the respective ages at adoption of a vegetarian diet and onset of a mental disorder showed that the adoption of the vegetarian diet tends to follow the onset of mental disorders.

"Conclusions: In Western cultures vegetarian diet is associated with an elevated risk of mental disorders. However, there was no evidence for a causal role of vegetarian diet in the etiology of mental disorders."

~~~

[45] Arachidonic acid (AA [or ARA]): A liquid unsaturated fatty acid that occurs in most animal fats and some vegetable oils. It's a precursor of prostaglandins, and is considered essential in animal nutrition, including human nutrition. ARA is a form of omega-6 fatty acid. And although we need ARA, getting too much "could be problematic". (Erin Coleman, 2017). It seems we need both omega-6 and omega-3 fatty acids in our diets, in roughly equal proportions; but too much omega-6 causes (too much) inflammation, which is the basis of most chronic disease, and is also linked to depression and perhaps also to anxiety and anger, etc. The biochemistry of ARA, and omega-6/omega-3 is very complex, and highly contested, and unresolved at this point (2017) in time.

[46] Watch the movie: 'All Jacked Up': The explosive junk food documentary the food companies hope you never see; by Mike Adams, 2008: https://www.naturalnews.com/022510.html

[47] And see also Morgan Spurlock's documentary - ('Super Size Me', 2004) - about trying to live on McDonald's burgers for 30 days, and the medically confirmed negative impact on his physical and mental health! Source: http://watchdocumentaries.com/super-size-me/. Accessed: 21st November 2017.

[48] Coenzyme Q10 may be important for general health. According to the Mayo Clinic: "Coenzyme Q10 (CoQ10) is an antioxidant that your body produces naturally. Your cells use CoQ10 for growth and maintenance.

"Levels of CoQ10 in your body decrease as you age. CoQ10 levels have also been found to be lower in people with certain conditions, such as heart disease.

"CoQ10 is found in meat, fish and whole grains. The amount of CoQ10 found in these dietary sources, however, isn't enough to significantly increase CoQ10 levels in your body.

"As a supplement, CoQ10 supplement is available as capsules, tablets and by IV. CoQ10 might help treat certain heart conditions, as well as migraines and Parkinson's disease." Source: https://www.mayoclinic.org/ drugs-supplements- coenzyme-q10/ art-20362602. Accessed: 30th October 2017.

~~~

[49] According to NHS choices: "Probiotics (like Acidophilus) are live bacteria and yeasts promoted as having various health benefits. They're usually added to yoghurts or taken as food supplements, and are often described as 'good' or 'friendly' bacteria.

"Probiotics are thought to help restore the natural balance of bacteria in your gut (including your stomach and intestines) when it has been disrupted by an illness or treatment." (Source: https://www.nhs.uk/Conditions/probiotics/Pages/Introduction.aspx. Accessed: 30th October 2017.

According to Enders (2015) changing the variety of live bacteria in the guts of lab mice can change their behaviour so radically that it is thought they could change character and temperament (in human terms)." And gut bacteria have been shown to be involved in communication between the gut and the brain in humans. (Enders, 2015).

~~~

[50] Cunningham, J. B. (2001) *The Stress Management Sourcebook. Second edition*. Los Angeles: Lowell House.

[51] Yu, W. (2012) High trans-fat diet predicts aggression: People who eat more hydrogenated oils are more aggressive. *Scientific American Mind*, July 2012. Available online: http://www.scientificamerican.com/article/high-trans-fat-diet-predicts-aggresion/

[52] Stress Management Society (2012/2016) 'Nutritional stress and health': The "Think 'nervous'" box. Available online: http://www.stress.org.uk/Diet-and-nutrition.aspx

[53] Dr Michael Greger quotes the following paper in defence of his view that vegetarian diets are better for emotional health:

Beezhold, B. L., Johnston, C. S., & Daigle, D. R. (2010) 'Vegetarian diets are associated with healthy mood states: a cross-sectional study in Seventh Day Adventist adults'. *Nutrition Journal*, 9, 26. http://doi.org/10.1186/1475-2891-9-26

[54] Perretta, L. (2001) *Brain Food: the essential guide to boosting brain power*. London: Hamlyn.

[55] Cordain, L. (2011) *The Paleo Diet Cookbook*. Hoboken, NJ: John Wiley and Sons.

[56] Fife, B. (2005) *Coconut Cures: Preventing and treating common health problems with coconut*. Colorado Springs, CO: Piccadilly Books Ltd.

[57] Andrew (2017) 'Grains and Inflammation: What is the relationship between grains and inflammation?' the PaleoMunch! Blog. Available online at: http://paleomunch.com/the-paleo-diet/grains-and-inflammation/. Accessed: 4th October 2017.

[58] "What is the Whole30?" "Founded by Melissa Hartwig (and Dallas Hartwig) in April 2009, the Whole30® is designed to change your life in 30 days. Think of it as a short-term nutrition reset, designed to help you put an end to unhealthy cravings and habits, restore a healthy metabolism, heal your digestive tract, and balance your immune system".

"Certain food groups (like sugar, grains, dairy and legumes) could be having a negative impact on your health and fitness without you even realizing it. Are your energy levels inconsistent or non-existent? Do you have aches and pains that can't be explained by over-use or injury? Are you having a hard time losing weight no matter how hard you try? Do you have some sort of condition (like skin issues, digestive ailments, seasonal allergies or fertility issues) that medication hasn't helped? These symptoms may be directly related to the foods you eat—even the "healthy" stuff."

Source: https://whole30.com/step-one/

~~~

[59] St. Pierre, B. (2017) 'Settling the great grain debate. Can wheat and other grains fit into a healthy — and sane — diet?' Precision Nutrition Blog. Online: http://www.precisionnutrition.com/grain-wheat-debate. Accessed: 4th October 2017.

~~~

[60] "What Is Candida Albicans?" "Candida Albicans is an opportunistic fungus (or form of yeast) that is the cause of Candida Related Complex and many undesirable symptoms including fatigue, weight gain, joint pain, and gas." "The Candida Albicans yeast is a normal part of your gut flora, a group of microorganisms that live in your digestive tract."

"Most people have some level of Candida Albicans in their intestines, and usually it coexists peacefully with the other bacteria and yeasts that live there. But a combination of factors can lead to the Candida Albicans population getting out of control, establishing fast growing colonies and biofilms, and starting to dominate your gut." Source: https://www.thecandidadiet.com/what-is-candida-albicans/

~~~

"When toxic Candida by-products enter the bloodstream, they can affect the brain. This yeast toxin hypersensitivity has a number of negative neurological effects.

"Some of those effects are: memory issues, anxiety and reduction in reasoning ability. In order to get relief, the Candida needs to be controlled and minimized.

"Dealing with Depression" "Since depression can be directly caused by Candida, you should start on one of the Candida elimination programs. Both programs use a multi-step program to get the Candida under control." Source: http://www.candida-albicans-cure.com/depression.html

~~~

[61] Stress Management Society (2012/2016) Nutritional stress and health: The "Think 'nervous'" box. Available online: http://www.stress.org.uk/Diet-and-nutrition.aspx

[62] Source: http://annewigmore.org

[63] Stanfield, M. (2008) *Trans Fat: The Time Bomb in your Food: The Killer in the Kitchen*. Souvenir Press: London.

[64] **Definition of inflammation**: A localized physical condition, normally inside the body, in which part of the body becomes reddened, swollen, hot, and often painful, especially as a reaction to injury or infection. Inflammation may be responsible for most serious modern diseases. And inflammation can be caused in the guts by grains, dairy, legumes, and other apparently 'harmless' foods.

[65] 'A study performed at the University of California surveyed 945 men and women about their trans-fat intake, as well as their levels of aggression. When the survey results were adjusted for outlying factors,

such as age and use of alcohol and tobacco, researchers found a strong link between aggressive behaviour and the consumption of high levels of trans fats.'

'Lead author Beatrice Golumb says, "We found that greater trans fatty acids were associated with greater aggression. This adds further rationale to recommendations to avoid eating trans fats as their detrimental effects may extend beyond the person who consumes them."

'The connection between trans fats and anger is thought to have to do with their inhibition of the body's ability to metabolize omega-3 fatty acids. Past studies have linked a lack of omega-3 with antisocial behaviour and depression, so the anger connection is not too surprising.' Sources: A University of California study, cited here: http://www.thealternativedaily.com/pissed-off-all-the-time-study-says-it-could-be-trans-fats/. And here:
http://www.theguardian.com/lifeandstyle/wordofmouth/2013/apr/24/can-food-make-you-angry - Accessed: 11th June 2016

~~~

[66] Mercola, J. (2010) Scientists Unlock How Trans Fats Harm Your Arteries. (Health Blog). Available online: http://articles.mercola.com/sites/articles/archive/2010/11/16/scientists-unlock-how-trans-fats-harm-your-arteries.aspx. Accessed: 20th May 2016.

[67] Ross, J. (2002) *The Mood Cure: Take charge of your emotions in 24 hours using food and supplements.* London: Thorsons.

[68] Amen, D.G. (2013) *Use Your Brain to Change your Age: Secrets to look, feel, and think younger every day.* London: Piatkus.

[69] According to Adda Bjarnadottir, MS, an online nutritionist: "Refined carbs have been stripped of almost all fibre, vitamins and minerals. For this reason, they can be considered as "empty" calories. They are also digested quickly, and have a high glycaemic index. This means that they lead to rapid spikes in blood sugar and insulin levels after meals" which is very bad for our physical health and emotional well-being. (Source: Authority Nutrition - An Evidence-Based Approach (an online blog). Blog title: 'Why Refined Carbs Are Bad For You'. By Adda Bjarnadottir, MS | September, 2015. Available online: https://authoritynutrition.com/why-refined-carbs-are-bad/. Accessed: 10th June 2016

[70] Boyd, D.B. (2003) Insulin and Cancer. *Integrative Cancer Therapies. Dec 2003. Vol. 2 (4):* Pages 315-329.

[71] Collagen is the most abundant protein in the human body and is the substance that holds the whole body together. It is found in the bones, muscles, skin and tendons, where it forms a scaffold to provide strength and structure.

[72] **Definition of adrenaline (or 'epinephrine' in the US):** "...a substance that is released in the body of a person who is feeling a strong emotion (such as excitement, fear, or anger) and that causes the heart to beat faster and gives the person more energy". It helps to fuel the fight or flight response.

[73] Patrick Holford (2010) *Optimum Nutrition for the mind.* London: Piatkus.

[74] Natural Health 365: *The link between gum disease and Alzheimer's.* Available online at: http://www.naturalhealth365.com/alzheimers-disease-oral-health-1552.html Accessed 20th May 2016

[75] Perricone, N. (2002) *Dr Nicolas Perricone's Programme: Grow young, get slim, in days.* London: Thorsons.

[76] NHS (2007) NHS Quality Improvement Scotland, Understanding alcohol misuse in Scotland: Harmful drinking 3 – Alcohol and self-harm'. 2007. Available online at: http://bit.ly/TbBYAX. Accessed: 28th May 2016.

[77] **Definition of alkaloid:** "Any of a class of nitrogenous organic compounds of plant origin which have pronounced physiological actions on humans. They include many drugs (morphine, quinine) and poisons (atropine, strychnine)." Source: http://www.oxforddictionaries.com/definition/english/alkaloid#alkaloid__2. Accessed: 11th June 2016.

[78] Ephedra and Ma Huang are used in widely banned or restricted supplements which are used as 'diet pills' and in illegal weight training and sports training (and which are banned by the International Olympic committee). These substances mimic adrenaline in speeding up the cardiovascular system (or heart and lungs), and (potentially) creating feelings of anxiety.

[79] Van der Veen, F. M., Evers, E.A.T., Deutz, N.E.P., Schmitt, J.A.J. (2006) Effects of Acute Tryptophan Depletion on Mood and Facial Emotion Perception Related Brain Activation and Performance in Healthy Women with and without a Family History of Depression. *Neuropsychopharmacology, Vol.32, Issue 1*, Pages 216-224.

[80] Christensen, L. (1991) The roles of caffeine and sugar in depression, *The Nutrition Report 1991*: 9(5 Pt.1): Pages 691-698. Quoted by Ross (2002; page 135).

[81] Gilliland, K. and Andress, D. (1981) Ad Lib caffeine consumption, symptoms of caffeinism and academic performance. *American Journal of Psychiatry, Vol 138 (4),* Pages. 512-514.

[82] **Definitions of junk food:** 1. "Pre-prepared or packaged food that has low nutritional value". Source: Google search for 'junk food'. Or: 2. "Food that is not good for your health because it contains high amounts of fat or sugar": (Merriam-Webster Dictionary). Or 3. "Food that is high in calories but low in nutritional content" (Merriam-Webster Dictionary). Online Merriam-Webster Dictionary: http://www.merriam-webster.com/ dictionary/ junk%20food. Accessed: 11th June 2016.

[83] Lawrence, F. (2004) *Not on the Label: What really goes into the food on your plate.* London: Penguin Books.

[84] Daily Mail (2016) Don't eat our pasta sauce more than once a week. Pages 1 and 2, Friday April 15th (2016).

[85] Coffman, M.A. (2016) The Disadvantages of Junk Food. A blog post at the 'Healthy Eating' website. Available online at this url: http://healthyeating.sfgate.com/ disadvantages-junk-food-1501.html. Accessed: 30th April 2016.

[86] Hadjivassiliou, M., & A. Gibson, & G.A.B. Davies-Jones & A.J. Lobo, et al (1996) 'Does cryptic gluten sensitivity play a part in neurological illness?' The Lancet, Volume 347, Issue 8998, 10 February 1996, Pages 369-371

Hadjivassiliou, M., & David S Sanders, Richard A. Grünewald, et al (2010) 'Gluten sensitivity: from gut to brain'. The Lancet Neurology, Volume 9, Issue 3, Pages 318 - 330.

(Extract from summary: "Although neurological manifestations in patients with established coeliac disease have been reported since 1966, it was not until 30 years later that, in some individuals, gluten sensitivity was shown to manifest solely with neurological dysfunction. Furthermore, the concept of extra-intestinal presentations without enteropathy has only recently become accepted.") This means...

This means that neurological damage can be caused by gluten, without leaving any traces in the gut! So, seeking a diagnosis of celiac disease, or freedom from this disease, does not mean you can then safely eat foods containing gluten!

~~~

One of the 20 sources cited by Dr David Perlmutter (2014) was this one:

Ford, R.P.K. (2009) 'The gluten syndrome: A neurological disease'. *Medical Hypotheses, Volume 73, Issue 3*: Pages 438 - 440.

Here is the summary of Ford's paper on the gluten syndrome:

"Summary

"Hypothesis: Gluten causes symptoms, in both celiac disease and non-celiac gluten-sensitivity, by its adverse actions on the nervous system.

"Many celiac patients experience neurological symptoms, frequently associated with malfunction of the autonomic nervous system. These neurological symptoms can present in celiac patients who are well nourished. The crucial point, however, is that gluten-sensitivity can also be associated with neurological symptoms in patients who do not have any mucosal gut damage (that is, without celiac disease).

"Gluten can cause neurological harm through a combination of cross reacting antibodies, immune complex disease and direct toxicity. These nervous system affects include: dysregulation of the autonomic nervous system, cerebella ataxia, hypotonia, developmental delay, learning disorders, depression, migraine, and headache.

"If gluten is the putative harmful agent, then there is no requirement to invoke gut damage and nutritional deficiency to explain the myriad of the symptoms experienced by sufferers of celiac disease and gluten-sensitivity. This is called "The Gluten Syndrome"."

~~~

And here are another 14 relevant sources:

Di Sabatino, A and Corazza, GR. (2009) 'Coeliac disease'. Lancet. 2009; 373: 1480–1493

Hadjivassiliou, M, Williamson, CA, and Woodroofe, N. (2004) The immunology of gluten sensitivity: beyond the gut. Trends Immunol. 2004; 25: 578–582

Hadjivassiliou, M, Sanders, DS, Grünewald, RA, Woodroofe, N, Boscolo, S, and Aeschlimann, D. (2010) 'The neurology of gluten sensitivity'. Lancet Neurol. 2010; 9: 330–342

Gobbi, G, Bouquet, F, Greco, L et al. (1992) 'Coeliac disease, epilepsy and cerebral calcifications'. Lancet. 1992; 340: 439–443

Volta, U, De Giorgio, R, Petrolini, N et al. (2002) 'Clinical findings and anti-neuronal antibodies in coeliac disease with neurological disorders'. Scand J Gastroenterol. 2002; 37: 1276–1281

Hadjivassiliou, M, Gibson, A, Davies-Jones, GAB, Lobo, A, Stephenson, TJ, and Milford-Ward, A. (1996) 'Is cryptic gluten sensitivity an important cause of neurological illness?' Lancet. 1996; 347: 369–371

Lock, RJ, Tengah, DS Pengiran, Unsworth, DJ, Ward, JJ, and Wills, AJ. (2005) 'Ataxia, peripheral neuropathy, and anti-gliadin antibody. Guilt by association?' J Neurol Neurosurg Psychiatry. 2005; 76: 1601–1603

Volta, U, Granito, A, Parisi, C et al. (2009) 'De-amidated gliadin peptide antibodies as a routine test for celiac disease: a prospective analysis'. J Clin Gastroenterol. 2009;

Hadjivassiliou, M, Aeschlimann, P, Strigun, A, Sanders, DS, Woodrofe, N, and Aeschlimann, D. (2008) 'Autoantibodies in gluten ataxia recognise a novel neuronal trans-glutaminase'. Ann Neurol. 2008; 64: 332–343

Koskinen, O, Collin, P, Lindfors, K, Laurila, K, Mäki, M, and Kaukinen, K. (2009) 'Usefulness of small-bowel mucosal transglutaminase-2 specific autoantibody deposits in the diagnosis and follow-up of celiac disease'. J Clin Gastroenterol. 2009;

Karell, K, Louka, AS, Moodie, SJ et al. (2003) 'HLA types in celiac disease patients not carrying the DQA1*05-DQB1*02 (DQ2) heterodimer: results from the European Genetics Cluster on Celiac Disease'. Hum Immunol. 2003; 64: 469–477

Volta, U, De Giorgio, R, Granito, A et al. (2006) 'Anti-ganglioside antibodies in coeliac disease with neurological disorders'. Dig Liver Dis. 2006; 38: 183–187

Cervio, E, Volta, U, Verri, M et al. (2007) 'Sera from patients with celiac disease and neurologic disorders evoke a mitochondrial-dependent apoptosis in vitro'. Gastroenterology. 2007; 133: 195–206

Hadjivassiliou, M, Mäki, M, Sanders, DS et al. (2006) Autoantibody targeting of brain and intestinal transglutaminase in gluten ataxia. Neurology. 2006; 66: 373–377

~~~

[87] Leaky gut allows whole molecules to pass through the gut wall and cause inflammation throughout the body. But what is the link between leaky gut and the blood/brain barrier?

"Gluten sensitivity research identifies a connection between gluten induced leaky gut, and leaky brain. The ramifications of these findings are important to understand the broad scope of the impact gluten has in many diseases.

"We were able to identify an intestinal Zot analogue, which we named **zonulin**. It is conceivable that the zonulins participate in the physiological regulation of intercellular tj (tight junctions) not only in the small intestine, but also throughout a **wide range of extraintestinal epithelia as well as the ubiquitous vascular endothelium, including the blood-brain barrier.** Dysregulation of this hypothetical zonulin model may contribute to disease states that involve disordered intercellular communication, including developmental and intestinal disorders, tissue inflammation, malignant transformation, and metastasis.

Sources: *Journal of Pediatric Gastroenterology and Nutrition.* 2010 Oct; 51(4):418-24. And:

Annals of the New York Academy of Sciences. 2000; 915: Pages 214-222.

You can read more at: https://www.glutenfreesociety.org/leaky-gut-leaky-brain-gluten-is-an-equal-opportunity-destroyer/#7gRJBhGGWIVEj6iX.99

~~~

[88] Source: https://www.agmrc.org/commodities-products/grains-oilseeds/wheat/; which seems to suggest that 60% of US wheat production is of the hard red variety, which has a higher gluten content!

[89] Online source: http://www.nhs.uk/conditions/vitamins-minerals/Pages/vitamins-minerals.aspxx. Accessed 4th May 2016

Mercola, J. (2013) Vitamin D — One of the Simplest Solutions to Wide-Ranging Health Problems. Available online: http://articles.mercola.com/sites/articles/archive/2013/12/22/dr-holick-vitamin-d-benefits.aspx. Accessed 15 June 2016.

[91] Food Standards Agency (2004) 'National Diet & Nutrition Survey: Adults aged 19 to 64'. Volume 5.

[92] Ballantyne, C. (2007) 'Fact or Fiction?: Vitamin Supplements Improve Your Health'. *Scientific American* (Online): http://www.scientificamerican.com/article/fact-or-fiction-vitamin-supplements-improve-health/ May 17, 2007. Accessed 26th April 2016.

[93] Benton, D. and G Roberts (1988) Effects of vitamin and mineral supplementation on intelligence in schoolchildren. *The Lancet, Vol 1 (8578),* Pages 140-143.

[94] "...**amino acids** in food make up protein. When protein is digested it is once again broken down into specific amino acids that are then selectively put together for different uses. These new proteins formed in the body are what make up most solid matter in the body: skin, eyes, heart, intestines, bones and, of course, muscle." Source: https://www.bodybuilding.com/fun/catamino.htm

And one of those amino acids, tryptophan, is helpful in reducing depression, and indeed, tryptophan used to be used for that purpose by physicians before antidepressant drugs, (like SSRI's), were marketed into medical practices.

~~~

[233] Goldacre, B. (2007) Patrick Holford's untruthful and unsubstantiated claims about pills: http://www.badscience.net/2007/09/patrick-holdford-unsubstantiated-untruthful/ Accessed 14th April 2016.

[96] Goldacre, B. (2012) *Bad Pharma: How drug companies mislead doctors and harm patients.* London: Fourth Estate.

[97] Perlmutter, D. (2015) *Brain Maker: The power of gut microbes to heal and protect your brain – for life.* London: Hodder and Stoughton.

[98] **Definition of probiotics**: 'Probiotics are live bacteria and yeasts that are good for your health, especially your digestive system. We usually think of bacteria as something that causes diseases. But your body is full of bacteria, both good and bad. Probiotics are often called "good" or "helpful" bacteria because they help keep your gut healthy.' (By Mary Jo DiLonardo. WebMD Feature. Available online: http://www.webmd.com/digestive-disorders/features/what-are-probiotics. Accessed 12th June 2016)

What is BDNF? "Brain-derived neurotrophic factor, also known as BDNF, is a protein that, in humans, is encoded by the BDNF gene. BDNF is a member of the neurotrophin family of growth factors, which are related to the canonical Nerve Growth Factor. Neurotrophic factors are found in the brain and the periphery." Source: https://en.wikipedia.org/wiki/Brain-derived_neurotrophic_factor).

Furthermore: "When BDNF levels are high, acquiring new knowledge is easy, memories are retained, and people feel happier. Indeed, BDNF can even be thought of as a natural anti-depressant." (Dr John Day's blog: http://drjohnday.com/10-ways-to-boost-brain-function-with-bdnf/)

~~~

[100] Written on 5 Jun 2015 by Max Kohanzad. For more by Max, please see Max's web page, here: http://max.coach/happiness-diet-hack/

[101] Byrne, J.W. (2016) *Holistic Counselling in Practice: An introduction to the theory and practice of Emotive-Cognitive Embodied-Narrative Therapy.* Hebden Bridge: The Institute for E-CENT Publications.

In particular, see the Holistic SOR model, in Byrne (2016), which lists several factors which affect the ability of the human organism to cope with environmental stressors.

~~~

[102] Hayes, N. (2003) *Applied Psychology (Teach Yourself Books)*. London: Hodder and Stoughton.

[103] Pinnock, D. (2015) *Anxiety and Depression: Eat your way to better health*. London: Quadrille Publishing Ltd.

[104] Kiecolt-Glaser, J.K., Belury M.A., Andridge, R., Malarkey, W.B., Glaser, R. (2011) Omega 3 supplementation lowers inflammation and anxiety in medical students: a randomised, controlled trial. *Brain, Behaviour, Immunity, Vol.25 (8)*. Pages 1725-1734

[105] Perretta, L. (2001) *Brain Food: the essential guide to boosting brain power*. London: Hamlyn.

[106] Lazarides, L. (2002) *Treat Yourself: With nutritional therapy*. London: Waterfall 2000.

[107] "The **blood glucose level** is the amount of **glucose** in the **blood**. **Glucose** is a **sugar** that comes from the foods we eat, and it's also formed and stored inside the body. It's the main source of energy for the cells of our body, and it's carried to each cell through the bloodstream". (Source: Google search). "Blood sugar that is too high or too low can make you very sick. Here's how to handle these emergencies." WebMD blog: http://www.webmd.com/diabetes/blood-sugar-levels).

[108] Unrefined carbohydrates: "Carbohydrates are essential nutrients that are responsible for the production of energy in the body. They form part of the three main macronutrients, which also include proteins and fats. While carbohydrates are commonly classified into simple and complex carbohydrates, they can also be categorized as unrefined and refined carbohydrates. Refined carbohydrates are ones that have been processed or altered with the addition of artificial chemicals and sugars, and their natural nutrients such as fibres, vitamins and minerals have been reduced or eliminated. Unrefined carbohydrates are in their natural state, and they contain all the naturally occurring nutrients that are beneficial to the body.

"Unrefined Carbohydrates" - "Unrefined carbohydrates are rich in fibre, vitamins and minerals, which are necessary for the production of energy in the human body. Natural food fibre is responsible for maintaining healthy blood sugar levels, and it acts as a barrier to the digestive system by controlling appetite. The recommended daily intake of natural fibre is between 20 to 45 grams. This amount of fibre can only be found in unrefined carbohydrates, especially wholegrain bread and cereals. Other examples that contain unrefined carbohydrates include brown rice, beans, oatmeal, bran cereal, millet, barley, couscous, wheat, vegetables, lentils, herbs, lamb, poultry and other wholegrain products.

"The consumption of unrefined carbohydrates is highly recommended due to their high nutritional value. When buying foods in a store or supermarket, you should choose products that have a high percentage of fibre and minerals. When selecting cereals and bread, the ingredients should include wholegrain or whole wheat." (But watch out for gluten intolerance. Source: http://www.fitday.com/fitness-articles/nutrition/carbs/the-difference-between-unrefined-and-refined-carbohydrates.html

[109] Refined carbohydrates: "Refined carbohydrates have undergone manufacturing or repackaging processes, and they are the worst form of carbs available. Moreover, some refined carbohydrates contain dangerous chemicals that may spike the blood sugar levels and trigger other health problems.

"Refined carbohydrates do not contain the necessary nutrients that are beneficial to your health. Despite the fact that they have a sweet taste and are delightful to consume, they have very low nutritional value. These products will cause more harm than good to the body. Research shows that consumption of refined products is the leading cause of diseases and disorders such as obesity, heart disease, diabetes and cardiovascular problems.

"The main problem associated with refined carbohydrates is that artificial sugar products are often added in abundance. These additives are not only addictive, but they're also detrimental to the general health of the body, and therefore, it's best that you refrain from consuming high quantities. Examples of food products that contain refined carbohydrates include packaged cereals, white bread, white rice, pasta, cakes, biscuits, sweets, candy, pastries, pies, white flour, beer, sweet white wine, sherry and many others.

"In comparison, unrefined carbohydrates take a much longer time to be absorbed by the body than refined carbohydrates. This is because refined carbs contain a lot of sugar, which makes them easier for the body to absorb. Other than containing beneficial natural nutrients, unrefined carbohydrates are also known to be the best source of sustainable energy." Refined carbs are linked to mood disorders. Source: http://www.fitday.com/fitness-articles/nutrition/carbs/the-difference-between-unrefined-and-refined-carbohydrates.html

~~~

[110] Dr Michael Greger (2015) argues against high-meat diets, in favour of high whole grains, beans, nuts and seeds. Cut down on all meats, he says, including white meats, and eat lots more plants (meaning vegetables and fruit):

Greger, M. (2015) *How not to Die: Discover the foods scientifically proven to prevent and reverse disease*. London: Macmillan.

[111] Bravo, J.A., P. Forsythe, M.V. Chew, E. Escaravage, H.M. Savignac, T.G. Dinan, J. Bienenstock, and J.F. Cryan (2011) Ingestion of Lactobacillus strain regulates emotional behaviour and central GABA receptor expression in a mouse via the vagus nerve. PNAS 2011 108 (38) 16050-16055; published ahead of print. August 29, 2011, doi:10.1073/pnas.1102999108

[112] Schmidt, K., Cowen, P.J., Harmer, C.J., Tzortzis, G., Errington, S., and Burnet, P.W. (2014) Prebiotic intake reduces the waking cortisol response and alters emotional bias in healthy volunteers. *Psychopharmacology* (Berl.) (December 3rd 2014) [Epub ahead of print]

[113] "Gluten is the number one cause of leaky gut. Other inflammatory foods like dairy, or toxic foods, such sugar and excessive alcohol, are suspected as well. The most common infectious causes are candida overgrowth, intestinal parasites, and small intestine bacterial overgrowth (SIBO)" (Source: 9 Signs you have a leaky gut, by Dr Amy Myers, Mindbodygreen Blog: http://www.mindbodygreen.com/0-10908/9-signs-you-have-a-leaky-gut.html. Accessed: 13th June 2016). And:

"NSAIDs (like Ibuprofen) can damage your gut lining, causing a condition responsible for a whole range of ailments, from allergies to autoimmune disease. It's called leaky gut." (Source: 5 Steps to Heal a Leaky Gut Caused By Ibuprofen, by Aviva Romm, Practicing Family Physician. *Huffpost Healthy Living*: Available online: http://www.huffingtonpost.com/aviva-romm/5-steps-to-heal-a-leaky-g_b_5617109.html. Accessed: 13th June 2016)

~~~

[114] Sansouci, J. (2011) Nutrition and anxiety. Healthy Crush Blog post. Available online: http://healthycrush.com/nutrition-and-anxiety/. Accessed 20th May 2016.

[115] Ross, J. (2003) *The Mood Cure*. London: Thorsons.

[116] "The research revealed that low brain serotonin made communications between specific brain regions of the emotional limbic system of the brain (a structure called the amygdala) and the frontal lobes weaker compared to those present under normal levels of serotonin. The findings suggest that when serotonin levels are low, it may be more difficult for the prefrontal cortex to control emotional responses to anger that are generated within the amygdala." University of Cambridge, Online News: http://www.cam.ac.uk/research/news/serotonin-levels-affect-the-brain%E2%80%99s-response-to-anger

[117] Virrkunen, M. (1986) Reactive hypoglycaemic tendency among habitually violent offenders. *Nutrition Reviews, Vol.44 (Suppl).* Pages 94-103

[118] **Definition:** "Reactive hypoglycaemia is the general term for having a hypo after eating, which is when blood glucose levels become dangerously low following a meal." *Reactive Hypoglycaemia - Hypos After Eating.* Diabetes blog: http://www.diabetes.co.uk/reactive-hypoglycemia.html. Accessed: 13th June 2016.

How does this happen? Sugary food pushes blood-sugar levels too high. Adrenalin sends out a warning signal. An emergency supply of insulin is sent around the body to mop up the blood-sugar excess; but it goes *too far*. This reduces the blood sugar level below what the body needs. Then cortisol is released to get glucose out of storage in your liver and muscles. Before that glucose arrives, you experience 'a hypo'.

~~~

[119] Schoenthaler, S.C. (1983) The Northern California diet-behaviour program: An empirical evaluation of 3,000 incarcerated juveniles in Stanislaus County Juvenile Hall. *International Journal of Biosocial Research, Vol 5(2),* Pages 99-106.

[120] Schoenthaler, S.C. (1983) The Los Angeles probation department diet behaviour program: An empirical analysis of six institutional settings', *International Journal of Biosocial Research, Vol 5(2),* Pages 107-17.

[121] Yu, W. (2012) High trans-fat diet predicts aggression: People who eat more hydrogenated oils are more aggressive. *Scientific American Mind,* July 2012. Available online: http://www.scientificamerican.com/article/high-trans-fat-diet-predicts-aggresion/

[122] Schoenthaler, S., and Bier I. D. (2002) Food addiction and criminal behaviour – The California randomized trial. *Food Allergy and Intolerance. 731–746.* Saunders.

Schoenthaler S et al (1997) The effect of randomized vitamin-mineral supplementation on violent and non-violent antisocial behaviour among incarcerated juveniles. *Journal of Nutritional & Environmental Medicine 7:* Pages 343–352.

Gesch, C B. et al (2002) Influence of supplementary vitamins, minerals and essential fatty acids on the antisocial behaviour of young adults. *British Journal of Psychiatry 81*: Pages 22–28.

Associate Parliamentary Food and Health Forum (2008) The Links between Diet and Behaviour. The influence of nutrition on mental health. Report of an inquiry held by the Associate Parliamentary Food and Health Forum. London: All Party Parliamentary Food and Health Forum.

~~~

[123] Sandwell, H. and Wheatley, M. (2008) Healthy eating advice as part of drug treatment in prisons. *Prison Service Journal, Issue 182.*

[124] Colman, A. (2002) *Dictionary of Psychology.* Oxford: Oxford University Press.

[125] Brogan, K. (2016) *A mind of your own: The truth about depression and how women can heal their bodies to reclaim their lives.* London: Thorsons.

[126] Lipitor is a drug commonly prescribed for reducing high cholesterol.

[127] Advil (ibuprofen) is a nonsteroidal anti-inflammatory drug (NSAID). Ibuprofen works by reducing hormones that cause inflammation and pain in the body.

[128] For example: "If low serotonin levels were responsible for depressed mood, then we should be able to induce depression in people by decreasing serotonin, and we should find low levels of serotonin in patients with depression. But neither of those things exist. Decreasing serotonin in humans can lower your mood, but it doesn't always work. And studies looking for low serotonin in depressed patients have been inconclusive. It appears that even though antidepressants increase serotonin, a lack of serotonin doesn't cause depression (kind of like aspirin treats a headache, but headaches are not caused by a lack of aspirin). Strike three. Serotonin is out." (*The Guardian*: Blog post: *If low serotonin levels aren't responsible for depression, what is?* Online: https://www.theguardian.com/science/blog/2010/sep/28/depression-serotonin-neurogenesis. Accessed: 13th June 2016)

~~~

[129] "...there is no evidence that serotonin directly underpins happiness". "How we know that serotonin doesn't make you happy". "Many studies have explored whether rapidly lowering serotonin levels makes healthy individuals feel less happy, and have consistently found that this is not the case. One common method used for this purpose is acute tryptophan depletion (ATD), which effectively and temporarily lowers brain serotonin levels by 50-90% over the course of several hours. Participants of ATD studies are given a drink containing a variety of essential amino-acids except for tryptophan – an essential molecule which is processed in the central nervous system to produce serotonin. These consumed amino-acids compete with the relatively fewer tryptophan molecules to access the brain from the bloodstream, and naturally win. As a result of this, serotonin synthesis goes down and levels of the neurochemical drop dramatically within 5-7 hours. Using this method, researchers find that healthy individuals don't actually report feeling any less happy when deprived of serotonin (Footnotes 9 and 20)".

"Footnote 9: Evers, E. A. T., Tillie, D. E., van der Veen, F. M., Lieben, C. K., Jolles, J., Deutz, N. E. P., Schmitt, J. A. J. (2005) Effects of a novel method of acute tryptophan depletion on plasma tryptophan and cognitive performance in healthy volunteers. *Journal of Psychopharmacology*, Vol 178, No. 1. Pages 1432-2072.

"Footnote 20: Van der Veen, F. M. et al. (2007). Effects of acute tryptophan depletion on mood and facial emotion perception related brain activation and performance in healthy women with and without a family history of depression. *Neuropsychopharmacology 32*, 216-224.Source: Deleniv, S. (2015) Is serotonin the happy brain chemical, and do depressed people just have too little of it? *The Neuropshere*. Online: https://theneurosphere.com/2015/11/14/is-serotonin-the-happy-brain-chemical-and-do-depressed- people-just-have-too-little-of-it/

~~~

[130] Redfern, R. (2016) The importance of Nutrition for mental health. *Naturally Healthy News, issue 30*.

[131] "Folate is a water-soluble B vitamin that is naturally present in some foods, added to others, and available as a dietary supplement. Folate, formerly known as folacin, is the generic term for both naturally occurring food folate and folic acid, the fully oxidized monoglutamate form of the vitamin that is used in dietary supplements and fortified foods... Folate is found naturally in a wide variety of foods, including vegetables (especially dark green leafy vegetables), fruits and fruit juices, nuts, beans, peas, dairy

products, poultry and meat, eggs, seafood, and grains (Table 2) [3,7]. Spinach, liver, yeast, asparagus, and Brussels sprouts are among the foods with the highest levels of folate." Extracted from 'Folate: Dietary Supplement Fact Sheet'; Published by the US Department of Health's National Institutes of Health, Office of Dietary Supplements. Available online: https://ods.od.nih.gov/factsheets/Folate-HealthProfessional/. Accessed: 14th June 2016.

[132] Sanchez-Villegas, A., Almudena, M.A., et al. (2013) Mediterranean dietary pattern and depression: the PREDIMED randomized trial. *BMC Medicine* 2013, Vol.11: Article 208. The conclusion of this study follows:

Conclusion: "In conclusion, results from this analysis are suggestive of a beneficial effect of a long-term intervention with a Mediterranean diet on depression for patients with DM2. Nevertheless, to definitely assess the role of Mediterranean diet in the prevention of depression, longer follow-up of this trial and further experimental investigations are needed."

And see also: Sánchez-Villegas A, Verberne L, De Irala J, Ruíz-Canela M, Toledo E, Serra-Majem L, et al. (2011) Dietary Fat Intake and the Risk of Depression: The SUN Project. PLoS ONE 6(1): e16268. doi:10.1371/journal.pone.0016268

~~~

[133] Warwick University (2016) '7 a day for happiness and mental health'. Press release: http://www.2.warwick.ac.uk/newsandevents/presssreleases/7-a-day_for_happiness/ Accessed 2nd May 2016

[134] The study was entitled: 'Psychological Well-being Linked to the Consumption of Fruit and Vegetables', by David G. Blanchflower, Andrew J. Oswald and Sarah Stewart-Brown. (2016).

~~~

[135] Hellmich, N. (2013) The best preventative medicine? Exercise. Online: dailycomet.com. Accessed: 18th June 2016

[136] Atkinson (2007), page 355.

[137] Source: Just Swim (2016) 'How swimming improves mental health'. An online blog: http://www.swimming.org/justswim/swimming-improves-mental-health/

[138] Source: Women's Running (2015) 'THE MENTAL HEALTH BENEFITS OF RUNNING: How running can alleviate symptoms of depression'. Online: http://womensrunninguk.co.uk/health/mental-health-benefits-running/. Accessed: 23rd November 2017

[139] Source: O'Connor, P.J., Herring, M.P. and Carvalho, A. (2010). 'Mental health benefits of strength training in adults'. *American Journal of Lifestyle Medicine, 4(5),* Pages 377-396.

[140] Perlmutter, D. (2015) *Brain Maker: The power of gut microbes to heal and protect your brain – for life.* London: Hodder and Stoughton.

[141] Office for National Statistics (ONS) (1995) Surveys of Psychiatric Morbidity in Great Britain. Report 1 – The prevalence of psychiatric morbidity among adults living in private households. London: The Stationery Office. Cited on: https://www.anxietyuk.org.uk/. Accessed 13th June 2016.

[142] Source: www.nhs.uk/Conditions/Anxiety/Pages/Introduction.aspx. Accessed 23rd February 2016

[143] The distinction here is between the 'sympathetic' nervous system (which activates our bodily systems to fight or flee) and the 'parasympathetic' nervous system (which calms us down again).

[144] Ratey, J., and Hargerman, E. (2009) *Spark: The revolutionary new science of exercise and the brain.* London: Quercus.

[145] LeDoux, J.E., and Gorman, J.M. (2001) A call to action: Overcoming anxiety through active coping. Volume 158, Issue 12, December 2001, Pages 1953-1955. Available online at: psychiatry*online.org*/doi/10.1176/appi.ajp.158.12.1953.

[146] "Muscle spindles are sensory receptors within the belly of a muscle that primarily detect changes in the length of this muscle...The responses of muscle spindles to changes in length also play an important role in regulating the contraction of muscles, by activating motor neurons via the stretch reflex to resist muscle stretch... Muscle spindles are found within the belly of muscles, embedded in extrafusal muscle fibres... Muscle spindles are composed of 3-12 intrafusal muscle fibres..." (Wikipedia, Muscle Spindle: Available online: https://en.wikipedia.org/wiki/Muscle_spindle. Accessed: 17th June 2016).

[147] Blumenthal, J.A., Smith, P.J., and Hoffman, B.M. (2012) Is exercise a viable treatment for depression? *American College of Sports Medicine Health & Fitness Journal.* July/August; Vol.16 (4): Pages 14–21. doi: 10.1249/01.FIT.0000416000.09526.eb. Cited in: Ratey, J., and Hagerman, E. (2009) *Spark: The revolutionary new science of exercise and the brain.* London: Quercus.

[148] Hoffman, B.M., Babyak, M.A., Craighead, W.E., Sherwood, A., Doraiswamy, P.M., Coons, M.J., and Blumenthal, J.A. (2011) Exercise and pharmacotherapy in patients with major depression: one-year follow-up of the SMILE study. 2011 Feb-Mar; Vol.73 (2): Pages 127-133. doi: 10.1097/PSY.0b013e31820433a5. Cited in: Evans, J. (2016) Natural vs medical. *What Doctors don't tell you.* (Alternative health magazine). London: WDDTY Publishing. April 2016 (Page 70).

[149] National Health Service (NHS) (2016) Exercise for depression. Available online: http://www.nhs.uk/conditions/stress-anxiety-depression/pages/exercise-for-depression.aspx. Accessed: 23rd February 2016.

[150] Mayo Clinic: Exercise and stress: Get moving to manage stress. Available online: http://www.mayoclinic.org/healthy-lifestyle/stress-management/in-depth/exercise-and-stress/art-20044469) Accessed: 23rd February 2016.

[151] Mayo Clinic Staff (2014) Depression (major depressive disorder). Depression and anxiety: Exercise eases symptoms. Available online: http://www.mayoclinic.org/diseases-conditions/depression/in-depth/depression-and-exercise/art-20046495. Accessed: 19th June 2016.

[152] NHS Choices (2016) Stress, anxiety and depression: How to control your anger – Available online: www.nhs.uk/conditions/anger-management. Accessed 16th June 2016.

[102] Mayo Clinic Staff (2014) Anger management: 10 tips to tame your temper: Available online: http://www.mayoclinic.org/healthy-lifestyle/adult-health/in-depth/ anger-management/art-20045434. Accessed 16th June 2016.

[154] Isold, K. (2010) Anger and exercise: Anger is a normal, adaptive human emotion. *Psychology Today blog.* Available online: https://www.psychologytoday.com/blog/hidden-motives/201008/anger-and-exercise. Accessed: 16th June 2016.

[155] Reynolds, G. (2010) Phys Ed: Can Exercise Moderate Anger? August 11, 2010. Available online, here: http://well.blogs.nytimes.com/2010/08/11/phys-ed-can-exercise-moderate-anger/?_r=0. Accessed: 16th June 2016.

~~~

[156] Here are some of the sources:

(a) Broderick J, Knowles A, Chadwick J, Vancampfort D. (2015) Yoga versus standard care for schizophrenia. Cochrane Database of Systematic Reviews 2015, Issue 10. Art. No.: CD010554. DOI: 10.1002/14651858.CD010554.pub2 - (Further research is required).

(b) Bangalore NG, Varambally S. (2012) Yoga therapy for schizophrenia. *International Journal of Yoga* 2012; **5**(2):85-91. [PUBMED: 22869990]

(c) Behere RV, Arasappa R, Jagannathan A, Varambally S, Venkatasubramanian G, Thirthalli J, Subbakrishna DK, Nagendra HR, Gangadhar BN (2011). Effect of yoga therapy on facial emotion recognition deficits, symptoms and functioning in patients with schizophrenia. Acta Psychiatrica Scandinavia, Vol 123 (2); pp: 147 -53

(d) Duraiswamy G, Thirthalli J, Nagendra HR and Gangadhar BN (2007). Yoga therapy as an add-on treatment in the management of patients with schizophrenia – a randomized controlled trial. Acta Psychiatrica Scandinavia, 116 (3); pp: 226-32

(e) Radhakrishna S (2010). Application of integrated yoga therapy to increase imitation skills in children with autism spectrum disorder. *International Journal of Yoga, 3 (1);* pp: 26-30.

(f) Radhakrishna S, Nagarathna R and Nagendra HR (2010). Integrated approach to yoga therapy and autism spectrum disorders. Journal of Ayurveda and *Integrative Medicine, 1 (2);* pp: 120-4.

(g) Sadock BJ and Sadock VA (2000). *Kaplan and Sadock's Synopsis of Psychiatry: Behavioural Sciences/Clinical Psychiatry, 7th Edition*. Lippincott Williams & Wilkins. USA

(h) Shapiro D, Cook IA, Davydov DM, Ottaviani C, Leuchter AF and Abrams M (2007). Yoga as a Complementary Treatment of Depression: Effects of Traits and Moods on Treatment Outcome. *Evidence based complementary and alternative medicine, 4(4),* pp: 493-502.

(i) Sharma VK, Das S, Mondal S, Goswami U and Gandhi A, (2006). Effect of Sahaj Yoga on neuro-cognitive functions in patients suffering from major depression. Indian *Journal of Physiological Pharmacology*, Oct-Dec, 50(4); pp: 375-83.

(j) Sharma VK, Das S, Mondal S, Goswami U and Gandhi A (2005). Effect of Sahaj Yoga on depressive disorders. Indian *Journal of Physiological Pharmacology*, Oct-Dec, 49(4); pp: 462-8.

(k) Uebelacker LA, Tremont G, Epstein-Lubow G, Gaudiano BA, Gillette T, Kalibatseva Z and Miller IW (2010). Open trial of Vinyasa yoga for persistently depressed individuals: evidence of feasibility and acceptability. *Behaviour Modification*, May, 34(3); pp: 247-64.

(l) Vancampfort D, De Hert M, Knapen J, Wampers M, Demunter H, Deckx S, Maurissen K and Probst M (2011). State anxiety, psychological stress and positive well-being responses to yoga and aerobic exercise in people with schizophrenia: a pilot study. *Disability Rehabilitation, 33(8);* pp: 684-9.

(m) Visceglia E and Lewis S (2011). Yoga therapy as an adjunctive treatment for schizophrenia: a randomized, controlled pilot study. *Journal of Alternative and complementary Medicine, 17(7),* pages: 601-7

~~~

[157] **Definition**: Restorative postures are basically supported reposes, like the Death Pose. 'Let's face it: Some yoga poses taste a little bit sweeter than others. And if yoga were a smorgasbord, restorative postures would most definitely be at the dessert table. These...

These soothing and well-supported poses offer us the opportunity to linger quietly for a few moments and savor the simple sweetness of life.' (Claudia Cummins, (2007) How to Start a Restorative Yoga Practice. *Yoga Journal*, Aug 28, 2007. Available online: http://www.yogajournal.com/article/beginners/restorative-yoga/. Accessed: 17th June 2016.

[158] Reder, A. (2007) Unmasking Anger. *Yoga Journal*. August 28th 2007. Available online: http://www.yogajournal.com/article/yoga-101/unmasking-anger/. Accessed: 17th June 2016.

[159] Medina, J. (2015) How Yoga is Similar to Existing Mental Health Therapies. Source: Psych Central website: http://psychcentral.com/lib/how-yoga-is-similar-to-existing-therapies/. Accessed: May 2016.

[160] Santer, M.J. Why Qigong Is So Effective Against Emotional Illnesses. Source: http://qigong15.com/blog/qigong-exercises/why-qigong-is-so-effective-against-emotional-illnesses/. Accessed May 2015.

[161] Tse, M. (1995) *Qigong for Health and Vitality*. London: Piatkus.

[162] Linder *and colleagues* conducted a randomized controlled trial to assess the ability of Qi Gong to relieve stress. See: Linder K. and Svardsudd, K. (2006) Qigong has a relieving effect on stress. *Lakartidningen*. (A Swedish Medical Journal) *2006; Vol.103 (24-25):* Pages 1942-1945.

[163] Jahnke, R. Larkey, L. Rogers, C. Etnier, J. and Lin, F. (2012) A Comprehensive Review of Health Benefits of Qigong and Tai Chi. *American Journal of Health Promotion, Jul-Aug; Vol.24 (6),* Pages e1-e25.

[164] Larkey L, Jahnke R, Etnier J, Gonzalez J. (2009) Meditative movement as a category of exercise: Implications for research. *Journal of Physical Activity & Health. 2009*; Vol.6: Pages 230–238.

[165] Jahnke R. (2002) *The Healing Promise of Qi: Creating Extraordinary Wellness through Qigong and Tai Chi*. Chicago, IL: Contemporary Books.

[166] Ratey, J. and Hagerman, E. (2010) *Spark! How exercise will improve the performance of your brain*. London: Quercus.

[167] Sapolsky R. (2010) *Why Zebras don't get Ulcers*. Third Ed. New York: St Martin's Griffin.

[168] Bryant, C.W. (2010) Does running fight depression? 14th July 2010. HowStuffWorks.com. Available online: http://adventure.howstuffworks.com/outdoor-activities/running/health/running-fight-depression.htm. Accessed 16th June 2016.

~~~

[169] Here is the reference for a much later book by Chaitow: Chaitow, L. (2003) *Candida Albicans: The non-drug approach to the treatment of Candida infection*. London: Thorsons.

[170] Two additional sources on Candida Albicans and the link to physical illness and emotional distress:

Jacobs, G. (1994) *Candida Albicans: A user's guide to treatment and recovery*. London: Optima. And:

Trowbridge, J.P. and Walker, M. (1989) *The Yeast Syndrome*. London: Bantam Books.

[171] Golomb, B.A., Evans, M.A., White, H.L., and Dimsdale, J.E. (2012) Trans-fat consumption and aggression. Online: PLoS One. 2012; 7(3):e32175. doi: 10.1371/journal.pone.0032175. Epub 2012 Mar 5.

[172] **Definition** of Mediterranean diet: A diet of a type traditional in Mediterranean countries, characterized especially by a high consumption of vegetables and olive oil and moderate consumption of protein, and thought to confer health benefits.

[173] Definition of Paleo diet: A diet based on the types of foods presumed to have been eaten by early humans, consisting chiefly of meat, fish, vegetables, and fruit and excluding dairy or cereal products and processed food.

[174] Simopoulos (2002) produced a study which argues for a low ratio of omega-6 to omega-3 fatty acids. Here is the abstract from that paper:

"Abstract:

"Several sources of information suggest that human beings evolved on a diet with a ratio of omega-6 to omega-3 essential fatty acids (EFA) of approximately 1 whereas in Western diets the ratio is 15/1-16.7/1. Western diets are deficient in omega-3 fatty acids, and have excessive amounts of omega-6 fatty acids compared with the diet on which human beings evolved and their genetic patterns were established. Excessive amounts of omega-6 polyunsaturated fatty acids (PUFA) and a very high omega-6/omega-3 ratio, as is found in today's Western diets, promote the pathogenesis of many diseases, including cardiovascular disease, cancer, and inflammatory and autoimmune diseases, whereas increased levels of omega-3 PUFA (a low omega-6/omega-3 ratio) exert suppressive effects. In the secondary prevention of cardiovascular disease, a ratio of 4/1 was associated with a 70% decrease in total mortality. A ratio of 2.5/1 reduced rectal cell proliferation in patients with colorectal cancer, whereas a ratio of 4/1 with the same amount of omega-3 PUFA had no effect. The lower omega-6/omega-3 ratio in women with breast cancer was associated with decreased risk. A ratio of 2-3/1 suppressed inflammation in patients with rheumatoid arthritis, and a ratio of 5/1 had a beneficial effect on patients with asthma, whereas a ratio of 10/1 had adverse consequences. These studies indicate that the optimal ratio may vary with the disease under consideration. This is consistent with the fact that chronic diseases are multigenic and multifactorial. Therefore, it is quite possible that the therapeutic dose of omega-3 fatty acids will depend on the degree of severity of disease resulting from the genetic predisposition. A lower ratio of omega-6/omega-3 fatty acids is more desirable in reducing the risk of many of the chronic diseases of high prevalence in Western societies, as well as in the developing countries, that are being exported to the rest of the world." Source: Simopoulos, A.P. (2002) 'The importance of the ratio of omega-6/omega-3 essential fatty acids'. *Biomedical Pharmacotherapy, Oct 2002, Vol.56 (8):* Pages 365-379.

~~~

[175] Cunningham, J. B. (2001) The Stress Management Sourcebook. Second edition. Los Angeles: Lowell House.

[176] Winnie Yu (2012) High trans-fat diet predicts aggression: People who eat more hydrogenated oils are more aggressive. *Scientific American Mind*, July 2012. Available online:
http://www.scientificamerican.com/article/high-trans-fat-diet-predicts-aggresion/

[177] Stress Management Society (2012/2016) Nutritional stress and health: The "Think 'nervous'" box. Available online: http://www.stress.org.uk/Diet-and-nutrition.aspx

[178] "A diet high in refined carbohydrates may lead to an increased risk for new-onset depression in postmenopausal women, according to a study published in The American Journal of Clinical Nutrition.

"The study by James Gangwisch, PhD and colleagues in the department of psychiatry at Columbia University Medical Centre (CUMC) looked at the dietary glycaemic index, glycaemic load, types of carbohydrates consumed, and depression in data from more than 70,000 postmenopausal women who participated in the National Institutes of Health's Women's Health Initiative Observational Study between 1994 and 1998."

Available online: https://www.sciencedaily.com/releases/2015/08/150805110335.htm. Accessed: 3rd October 2017.

~~~

[179] Perretta, Lorraine (2001) *Brain Food: the essential guide to boosting brain power*. London: Hamlyn.

[180] Cunningham, J. B. (2001) *The Stress Management Sourcebook*. Second edition. Los Angeles: Lowell House.

[181] Woodward, N. (2006) Stress, Diet and Body Acidification. Listed in *Cellular Chemistry*, originally published in issue 130 - December 2006. http://www.positivehealth.com/article/alkaline/stress-diet-and-body-acidification

[182] The research on milk and the emotional and behavioural effects upon a group of children, in a double blind study, published in the Lancet in the UK, has been largely ignored by policy makers. Here is a flavour of the problem, from the opening of a blog by Dr H Morrow Brown MD, FRCP (Edin), FAAAAI (USA):

"The emotional aspects of milk intolerance are so variable and so bizarre that it is difficult to select the most interesting and illustrative cases seen over the years. Emotional effects along with gastro-intestinal symptoms are commonly associated with migraine. Milk intolerant children often have a short attention span, cannot sit still, and have tantrums and poor coordination. A tendency to self-injury and destructiveness sometimes occurs repeatedly after drinking milk. Their poor coordination is obvious in their writing and "art work", because meaningless squiggles become recognizable objects or people after withdrawal of the relevant foods."

We believe it is important, because of this research, to limit the amount of dairy milk that we consume, and to substitute nut or rice milk where possible.

~~~

[183] Source: Campbell, T. (2014) Are smoothies good or bad? Newsletter, Centre for Nutrition Studies. Available online: http://nutritionstudies.org/are-smoothies-good-or-bad/. Accessed: 16th October 2017.

[184] Source: The Real Food Guide (2017) 'What is margarine and why is it bad for you?' An online blog: http://therealfoodguide.com/what-is-margarine-and-why-is-it-bad-for-you/

[185] Mosley, M. (2015) 'Which oils are best to cook with?' 28th July 2015. BBC: News: Magazine, 28th July 2015. Online: http://www.bbc.co.uk/news/magazine-33675975

[186] Dr John Briffa, 'High Anxiety', *Observer Magazine,* 19th June 2005, page 61.

[187] Perretta, L. (2001) *Brain Food: the essential guide to boosting brain power*. London: Hamlyn.

[188] Lettuce and anxiety are mentioned in this blog: http://www.organicfacts.net/health-benefits/vegetable/health-benefits-of-lettuce.html

[189] Chamomile tea for anxiety and insomnia; mentioned in this blog: http://naturalsociety.com/9-amazing-health-benefits-of-chamomile-tea/

[190] Blog address for Health Unblocked post about Chamomile tea and SSRI's: https://healthunlocked.com/anxietysupport/posts/132860526/can-camomile-tea-interfere-with-anti-depressants-and-antibiotics

[191] Here's one online address where you can watch the video: To study this material for CE credits, then please go to the Mad in America site, here: https://app.ruzuku.com/courses/

~~~

[192] **Wernicke's encephalopathy** (or **Wernicke's** disease) is the presence of neurological symptoms caused by biochemical lesions of the central nervous system after exhaustion of B-vitamin reserves, in particular thiamine (vitamin B1).

[193] **Korsakoff** syndrome is a chronic memory disorder caused by severe deficiency of thiamine (vitamin B-1). Korsakoff syndrome is most commonly caused by alcohol misuse, but certain other conditions also can cause the syndrome.

~~~

[194] Psychiatric manifestations of vitamin B12 deficiency: a case report.

Abstract

Psychiatric manifestations are frequently associated with pernicious anaemia including depression, mania, psychosis, and dementia. We report a case of a patient with vitamin B12 deficiency, who has presented severe depression with delusion and Capgras* syndrome, delusion with lability of mood and hypomania successively, during a period of two Months. Source: https://www.ncbi.nlm.nih.gov/pubmed/ 15029091

(*Capgras Syndrome, also known as **Capgras** Delusion, is the irrational belief that a familiar person or place has been replaced with an exact duplicate — an imposter (Ellis, 2001, Hirstein, and Ramachandran, 1997).)

~~~

[195] Myxoedema psychosis, more colloquially known as myxoedema madness, is a relatively uncommon consequence of hypothyroidism, such as in Hashimoto's thyroiditis or in patients who have had the thyroid surgically removed and are not taking thyroxine. Source: https://en.wikipedia.org/ wiki/ Myxedematous_psychosis

~~~

[196] pellagra (pɛˈlagrə, pɛˈleɪgrə/) *noun:*

1. A deficiency disease caused by a lack of nicotinic acid* or its precursor tryptophan in the diet. It is characterized by dermatitis, diarrhoea, and mental disturbance, and is often linked to over-dependence on maize as a staple food. Source: http://www.webmd.com/diet/niacin-deficiency-symptoms-and-treatments#1

   (*Nicotinic acid *noun* BIOCHEMISTRY: A vitamin of the B complex which is widely distributed in foods such as milk, wheat germ, and meat, and can be synthesized in the body from tryptophan. Its deficiency causes pellagra.)

~~~

[197] Brogan, K. (2016) *A mind of your own: The truth about depression and how women can heal their bodies to reclaim their lives.* London: Thorsons.

[198] Perlmutter, D. (2015) *Brain Maker: The power of gut microbes to heal and protect your brain – for life.* London: Hodder and Stoughton.

[199] Ross, J. (2003) *The Mood Cure: Take charge of your emotions in 24 hours using food and supplements.* London: Thorsons.

[200] Enders, G. (2015) *Gut: The inside story of our body's most under-rated organ.* Scribe Publications.

~~~

[201] Kaplan, B.J., Susan G. Crawford, Catherine J. Field and J. Steven A. Simpson (2007) Vitamins, minerals, and mood. *Psychological Bulletin, Sept; 133(5):* Pages 747-760.

~~~

[202] Source: Available online at NCBI: https://www.ncbi.nlm.nih.gov/pubmed/17723028

~~~

[203] Keys, A., Brozek, J., Henshel, A., Mickelson, O., & Taylor, H.L. (1950). *The biology of human starvation,* (Vols. 1–2). Minneapolis, MN: University of Minnesota Press.

~~~

[204] Kaplan, B.J., Julia J. Rucklidge, Amy Romijn, and Kevin Flood (2015) The emerging field of nutritional mental health: Inflammation, the microbiome, oxidative stress, and mitochondrial function. *Clinical Psychological Science, Vol.3 (6):* 964-980.

[205] American Psychological Association: The psychology of hunger. By Dr. David Baker and Natacha Keramidas, October 2013, Vol 44, No. 9.
Online: http://www.apa.org/monitor/2013/10/hunger.aspx

[206] Kaplan, B.J., Julia J. Rucklidge, Amy Romijn, and Kevin Flood (2015) The emerging field of nutritional mental health: Inflammation, the microbiome, oxidative stress, and mitochondrial function. *Clinical Psychological Science, Vol.3 (6):* 964-980.

[207] American Psychological Association (2013): 'The psychology of hunger'. By Dr. David Baker and Natacha Keramidas, October 2013, Vol 44, No. 9. Online: http://www.apa.org/ monitor/ 2013/ 10/hunger.aspx

[208] Keys, A., Brozek, J., Henshel, A., Mickelson, O., & Taylor, H.L. (1950). *The biology of human starvation,* (Vols. 1–2). Minneapolis, MN: University of Minnesota Press.

[209] American Psychological Association: The psychology of hunger. By Dr David Baker and Natacha Keramidas, October 2013, Vol 44, No. 9.
Online: http://www.apa.org/monitor/2013/10/hunger.aspx

[210] Kaplan, B.J., Julia J. Rucklidge, Amy Romijn, and Kevin Flood (2015) The emerging field of nutritional mental health: Inflammation, the microbiome, oxidative stress, and mitochondrial function. *Clinical Psychological Science, Vol.3 (6):* 964-980.

[211] Here's one online address where you can watch the video:
https://www.hardynutritionals.com/videos/36-continuing-medical-education-series-nutrition-and-mental-health-part-1

To study this material for CE credits, then please go to the Mad in America site, here: https://app.ruzuku.com/courses/

[212] Berk et al. (2013) 'So depression is an inflammatory disease, but where does the inflammation come from?' BMC Medicine 2013, 11:200 Available online: http://www.biomedcentral.com/1741-7015/11/200. Downloaded: 8th September 2017

[213] Bonnie J. Kaplan, Julia J. Rucklidge, Amy Romijn, Kevin McLeod (2015) 'The Emerging Field of Nutritional Mental Health'. *Clinical Psychological Science, Vol 3*, Issue 6, pp. 964 - 980

~~~

[214] "Essential fatty acids are, as they sound, fats that are necessary within the human body. Though you've probably often heard the word "fats" and associated it with bad health, there are some essential fatty acids that are necessary for your survival. Without them, you could cause serious damage to different systems within the body. However, essential fatty acids are also not usually produced naturally within the body. This means that you have to obtain essential fatty acids by adding them to your diet. There are two basic types of essential fatty acids": Omega-3 and Omega-6. And it is argued that we need more of the 3's than the 6's; or, at least, we have to get the balance right (which could be as low as 1:1). Too much omega-6 seems to be bad for our health (and western diets currently include too much omega-6). Sources: Friday Editor (2017) 'What are essential fatty acids?' The Fit Day Blog. Available online at: http://www.fitday.com/fitness-articles/nutrition/fats/what-are-essential-fatty-acids.html. And, Dr Michael Greger (2016).

[215] Dr Michael Greger (2016) gives the following source for his conclusion that eating more vegetables may help to reduce depression:

Agarwal, U, Suruchi Mishra, Jia Xu, Susan Levin, Joseph Gonzales, and Neal D. Barnard (2015) 'A Multicentre Randomized Controlled Trial of a Nutrition Intervention Program in a Multi-ethnic Adult Population in the Corporate Setting Reduces Depression and Anxiety and Improves Quality of Life: The GEICO Study. *American Journal of Health Promotion, Vol 29, Issue 4*, pp. 245 - 254.

~~~

[216] **E-CENT** stands for Emotive-Cognitive Embodied Narrative therapy. The **emotive** component of the human being, and of our approach to counselling, is emphasized, by being given first place, because humans are **primarily** emotional beings. **Cognition** (which includes attention, perception, language, and thinking), is in second place, because language and thinking are products of our socialization, rather than being innate or fixed. **Embodiment** is the physical stratum which underpins and sustains our innate feelings and our socialized language/thinking. **Narrative** is next, because we create our narratives (or stories of our experience) out of our socialized language and socially shaped thinking. And **therapy** is what we do with these insights into the social individual.

[217] Prochaska, J.O., Norcross, J.C. & DiClemente, C.C. (1998). *Changing for Good*. Reprint edition. New York: Morrow.

[218] Kaizen: A philosophy of continuous improvement, often in very small steps. In E-CENT we emphasize the importance of *gradual* change through *small* steps in personal habit change, because attempts at big steps often backfire, because the habit-based part of us rebels against the challenge of dramatic change.

[219] Bargh, J.A. and Chartrand, T.L. (1999) 'The unbearable automaticity of being'. *American Psychologist, 54(7)*: 462-479.

[220] Duhigg, C. (2013) *The Power of Habit: Why we do what we do and how to change*. London: Random House.

~~~

How to control your anger, anxiety and depression: